Digital Business Models

I0888182

By presenting the conditions, methods, and techniques of monetisation of business models in the digital economy, this book combines implementation of the theoretical aspects of monetisation with the presentation of practical business solutions in this field.

The scope of the book includes the relationship between the monetisation and scalability degree of business models. The book describes the place and role of the digital business ecosystem in the process of digital transformation. It demonstrates ideological and functional conditions for the use of the concept of sharing to design innovative business models while also presenting a multidimensional approach to the use of Big Data and their monetisation in the context of business models. *Digital Business Models* shows the place and role of ecological and social factors in building digital business models that are part of the concept of the circular economy and presents the contemporary conditions of a sustainability concept that meets the ethical challenges of doing digital business. It demonstrates how important are the social factors of business model design and the creation of social value in modern business. The book explores the servitisation of digital business models using digital technologies and features case studies on the effective solutions of business models that use servitisation as a factor supporting the monetisation of business models.

Written for scholars exploring the efficiency and effectiveness of business models related to contemporary concepts – Sharing Economy, Circular Economy, Network Economy, Big Data, and so on – and those designing business models taking into account social aspects, it will also be of direct interest to entrepreneurship courses.

Adam Jabłoński is Associate Professor and Head of Institute of Management in WSB University in Poznań, Poland. He is also Vice-President of the Board of a reputable management consulting company "OTTIMA plus" Ltd of Katowice, and President of the "Southern Railway Cluster" Association of Katowice.

Marek Jabłoński is Associate Professor in WSB University in Poznań, the Faculty in Chorzow, Poland. He is also President of the Board of a reputable management consulting company "OTTIMA plus" Ltd of Katowice and Vice-President of the Association "Southern Railway Cluster" in Katowice.

RIOT!

Routledge Studies in Innovation, Organizations and Technology

Frugal Innovation
A Global Research Companion
Edited by Adela J. McMurray and Gerrit A. de Waal

Digital Work and the Platform Economy
Understanding Tasks, Skills and Capabilities in the New Era
Edited by Seppo Poutanen, Anne Kovalainen, and Petri Rouvinen

The Future of Work in Asia and Beyond
A Technological Revolution or Evolution?
Edited by Alan R. Nankervis, Julia Connell and John Burgess

Society and Technology
Opportunities and Challenges
Edited by Ewa Lechman and Magdalena Popowska

Contextual Innovation Management
Adapting Innovation Processes to Different Situations
Patrick van der Duin and Roland Ortt

Research, Innovation and Entrepreneurship in Saudi Arabia
Vision 2030
Edited by Muhammad Khurram Khan and Muhammad Babar Khan

Developing Digital Governance
South Korea as a Global Digital Government Leader
Choong-sik Chung

Digital Business Models
Perspectives on Monetisation
Adam Jabłoński and Marek Jabłoński

For more information about this series, please visit: www.routledge.com/Routledge-Studies-in-Innovation-Organizations-and-Technology/book-series/RIOT

Digital Business Models

Perspectives on Monetisation

Adam Jabłoński and Marek Jabłoński

Routledge
Taylor & Francis Group
LONDON AND NEW YORK

First published 2021
by Routledge
2 Park Square, Milton Park, Abingdon, Oxon OX14 4RN

and by Routledge
605 Third Avenue, New York, NY 10017

First issued in paperback 2022

Routledge is an imprint of the Taylor & Francis Group, an informa business

Publisher's Note
The publisher has gone to great lengths to ensure the quality of this reprint but points out that some imperfections in the original copies may be apparent.

British Library Cataloguing-in-Publication Data
A catalogue record for this book is available from the British Library

Library of Congress Cataloging-in-Publication Data
Names: Jabłonski, Adam, author. | Jabłonski, Marek, author.
Title: Digital business models: perspectives on monetisation /
Adam Jabłonski, Marek Jabłonski.
Description: Abingdon, Oxon; New York, NY: Routledge, 2021. |
Series: Routledge studies in innovation, organizations and technology |
Includes bibliographical references and index.
Identifiers: LCCN 2020024064 (print) | LCCN 2020024065 (ebook)
Subjects: LCSH: Information technology–Economic aspects. |
Electronic commerce. | Business enterprises–Technological
innovations. | Money.
Classification: LCC HC79.I55 J34 2021 (print) |
LCC HC79.I55 (ebook) | DDC 658.4/012–dc23
LC record available at https://lccn.loc.gov/2020024064
LC ebook record available at https://lccn.loc.gov/2020024065

ISBN 13: 978-0-367-54852-0 (pbk)
ISBN 13: 978-0-367-33865-7 (hbk)
ISBN 13: 978-0-429-32267-9 (ebk)

DOI: 10.4324/9780429322679

Typeset in Bembo
by Newgen Publishing UK

Contents

Figures

Tables

Preface

The digital economy is currently the core area of global business development. Traditional management formulas are not applicable in many areas in both theoretical and practical terms. New scientific theories should be sought to better understand the economic and social processes taking place. The digitalisation of business resulting from the universality of mobile devices, computers, and the Internet means that most areas of people's lives are being transferred to the virtual world. The widespread digital transformation of world economies is underway. A transactional approach in economics is often replaced with a relational approach based on relationship networks. Communities focused on specific ideas and values are being developed and the modern perception of business is changing. Due to universal access to information, it is not only economic effects which are required of business ventures, but also widespread social acceptance. Business models as ontological entities and as a management concept have been recognised by scientists and practitioners. Without this concept, it is impossible to understand the laws governing modern business conditions. It is not easy to understand the concept of business models of companies operating in the digital economy. The digitalisation of business has a significant impact on the shape of modern business models, leading to opportunities to develop innovative, even revolutionary, formulas for doing business. The dynamic development of information technologies accelerates the possibility of creating new value propositions delivered through business models while rapidly shortening the life cycle of enterprises. The market competition is based on better (faster, cheaper, etc.) and more attractive (nicer, more pleasant, etc.) value delivery through digital solutions. The designers of digital business models are looking for new formulas for creating and delivering value using the potential inherent in complex technical systems supported by relationship networks. Complex business ecosystems are established through the combination of technology, social relationships and organisation of activities. They are based not only on various technologies but also on other ways of creating value. This creates an environment where many creators of digital business models can conduct their activity, often using the same resources as other network participants. Such conditions for the functioning of digital business mean that base technologies are often widely used, and the uniqueness of the delivered value lies mainly in the configuration of the designed digital business model. Hence, breakthrough solutions in the field of digital business models that significantly affect the composition of business ecosystems are constantly emerging. The digital world, its realities, and context are constantly forcing new operating conditions upon business entities. Opportunities for activity on these markets often become threats at the same time. It is more difficult to turn resources into money. Collecting resources and combining them into a coherent synthetic system is the first stage of designing digital business models. The biggest problems are revealed when the designer of a digital business model wants to financially monetise the created value through a specific pattern. At that point, there is a significant risk of users rejecting the carefully built business solution. Digital business models should be viewed in terms of monetisation. Economic factors are responsible for the company's ability to develop, which in turn is of the greatest importance to its recipients. A balanced approach to constructing monetisation formulas is a significant challenge for the designers of digital business models. The multitude of solutions in the field of the monetisation of digital business models means that it is not easy to choose the optimal solution, but it is also difficult to create a new, user-friendly payment charging formula. It is this aspect that digital business managers have the biggest problem with. The choice of technology, the development of an idea of value creation, the method of delivering value to the customer and a consistent monetisation formula are the biggest challenges for digital entrepreneurs. The authors of the monograph undertook the difficult task of identifying key aspects of the development and functioning of digital business models in the context of their monetisation. This issue is of key importance in terms of the expected success of innovative enterprises. The following theoretical assumptions were made.

The main objective of scientific discussion

The main purpose of scientific discussion is to present the mechanisms of the conceptualisation and operationalisation of digital business models in terms of their monetisation from a multidimensional and holistic perspective.

Establishing a scientific problem and identifying a cognitive gap

Within the set scientific objective, it is crucial to determine the scientific problem and identify the cognitive gap. This cognitive gap is an identifiable set of factors responsible for the effective use of the monetisation formulas of digital business models in the context of globalisation. This research area is part of the current conditions of the functioning of the global digital economy. Theoretical and practical factors which determine the level of effectiveness of the monetisation formulas of digital business models should emerge against the background of this concept.

The subject of scientific discussion

The subject of scientific discussion includes scientific and application reflections in the field of factors which determine the design of digital business models in terms of their effective monetisation.

Cognitive goals

Cognitive goals include:

1. Identification of key scientific theories, on the basis of which digital business models are designed.
2. Description of key concepts of the so-called new economy, their assumptions and limitations.
3. Assessment of the impact of the concept of the new economy on the emergence of digital business models.
4. Assessment of the relationship between the configuration of digital business models and the effectiveness of the monetisation formulas which they use.

Methodological goals

Methodological goals include:

1. Indication of the configuration of factors that describe digital business models.
2. Development of strategic recommendations for the development of digital business models in terms of their monetisation.

Utilitarian goals

Utilitarian goals include:

1. Development of the authors' original canvas for the description of digital business models, including their monetisation formulas.
2. Development of a set of factors responsible for the effectiveness of the adopted monetisation formulas as part of digital business model design.

Key research questions

The following research questions were posed within the defined research objectives:

1. Does the effectiveness of monetisation formulas result from the compilation of other components of digital business models?

2. Is there a synergy between the chosen concept of the new economy and the potential for the monetisation of the digital business model?
3. What set of components shapes a coherent digital business model which is capable of achieving the expected level of monetisation?

Embedding the subject in scientific theories

Due to the multidimensional and holistic nature of the functioning of digital business models, the subject of scientific discussion requires addressing both issues related to the theory of management science, economics and finance as well as the theory of technical sciences. The structure of the monograph is presented in Figure P.1.

The descriptions of monetisation formulas, key problems and approaches in this respect were preceded by the presentation of theoretical conditions for the functioning of digital business. The issues of building scientific theories in the field of the digital economy, with an indication of modern trends, tendencies and challenges in this area, are described in Chapter 1. It is important to present various concepts on the basis of which digital business models are designed to understand contemporary global business realities. Concepts such as the Sharing Economy, Big Data, the Circular Economy, the Platform Economy, Deep Learning, and others are core assumptions for the functioning of digital business models. These modern concepts of the so-called new economy are described in Chapter 2. Chapter 3 is devoted to a very important issue of the functioning of digital business models, namely the creation of social aspects. Digital business models, supported by modern ideas, support building a community of users

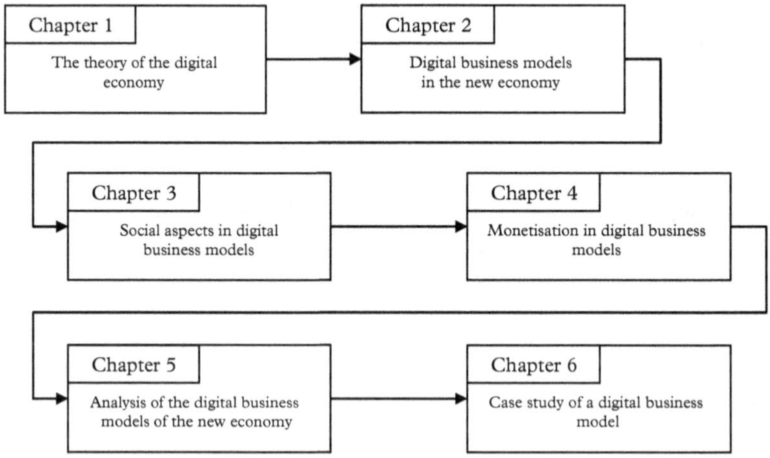

Figure P.1 Structure of the monograph.
Source: Own study.

who, in addition to receiving value from digital solutions, often unite around new ideas, leading to ideas that can affect economic, ethical and environmental issues. The carrier of the value of a digital business model can be such an idea, not just a technological solution or a value proposition itself. The social impact of digital business models on the world is an important factor of their success. Chapter 4 is the essence of the monograph because it reflects the conditions of designing the monetisation formulas of digital business models. It takes into account the issue of the scalability of digital business models, results management and monetisation controlling; it also describes various approaches to the classification of monetisation formulas. Chapter 5 refers to the process of the operationalisation of digital business models in the context of specific companies operating on global markets. An original model of presenting digital business models has been proposed to operationalise digital business models in the context of monetisation. An original canvas has been designed to present the characteristics of digital business models, which takes monetisation formulas into account. The canvas includes quantitative and qualitative aspects. Such a dual description of digital business models allowed for the identification of factors relating to the scalability of business models and determinants which characterise their configuration. To better illustrate the aspects of the functioning of digital business models in the conditions of global competition, a case study based on CD Projekt, which is an excellent example of the success of a digital business model, has been conducted. This company has achieved spectacular global market success in recent years. As a producer of iconic computer games, it has increased its value and volume of users above average levels. It launched the high-quality computer game Witcher (with sales of over 40 million copies), which became even more popular and widely recognised after the broadcast of the Netflix series. The last part of the monograph is the conclusion containing the presentation of key problems, comments, observations and conclusions resulting from theoretical, analytical and research works on the research questions posed.

Adam Jabłoński
Marek Jabłoński
Poznań 2020

1 The theory of the digital economy

Introduction

Changes in the global economy determine the new logic of understanding concepts that fall within the scope of management science. This is related, among others, to the emergence of new rules, not only in the area of theory but business practices as well. The creation of new spaces opens the way to new thinking, innovative reasoning and synthesising creative and entrepreneurial solutions. This results in the need for interdisciplinary modelling towards the emergence of new trends and directions in management. These trends depict a real picture of management science and become a source of reflection for scientists and managers, which generates new values, perspectives and ideas. The concept of business models, which have been developed in theory and practice for almost two decades, is helpful in the context of new ideas for creating value in the market. Ideological solutions which are relevant to the modern world are operationalised by means of business models. A new picture of economics is being created, whereby its earlier assumptions in many cases fell apart, building a path by which to create its new meanings.

The Internet undoubtedly shapes the new reality of business as well as the sphere of everyday life, building new opportunities for societies and individuals who have been excluded so far. It has a social dimension, whereby solutions built into IT platforms operated from the level of mobile applications are available to most citizens. Such business models supported by certain ideas generate the rapid growth of enterprises focused on exploiting their potential.

A holistic view of this issue should help identify these factors of digital business models and their functionality to create customer-friendly value propositions. Digitalisation is the use of digital technologies to change a business model and provide new revenue and value-producing opportunities; it is the process of moving to a digital business (Gardener Glossary, 2018).

Digitisation (i.e. the process of converting analogue data into digital data sets) is the framework for digitalisation, which is defined as the exploitation of digital opportunities. Digitalisation by means of combining different technologies (e.g.

cloud technologies, sensors, Big Data, 3D printing) opens unforeseen possibilities and offers the potential to create radically new products, services and BM (Rachinger et al., 2018).

Industry 4.0 is being encouraged by the introduction of digital technologies that push the specialisation of the value chain and also connectivity between actors. Industry 4.0 heralds greater operational efficiency and the development of new products, services and business models (Martín-Peña, Díaz-Garrido, and Sánchez-López, 2018, pp. 91–99).

The purpose of this chapter is to explain the broad context of the theory of the digital economy and the design of contemporary digital business models, as well as transforming services previously provided by analogue formula and currently created by digital economy solutions. The technological perspective opens new opportunities for creating effective business models used to provide such values that could not be delivered without this technology. Ecosystems will survive thanks to the adaptive abilities and resilience of individuals and their interactions (Boschma, 2015, pp. 733–751). Digital business ecosystems are the new forms of value creation in networks in which digital infrastructure streamlines self-organisation mechanisms (Süße et al., 2017, pp. 25–46).

While evolutionary theory encompasses natural systems, digital ecosystems are artificial. Potential participants in shared digital business ecosystems must first establish mechanisms similar to natural ecosystems. They touch upon the dual role of digital technology as an accelerator of environmental turbulence and allow one to deal with complex, dynamic and rapidly changing environments (El-Sawy and Pereira, 2013, pp. 1–12). Briscoe defines the digital business ecosystem as "a distributed, adaptive, open socio-technical system with properties of self-organisation, scalability and sustainability inspired by natural ecosystems" (Briscoe, 2010, pp. 39–46).

Digital business ecosystems can be understood as a group of companies or organisations linked by a common interest in the well-being of digital technology in order to materialise them for their own product or service innovation (Selander, Henfridsson, and Svahn, 2013, pp. 183–197).

When summarising this issue, it is worth paying attention to the fact that the digital ecosystem is a specific, new and increasingly important business ecosystem. A digital business ecosystem is constructed when the "adoption of Internet-based technologies for business" is on such a level that "business services and the software components are supported by a pervasive software environment, which shows an evolutionary and self-organising behaviour" (Nachira, 2002, p. 23). In this chapter, it will be particularly important to describe the place and role of the digital business ecosystem in the process of digital transformation. This will also be related to the definition of a digital strategy embedded in the digital business ecosystem. The digital strategy described will be based mainly on intangible and digital resources.

Creating theory in management sciences and its new tendencies

In theoretical terms, management mechanisms require researchers' insight and the ability to precisely deduce and draw conclusions. In practical terms, they require an understanding of market and business behaviours, as well as the ability to interpret and operationalise them. It becomes important to overtake practice by properly concluding based on facts and using interpretative prediction focused on creating new theories and concepts. In this picture, a number of questions, dilemmas and doubts arise. Thus, it is of particular importance to constantly raise scientific issues and define the related cognitive gaps. The adopted principles of theory of development provide a platform for dialogue with stakeholders of this theory – both researchers and managers, using these principles to achieve management goals in many dimensions. The essence of empirical sciences involves solving scientific problems in the context of two reference areas. The first consists of facts about phenomena or processes of the real and material world, and are related to practical activity. They are the foundation of every empirical science as they constitute the beginning of the practice of science and help to check its results. This is where observation is conducted, the observational situation is identified, the inductive generalisation of facts is carried out and the value of theory is confirmed by the verification or confirmation of hypotheses. … The second reference area consists of theoretical and methodological constructions which the theory is composed of. It is a peculiar system of laws and a necessary attribute of every scientific discipline (Lisiński, 2018, p. 5). In both the first and second cases, the adoption of an appropriate method is important. Method science plays the role of an atlas of inquiry, where all roads lead to the goal of learning about the reality that surrounds us. However, not all roads lead to it directly, as not all of them are clearly described or recognised by the research community. It is worth knowing how to choose the right road for the studied problem, context, conditions or cognitive attitude (Niemczyk, 2016, p. 17). If the area of epistemological issues is not suitable for creating a universal theory of cognition, it is a place for reflection on the cognitive assumptions underlying the development of various disciplines. Epistemology loses the value of a meta-theory of cognition, and becomes a cognitive self-reflection of a given discipline. The burden of analysis and inquiry is shifted to specialists in a specific field and scientific discipline, and even in a specific research field. When creating their own discourse, they should be able to "put it in parenthesis", criticise, question or discover cognitive assumptions (Sułkowski, 2012, p. 25). It is especially important when it is assumed that:

- management problems are empirical (they have their sources and occur inside and outside the organisation),
- management problems in a pragmatic sense evolve (change) under the influence of changes taking place in the environment (and inside the

organisation), which results in the loss of the assumed effectiveness of the methods of solving them (they require improvement),
- management problems emerge faster than science develops,
- science recognises emerging problems and adapts its research instruments to them,
- science recognises problems with a certain delay and develops methods to solve them (Szarucki, 2016, p. 47).

It should also be remembered that research in management sciences is often accompanied by, for example, theoretical, conceptual, research or statistical models (Zakrzewska-Bielawska, 2018, p. 11). They often reflect management trends. It is worth noting that a critical thread is also used to create the theory. The starting point is the lack of consent to existing forms of organisational orders as being exploitative, unfair, alienating or discriminating against one or another group. The research and development of theories consist of justifying these theses either through empirical research or through the appropriate reinterpretation of previous theories or concepts of organisation and management (Koźmiński and Latusek-Jurczak, 2017, p. 19). Current trends and concepts greatly undermine the achievements of classical economics. Understanding them requires a different perspective than was previously the case. The priority of profitability as a key goal of companies is increasingly not applicable, as the most important issue is to develop social aspects including community building. New possibilities resulting from the use of innovative technological solutions mean that modern concepts serve human beings in the first place – they are humanistic and subordinated to it. In this context, we are not talking only about the customer, but more broadly about the user who may or may not be the aforementioned customer. The classic value chain then has little use because the proposed solutions broaden the range of considerations and applications. In this way, new approaches and paradigms are developed.

Contemporary trends in management sciences from the perspective of new paradigms

Contemporary trends affecting the issues of business management and business creation are primarily based on two streams of knowledge development. The first of these is business digitalisation, which manifests itself in the transfer of traditional business sphere solutions to a virtual environment by means of innovative technologies which enable this process. The second is the development of opportunities to build communities in which the potential for both monetising business and generating social values has not yet been fully explored. These two areas generate opportunities for creating new solutions that are operationalised through the concept of business models.

The development of technology changes the rules of configuring business models because it is mainly the potential of technology that contains unexplored opportunities to create attractive value, which is a driver of transforming ideas into specific formulas for delivering value to customers and other groups of stakeholders. Business digitalisation and socialisation allows for the creation of financial and social profits with the reverse principle of building value by organisations.

In many cases, the first step of entrepreneurial activity is not winning customers as it was according to the traditional approach, but rather building the community and searching for opportunities to monetise the business. Emphasis in this approach is placed on building trust among the community, focused on the proposed projects, and then on creating opportunities to create financial value. The new era of business digitalisation introduces a whole range of technological solutions ranging from the use of social media in improving business models of enterprises to Artificial Intelligence solutions and business robotisation (Ross, 2016). The key question that can be asked in terms of these dynamic changes and emerging trends is: will digitalisation change the existing principles of strategic management? The question is not easy, and is certainly controversial. There is no doubt that it is currently the business model, usually embedded in and depending on technological solutions used, that increases its advantage over business strategies. A coherent solution based on the unique configuration of the business model used, and which is difficult for competitors to copy, creates new space for the development of the concept of strategic management. It should also be noted that, through the operationalisation of the business model, the boundary between traditionally understood areas of operational and strategic management is blurred. In this way, a monolithic arrangement of the joint implementation of the assumptions of the business model and strategy is developed, creating a uniform structure which is sometimes difficult to distinguish for customers, which seems to be a positive aspect. A customer, who is often also a user, co-creator and partner of a given solution, very often finds himself/herself in many places in the value chain alone or together with the supplier. In this situation, as a rule, it is not of a standard nature. The irrelevance of the Porterian value chain for digital applications is such a tangible example of changes in strategic management due to business digitalisation. In some industries, for example the business models of e-book publishing, the value chain is very limited, and it can even be considered to be disappearing in a sense. A book is now ready for sale when an electronic version is created. The entire analogue book production process does not take place, and logistics processes do not occur in the spheres of both core and supporting processes. The polarisation of business is reversed from suppliers and customers to co-creating business and/or social initiatives. Creating new markets in the digital economy has become the fundamental imperative of the dynamic activity of the organisation.

New business models based on a unique array of value delivered through digital technologies undermine the legitimacy of exploiting traditional solutions by displacing or even destroying them (Ng, 2014, p. 157). Social value is being developed, which provides for new opportunities for value exchange. Social, environmental and economic aspects should be balanced, which is manifested in the assumptions of the concept of sustainable business models, as well as the emergence of hybrid solutions based on combining the space of business and public activities. Digital identity enables people to increase their subjectivity and influence on shaping business. The treatment of people as objects is becoming a thing of the past. Individuals are becoming increasingly important in the age of universal access to the Internet and social media activity.

Digitalisation is becoming the benchmark for new paradigms. Until now, scientific revolutions in the humanities were rather immaterial, limited to the theories and methods of conceptualising and understanding cultural reality, which defined research practices and directives, but rarely designed tangible tools as in the exact sciences. Very often, discoveries made with the use of new tools were purely accidental, but they represented a significant breakthrough and often changed the entire discipline (Bomba, 2013). Nowadays digital economy tools change the ways of creating, delivering and capturing value, which is the logic of business models. These tools shape the new reality of economic activity. Digitalisation as a continuous process of convergence of the real and virtual worlds is becoming the main driver of innovation and change in most sectors of the economy. The key factors driving the development of the digital economy are now the Internet of Things (IoT) and Internet of Everything (IoE), hyperconnectivity, applications and services based on cloud computing, Big Data Analytics (BDA) and Big Data-as-a-Service (BDaaS), automation and robotisation, multi-channel and omni-channel distribution models for products and services. The radical, and in some cases disruptive, nature of the changes taking place is of particular importance, bringing completely different values to market entities and consumers than before (Gajewski, Paprocki, and Pieriegud, 2016, p. 11). The so-called economics of the digital economy includes the Sharing Economy, the remix economy, the access economy, the creative economy, the reputation economy, the gift economy, the experience economy, Wikinomics and the trust economy. Four processes triggered by the expansion of the digital economy take place against the background of these "economics", namely disintermediation, prosumption, amateur cult and the appreciation of emotional intelligence (in contrast to the rationality of the industrial era), as well as the appearance of the phenomenon of the so-called gig economy, that is, the short-term electronic economy … It is astonishing that, among a kind of explosion of new "economics", none of them refers to economic sciences, but looks for a foundation in sociology, social psychology and cultural anthropology. Instead of the commonly expected "technicalisation" in the digital age, multidimensional socio-cultural processes are triggered by digitalisation (Jung, 2017, pp. 128–129, p. 138). The indicated technological trends in the area of innovative digital solutions shape the determinants of new paradigms. The science development scheme, according to Kuhn, defines three periods:

1. Pre-paradigmatic.
2. Paradigmatic.
3. Change in the paradigm (Kuhn, 1968).

At the current stage of the dynamically defined concepts and trends of the digital economy, as well as their operationalisation by means of business models, which in many cases have achieved unimaginable economic successes, it can be pointed out that the subject of scientific research related to the digitalisation of business models should be assigned to the pre-paradigmatic period with an already noticeable process of revolutionary changes taking place as part of the transformation of paradigms from the traditional perception of an enterprise to their digital nature, along with a whole range of new concepts, rules and tools for practical implementation. At the same time, Kuhn suggested that the question of whether a given discipline is or is not a science can only be answered when members of the scientific community who doubt its status reach a consensus as to the assessment of their past and current achievements. This science has not yet achieved such a state in the field of the digital economy with the whole array of tools.

Innovative technologies and the concept of business models

The concept of business models has been developing dynamically in the last decade. This development, which should be highlighted, not only lies in this concept and the attractiveness thereof, but in trends that cause changes and are immediately operationalised with them. Different concepts overlap and thus create the formulas of running a business, which are simple in terms of design but result from iterative modelling. Nowadays, to create an attractive business model, it is necessary to embed it in strategic management logic, taking technological solutions into account. Teece described the relationship between a business model, strategy, dynamics of action, and technology in a clear way. Using the concept of dynamic capabilities of such abilities that are important for maintaining competitiveness in a changing environment (Teece, Pisano, and Shuen, 1997, pp. 509–533), he pointed out that dynamic capabilities and strategy combine to create and improve a defensible business model. This model drives organisational transformation and leads to the achievement of the expected level of profits which enable the company to maintain and increase its capabilities and resources (Teece, 2018, p. 44).

Dynamic capabilities are based on a future strategy based on predicting competitors' responses and protecting intellectual property. These two areas influence the shape of the resource-based business model that should be dynamically transformed through the impact of organisational culture and shared values.

Technology is of crucial importance in this context. Currently, innovative technologies and tools of the digital economy shape opportunities for creating an attractive and effective business model. In general, business models are the main topic and a source of novelty in the discussion about the digital market. The current emphasis on innovation is mainly based on business models dedicated to digital business. This is an important determinant of value creation (Keen and Williams, 2013, p. 646). This value is a fundamental aspect of designing business models based on contemporary concepts usually derived from non-management sciences such as psychology, sociology, technical sciences, and others. According to Adam Smith, the word value can have two meanings, namely value-in-use and value-in-exchange. Value-in-exchange is the number of goods and services that can be obtained on the market in exchange for a given item. In other words, it is the price of a given good that can be sold and bought on the market. Value-in-use is the desire for the satisfactory potency of a good. Satisfaction that is obtained by using a good is known as value-in-use. In the case of the digital economy, these general assumptions do not change, but their distribution of importance is very often reformulated from possessing value to other forms of disposition. Modern tools are used to create value-in-use as well as value-in-exchange, where these tools facilitate the effective flow of value.

Contemporary economic concepts and trends based on advanced information technologies are building a new environment of conducting business and social activity. Due to its attributes, it can be called a social business ecosystem. Simultaneously, economic and social results are generated, creating opportunities to shape new formulas for communication and building social bonds. The dynamics of contacts of people interested in a given topic is so large that in many cases it turns into a passion of not only the authors of these models, but above all their users and co-creators, namely communities. Modern business models are not effective without communities. The larger the community and the greater its involvement in a given project, the greater the impact of the model and hence the greater the ability to create value. Co-creation and an ideological layer are a feature of modern business models. Commonly shared values connect people; the communication platform is modern tools and Internet platforms focused on implementing the assumptions of these ideas. Business models that reflect these ideas by means of their operationalisation become an important aspect of the progress and growth dynamics of new areas of scientific exploration in the area of management and business. These concepts and trends that show progress in the field of technology change the approach to strategic management. In this approach, the business model is ahead of the strategy. Business models fully exploit the potential of technological solutions in the context of combining them with other resources and management intentions of managers. Researchers in management science do not have an easy task in this area because the intertwining of resources, management intentions, configurations and social factors of the interaction of business model actors is holistic and not easy to describe by means of simple models.

To demonstrate the wide scope and holistic cognitive nature of the digital economy, a list of theories related to defining the digital ecosystem by Senyo, Liu, and Effah (2019, p. 60) was used. They have been described critically. (See Table 1.1.)

To attempt to broadly describe the theoretical assumptions on the basis of which the digital economy functions, a list of contemporary methods, concepts and approaches to the so-called new economy has been developed (see Table 1.2).

Table 1.1 Critical description of key theories related to the digital economy

No.	*Theory name*	*Description*
1.	Ecology theory	The theory of ecological systems sets out assumptions through which community psychologists can examine the relationships between individuals in communities and society. This theory is also commonly referred to as ecological assumptions based on a system approach. This theory defines five environmental systems which a person interacts with. They are: The Micro System, The Mesosystem, The Exosystem, The Macrosystem, and The Chronosystem. The author of this theory is Urie Bronfenbrenner.
2.	Complex network theory	Complex network theory is focused on aspects related to identifying the features of network topology, the mechanisms of topology generation, and network dynamics. It includes relationships in computer networks, technology networks, network brain, and social networks. Key scientific questions include, but are not limited to, issues such as understanding the relationship between the network structure and its behaviour.
3.	Actor-network theory	Actor network theory (ANT) is a theoretical-methodological concept in the field of social sciences. Its assumptions are based on a constructivist approach. It combines the trends of science, technology, and sociology of scientific knowledge. It was originally created by the French scientists Latour and Callon as an attempt to understand the processes of technological innovation and the creation of scientific knowledge. The actor-network theory adopts the principle of generalised symmetry; that is what is human and non-human (e.g. artifacts, organisational structures) should be integrated into the same conceptual framework and assigned to an equal number of agencies. In this way, a detailed description of specific operating mechanisms that maintain the network as a whole while allowing for the impartial treatment of actors is obtained.
4.	Spectral graph theory	Spectral graph theory is derived from mathematics. It is the study of the properties of a graph in relation to the characteristic polynomial, eigenvalues, and eigenvectors of the matrices associated with the graph, such as its adjacency matrix or Laplacian matrix. The adjacency matrix of a simple graph is a real symmetric matrix and is therefore orthogonally diagonalisable; its eigenvalues are real algebraic integers. While the adjacency matrix depends on the vertex labelling, its spectrum is a graph invariant, although not a complete one. Spectral graph theory is also concerned with graph parameters that are defined via multiplicities of eigenvalues of matrices associated to the graph, such as the Colin de Verdière number.

(continued)

Table 1.1 Continued

No.	*Theory name*	*Description*
5.	Competing values theory	The Competing values theory of Quinn and Rohrbaugh is a theory that was developed on the basis of research on the main indicators of effective organisation. Based on statistical analyses of a comprehensive list of effectiveness indicators, Quinn and Rohrbaugh (1983) discovered two main dimensions underlying conceptions of effectiveness. The first dimension is related to organisational focus, from the internal focus on the well-being and development of people in the organisation to an external focus on the well-being and development of the organisation itself. The second dimension differentiates organisational preferences for structure and represents the contrast between stability and control and flexibility and change. Together, two dimensions form four quadrants, each quadrant of which represents one of the four main models of organisation and management theory (Quinn 1988): 1. Human relations model. 2. Open systems model. 3. Internal process model. 4. Rational goal model (Quinn, 1988).
6.	Claudio Ciborra's theory	C. Ciborra's concept focuses on ex-ante transaction costs. On the one hand, the role of IT as a tool which increases the amount of available and communicable information ("electronic communication effect") is emphasised while reducing the cost of communication – which is important for decision-makers, thus reducing uncertainty and improving the functioning of the market. Information infrastructure can shape not only work procedures and methods of operation, but also how people perceive these practices. In information science, the information infrastructure falls under three other concepts: "information environment", "infosphere", and "information space".
7.	Evolution theory	The theory of evolution includes a well-established scientific view that organic life on our planet has changed for a long time and continues to change in a process known as natural selection. Not only did Charles Darwin point out that evolution had occurred, but he also described the mechanism explaining this process of change.
8.	Resource-based theory	Resource-based theory assumes that having strategic resources gives the organisation a very good opportunity to achieve competitive advantage over competitors (Barney, 1991, pp. 99–120).
9.	Markov chain theory	Markov processes owe their name to their creator Andrei Markov, who first described this problem in 1906. A generalisation to countably infinite state spaces was developed by Kolmogorow in 1936. Markov chains are related to Brownian motion and ergodic hypothesis, which are two important subjects in physics, but arose as a generalisation of the law of large numbers to dependent events.

No.	*Theory name*	*Description*
10.	Architectural innovation theory	Architectural innovation is innovation that changes the way product components are combined, leaving core design concepts (and thus the basic knowledge underlying the components) unchanged. Architectural innovation refers to destroying the usefulness of a company's architectural knowledge, but preserving the usefulness of knowledge of product components. A component is defined as a physically distinct portion of a product that represents the core design concept and performs a well-defined function.
11.	Zachman framework	The premise of the Zachman Framework is to identify enterprise ontology, which is the fundamental structure for enterprise architecture that provides a formal and structured way of viewing and defining enterprise activity. Ontology is a two-dimensional classification schema that reflects the intersection between two historical classifications. The first are primitive interrogatives: What, How, When, Who, Where, and Why. The second is derived from the philosophical concept of reification, the transformation of an abstract idea into an instantiation. The Zachman framework reification transformations are: Identification, Definition, Representation, Specification, Configuration, and Instantiation.
12.	Boundary spanning practice	The concept of the role of boundaries is developed in the course of academic research into innovation systems. With the exception of closed systems, all systems cross their boundaries, and this process is facilitated by a boundary key. As innovation models developed, the role of the boundary key remained crucial in seeking and introducing new ideas into the system or subsystem. Boundary keys are needed to transfer explicit and tacit knowledge within an organisation in a process sometimes referred to as socialisation.
13.	Transaction cost theory	Transaction cost theory is part of corporate governance and agency theory. It is based on the principle that costs will arise when someone provides a service to another entity. It describes the management framework as based on the net effects of internal and external transactions, rather than as contractual relations outside the company (i.e. with shareholders).

Source: Own study.

While the theory of evolution is connected with natural systems, digital ecosystems are of artificial origin. Potential participants in shared digital business ecosystems must first establish mechanisms similar to natural ecosystems. They face the dual role of digital technology as an accelerator of environmental turbulence, which enables them to cope with complex, dynamic and rapidly changing environments (Lenkenhoff et al., 2018, pp. 167–172).

Table 1.2 List of approaches and concepts appropriate for the functioning of digital technology

No.	*Name of theory/ concept*	*Description*
1.	Network economy	The premise of the network economy is to change the seller-buyer relationship which is suitable for the market economy to the supplier-user relationship implemented in the network of connections.
2.	Social economy	The premise of the social economy is activity that is subordinated, in whole or in part, to social goals implemented using economic instruments. A social business model can be such an instrument.
3.	Artificial intelligence	The premise of artificial intelligence is the use of systems or machines that imitate human intelligence during the performance of tasks and that can iteratively improve on the basis of information collected over time.
4.	Cognitive computing	The premise of cognitive computing is to use a set of technologies that are the result of studying the operation of the human brain. It is a combination of artificial intelligence and signal processing. They combine a set of modern tools: self-learning machines, reasoning and inferring, natural language processing, speech, computer-human interactions, and many more. They are all aspects of cooperation between machines and man. It refers to technologies that mimic the way information is processed in the human brain and increase the quality of human decision-making.
5.	Augmented intelligence	The premise of augmented intelligence is to define technical and social conditions to ensure effective cooperation between man and machine.
6.	Internet of Things	The premise of the Internet of Things is to connect material objects with each other and with online resources using an extensive computer network. The Internet of Things involves connecting all devices that can be used to communicate with each other into one complex system.
7.	Remix economy	The premise of the remix economy is to use existing objects, e.g. songs (music, literature, etc.) and combine them in such a way that a completely new object is created – e.g. a new song.
8.	Sharing Economy – Access Economy	The premise of the Sharing Economy is business models in which activity is conducted through the intermediation of cooperation platforms, creating a publicly available market for the temporary use of goods or services provided by private individuals or institutions.

No.	*Name of theory/ concept*	*Description*
9.	Creative Economy	The premise of the Creative Economy is the development of creative industries focused on satisfying the needs and expectations of consumers, their experiences closely associated with the achievement of high quality and implementation of various lifestyles, e.g. music, film, entertainment, recreation, organisation of meetings and events, and processes of providing creative services for companies and business, e.g. industrial design, computer graphics, fashion design, software production, advertising industry, architectural services.
10.	Reputational Economy – Trust Economy	The premise of the Reputational Economy is to build trust capital in the network in order to break the digital anonymity of contact. It is a substitute for direct face-to-face experience.
11.	Experience Economy	The premise of the Experience Economy is to build an economic model in which the most important economic value in terms of generating demand is to build a positive customer experience.
12.	GIG Economy	The premise of the GIG Economy is to use the economy based on the performance of tasks and projects increasingly offered through digital platforms rather than on a full-time job. This form of employment, largely based on the principles of choice or freedom of choice, is used by freelancers or, more broadly, giggers – people who undertake various tasks for others without the participation of the traditional employer model.
13.	Platform Economy	The assumption of online platforms is to facilitate cooperation between entities interested in using a given good under the Sharing Economy, Big Data or the Circular Economy, using a mechanism based on an automated system of notifications, registration, or verification of users.

Source: Own study.

The digital age is changing social and economic activities. When questions like "Who are our customers? How to communicate with them? What to offer them and what transactions can happen?" remain the same, digital business models have changed the way these problems are solved (Härting, Reichstein, and Schad, 2018, pp. 1495–1506). In addition, a fundamental transformation of services is currently underway, which is key to increasing productivity and competition in the global economy. This transformation is fuelled by the development of information technology (IT) tools, the applications which they are used for, and the networks where they operate. The transformation of services changes the way companies add value, changing the core economic activity of countries around the world (Kushida and Zysman, 2009, p. 174). Transformation refers to cases when digital technologies are used to enable new ways of doing business in place of traditional ones. This is made possible, among others, by means of AET classification (automation, extension, and transformation), where research aims to systematically capture the role of digital technologies in business model innovations (Li, 2017). The attributes of business models that come from the literature review include, in part, attributes that refer to value proposition and dimension of delivery (offer, values, product/service, goal, and customers), others are part of creating the value of the model (key resources and activities), and the last ones represent the dimension of value capture (revenue and valuation model) (Täuscher and Laudien, 2018, pp. 319–329). The classification of business models which operate based on digital platforms shows how many solutions it is possible to create through the use of innovative technologies. There are many more of these solutions than in the context of using analogue solutions based on human-human interfaces. As regards the digital economy, we deal with human-machine interfaces, and with the use of the Internet of Things concept, the machine-machine interface. The attribute of cloud computing should not be overestimated, whereby large data sets and the use thereof allows for their directional application for commercial and social purposes. Table 1.3 presents the key features of digital business models.

The presented categorisation indicates the attributes of business models in relation to the volume of value creation, value delivery, and value capture from the market through a combination of technological solutions which create specific configurations of solutions. The multitude of options presented confirms the high level of development potential that lies behind digital economy solutions. In addition, an important element has been added to the presented features of digital business models, namely value monetisation. Within this criterion, three important elements have been identified – the monetisation scheme, user volume, and range of impact. By defining the scale for these items, it is possible to identify the potential of the digital business model in terms of this criterion.

The dynamics of modern management are definitely dominated by digital solutions. Digital transformation has opened the way for the creation of new businesses, the logic of which is completely different from previous analogue processes. From this perspective, e-business is particularly important; it is visible primarily in relation to concluded transactions used for the monetisation of company business models.

To understand and adopt the logic of digital business operations, it is important to define its core definitions and interpretative assumptions in relation to distinctive features as shown in Table 1.4.

The analysis of selected e-business definitions clearly indicates the orientation of transaction theory in creating economic value. This cognitive perspective indicates the relationship between the dimension of digitalisation and the

Table 1.3 Key features of digital business models

	Features of the business model	*Specification*				
Value creation dimension	Platform type	Internet platform	Mobile application			
	Core activity	Data transmission services	Community building	Content creation		
	Price fixing	Price fixing	Price fixing by sellers	Price fixing by buyers	Auction	Negotiations
	Rating system	User opinions	Market opinions	None		
Value delivery dimension	Value proposition	Price/Cost/Performance	Emotional value	Social value		
	Transaction content	Product	Service			
	Transaction type	Digital	Offline			
	Range of the industry	Vertical	Horizontal			
	Market participants	C2C	B2C	B2B		
	Geographical scope	Global	Regional	Local		
Value capture dimension	Revenue stream	Commissions	Prepayments	Advertising	Sale of services	
	Price policy	Fixed price list	Market valuation	Differentiated price list		
	Price-based discrimination	Based on the features	Based on the location	Based on quantity	None/Other	
	Source of revenue	Seller	Buyer	Third party	None/Other	
Value monetisation	Monetisation formula	Widely used	Combination of solutions	Unique/innovative		
	User volume	Small	Medium	Large		
	Range of the company's impact	Local/regional	National	International		

Source: Own study based on Täuscher and Laudien, 2018, pp. 319–329.

Table 1.4 List of selected e-business definitions in relation to its distinctive feature

Author	*Definition of e-Business*	*Distinctive feature*
IBM, 2008	A secure, flexible, and integrated approach to delivering diversified business value by combining systems and processes that conduct core business operations with simplicity and range, made possible thanks to Internet technology.	Connection, synergy of systems and processes
Price Waterhouse Coopers, 1999	From now on, e-business will be defined as the use of information technologies to facilitate the purchase and sale of products, services, and information based on public network standards.	Business transaction factor
Wirtz, 2000	[...] is defined as the initiation, negotiation and/or business transaction between economic entities that are carried out electronically via telecommunications networks.	Communication and transaction factor
Rayport, Jaworski, 2001	E-business can be formally defined as the mediation of exchange by technology between parties (persons, organisations, or both parties), as well as electronic intra- or inter-organisational activities facilitating such exchange.	Exchange factor
Jelassi, Enders, 2004	The use of electronic means to conduct the organisation's activities internally and/or externally.	Factor of entrepreneurship development
Chen, 2005	Activity conducted using electronic networks or electronic media. Sometimes used as a synonym for e-commerce and sometimes used more widely to include other business activities in addition to buying and selling.	Communication and transaction factor
Papazoglou, Ribbers, 2006	E-business can be defined as running an automated business, as transactions via electronic communications networks (e.g. via the Internet and/or possibly private networks) from beginning to end.	Factor of business process automation
Chaffey, 2009	All electronic information exchange, both within the organisation and with external stakeholders supporting the scope of business processes.	Stakeholder relationship factor
Laudon, Traver 2014	[...] It is the use of the Internet, websites, and mobile applications to conduct business transactions.	Business transaction factor
Schneider, 2017	The term e-commerce [...] covers all business activities which use Internet technologies. Internet technologies include the Internet, the network, and other technologies such as wireless transmissions in a mobile network.	Complex management factor

Source: Own study based on Wirtz, 2019.

commercialisation of business models with the strong impact of technology. Westerman, Bonnet, and McAfee (2014) suggest three areas in which managers can use new digital technologies:

- Customer experience: companies can apply information and communication digitalisation to engage their customers in an innovative way, for example, by creating digital user communities to provide added value.
- Operational processes: digital technologies significantly increase the operational efficiency of processes at all stages of the value chain.
- Business models: digitalisation enables the development of completely new forms of value creation and recording. This includes, for example, the entire reconfiguration of the value delivery model and completely innovative value propositions (Westerman, Bonnet, and McAfee, 2014).

This approach generates new business structures. Weill and Woerner classified four types of new generation enterprises on a matrix:

- Suppliers
- Omnichannels
- Modular producers
- Ecosystem drivers (Weill and Woerner, 2018).

New groups of enterprises are connected with thematic segments of creating digital business models. Internet industry business models in the B2C sector can be divided into the following segments based on the 4C-Net business model: content, context, commerce, and connection (Wirtz, 2000a).

As part of the content of the business model, content compilation and content display should be performed. In terms of the context, it is necessary to classify and systematise the information which is available on the Internet. In terms of commerce, it will be important to initiate and/or settle business transactions. As regards connections, opportunities should be provided for exchanging information in networks (Wirtz, 2000b).

It is also worth paying attention to hybrid solutions, which can be created in various combinations of both the type of organisation and their business process structure. Such mechanisms are particularly effective in achieving high business performance and methods of monetisation of their business model.

The widespread use of digitalisation means that it has a scope related to individual entities, small and medium-sized enterprises, international corporations, as well as authorities. Digital business models must also take into account this aspect of understanding the digital economy, as depicted in Table 1.5.

In addition to identifying scientific theories relevant to the digital economy, attention should be paid to differences in the understanding of individual components of digital business models. A popular model of business model description, the Business Model Canvas by A. Osterwalder and Y. Pigneur (Osterwalder and Pigneur, 2010), should be adapted to the specificity of the

Table 1.5 Potential impacts on value creation and capture in an expanding digital economy – components and actors

	Digital economy component	*Core, digital sector*	*Digital economy*	*Digitalised economy*
ACTORS	Individuals (as users/ consumers, and workers)	- New jobs for building and installing ICT infrastructure. - New jobs in the telecom and ICT sector, especially ICT services.	- New jobs in digital services, especially for highly skilled people. - New forms of digital work, including for the less skilled.	- New jobs in ICT occupations across industries. - Need for new skills as higher-value roles are redesigned using digital tools. - Greater efficiency of services received. - Job losses of transformation due to digitalisation. - Risk of worsened working conditions. - Improved connectivity. - More choice, convenience, customisation of products for users and consumers. - Lower consumer prices.
	MSMEs	- Greater inclusion under suitable circumstances or spillovers/domestic linkages. - Increased competition from cloud-service provides.	- New opportunities in digital ecosystems. - Increased competition from foreign digital firms.	- Platform-enabled market access. - Reduced transaction costs. - Risk of "race to the bottom" in markets vs. ability to find a niche. - Lost opportunities due to automation (e.g. logistics, business processes). - New roles in service provision. - New business opportunities for digitalised enterprises.
	Multinational enterprises/digital platforms	- Investment opportunities for companies that meet high capital, technological and skills requirements.	- Enhanced productivity from data-driven business models.	- Emergence of platform firms with data-driven models. - Gains from efficiency, productivity and quality. - Opportunities for the monetisation of data.

		- Greater control of value chains using platform-based business models. - New opportunities in the sharing economy.	- Increased competitive advantage of digital platforms. - Increased market power and control of data value chain. - Leading digitalisation in different sectors.
Governments	- Attracting investment. - Tax revenues from the economic activity created.	- More tax revenue resulting from increased economic activity and formalisation of enterprises. - Loss customs revenue from digitalisation of products.	- Increased efficiency of services through e-government. - Increased revenue from customs automation. - Unclear impact on tax revenue: increases from higher economic activity; losses from tax optimisation practices by digital platforms and MNEs. - Data-driven opportunities to meet various SDGs.
ECONOMY-WIDE IMPLICATIONS	- Increased growth, productivity, and value added. - Employment creation. - Investment and diffusion of technologies; R&D likely located in high-income countries. - Mixed trade impacts.	- Higher growth, productivity and value added. - Employment creation/losses. - Higher investment. - Aggregation of digital firms in some locations. - Mixed trade impacts. - Market concentration.	- Growth through improved efficiency in sectors and value chains. - Productivity improvements. - Innovation impacts. - Potential crowding out of local firms in digitally disrupted sectors. - Potential automation in low and medium-skill jobs. - Wider inequality. - Mixed trade impacts. - Impacts on structural change.

Source: Own study based on *Digital Economy Report, Value Creation and Capture: Implications for Developing Countries*, United Nations, New York, 2019, p. 5.

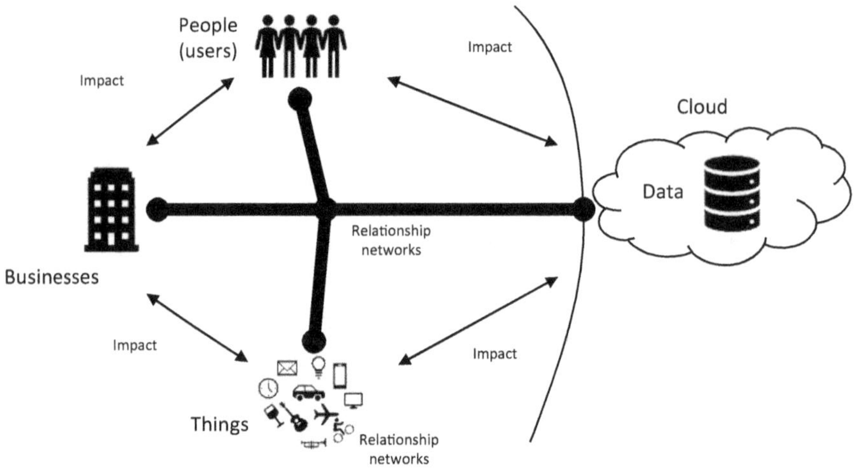

Figure 1.1 Digital key elements.
Source: Own study based on Blaschke et al., 2017, p. 126.

digital economy. A description of the key components of the digital business model was proposed by Blaschke and colleagues, as in Figure 1.1.

When undertaking a critical analysis of the proposed model, it seems reasonable to indicate the need to add a network of relationships that binds all related elements together to the model proposed by Blaschke and colleagues. People, business, cloud computing and things create the configuration of the ecosystem within which a network of relationships with a unique structure is developed. They are of organisational and technological nature. Technological relationships are built through interfaces and result from the technology used, while organisational relationships result from the designed component digital business model. The defined elements interact, making the digital business model dynamic. Interactions put the business model in motion in the sense that the level of knowledge increases as a result of experience in the interaction of these components. The level of maturity of the digital business model increases due to the interactions in the relationship network.

The more unique the structure of the digital business model – often designed with resources outside the organisation – the greater the chance to create an innovative position of value. Table 1.6 presents the digital components of the digital business model in the context of the nine-component business model template by Osterwalder and Pigneur.

There is a significant difference in the perception and description of digital business models in the context of the classical canvas of the business model by Pigneur and Osterwalder. The classical components of the business model,

Table 1.6 The two dimensions of digital value drivers

Business Model Components	Digital Key Elements
Value Proposition	Data
Customer Segments	Cloud
Revenue Streams	People
Channels	Business
Customer Relationships	Things
Key Partners	Network
Key Resources	
Key Activities	
Cost Structure	

Source: Own study based on Blaschke et al., 2017, p. 128.

as defined in the canvas of the business model, should be extended with six components belonging to the specificity of digital business models including components such as Data, Cloud, People, Business, Things and Network. The fundamental but key element is the network of relationships that unites all components into a coherent whole. Table 1.7 presents the characteristics of the components of the digital business model.

The described model of digital business model configuration is completely different from the traditional approach to business models. In their case, the key role is played by technology and the dynamics of interaction between actors in the network.

Referring to a different approach to defining the digital business model in a visual way, its configuration, which consists of digital value proposition, a digital organisation, necessary data, core digital ability, the demonstration of digital value and willingness to share data, has been presented. Key questions that digital business model designers should answer include value proposition, performance, customer needs, and how value is demonstrated in Figure 1.2.

In this context, it is worth paying attention to the need to supplement the presented scheme with the size of the user community centred around the digital business model. A condition of implementing an effective monetisation strategy will be having an appropriate community that will financially support the digital business model through its activities. The digital business ecosystem is not only based on the traditional value chain, but also on the complex system of relationships between network actors over time. It should be noted that the roles of individual actors result from the accepted logic of value delivery and the adopted monetisation scheme. An important role is also played by the aspect of building a community that makes mutual relationships dynamic and initiates actions and reactions

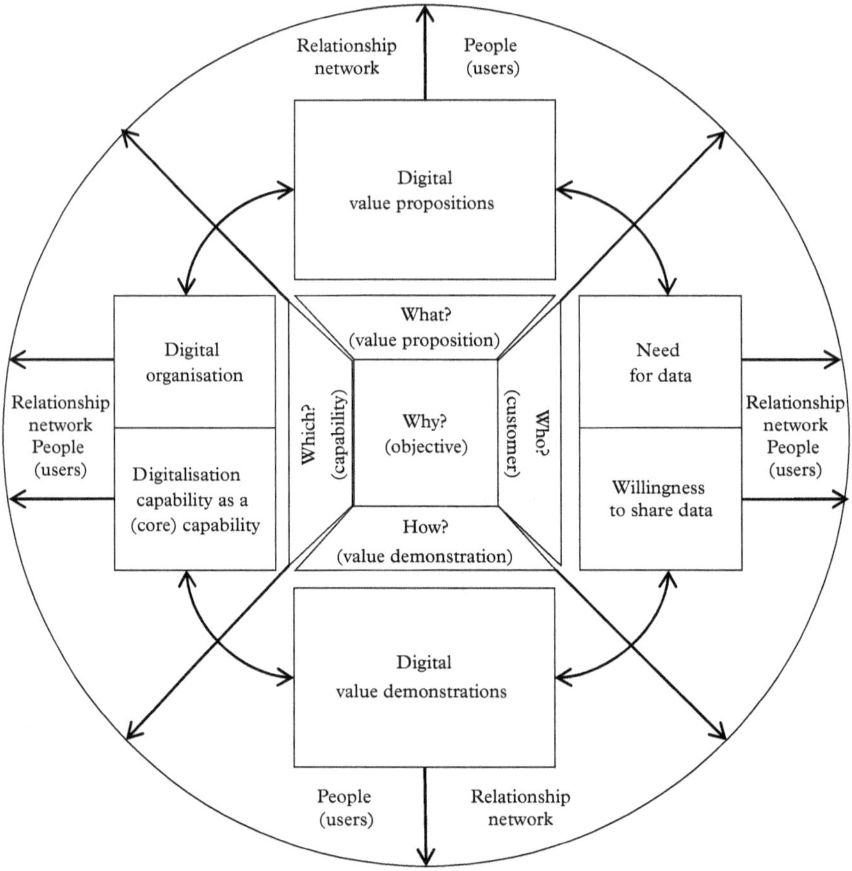

Figure 1.2 Digital business models.
Source: Own study based on Ritter and Pedersen 2019, p. 5.

Conclusions

The discussion presented in the chapter highlights the important role of the digital economy in creating new approaches and management theory. Previous theories and concepts of economics and management do not fully apply to the assumptions of the modern digital economy. Innovative technologies are conducive to the emergence of new formulas for doing business and creating economic and social value. Assumptions for designing digital business models also cannot be fully based on the popular canvas model, which should be expanded to include technological aspects and the network paradigm. In this context, a new perspective emerges on shaping business models functioning in the digital economy.

Table 1.7 Description of Digital Key Components

Key Component of the Digital Business Model	*Description*
Data	Data refer to records in databases and data management processes. Data can also build business assets that can be used in a digital business model. This data can be used for analysis, planning, and forecasting, including cognitive calculations. The data used may also include advanced analytical procedures that process small or large amounts of data and generate information which is useful to the creators of the digital business model. Data includes types such as Big Data and Smart Data.
Cloud	Cloud is a type of technical infrastructure. In the context of the digital business model, it is also a service that creates specific value. It supports digital content, on-demand services, business scaling services, and "pay for consumption" services. Moreover, services can be provided through cloud computing anywhere in the world.
People	The term People is used as an abbreviation for digitally connected people, i.e. communities, which leave specific marks through their activity in the digital world. People build communities using different types of devices. A condition for people to join the world of the digital economy is to have devices that ensure continuous access to services rendered at their disposal. In this way, open relationships with other people in the network are built.
Business	The term Business is used as an abbreviation for "digitally connected companies/groups of companies" that combine digital capabilities to create new and innovative solutions. Companies connect digitally with other companies, as well as individuals and resources, using various types of digital means: the Internet, XML standards, and other forms of building digital interfaces to create economic and social value.
Things	Things in the context of the digital economy are no longer static objects, but they become the foundation of the digital world. In this way, they interact intelligently with people, companies, or other objects. Things intelligently shape the network together with people and organisations. They can interact without people. Things also include intelligent robots, autonomous vehicles and drones, and other things as well. An example of things embedded in digital economy systems is the concept of the Internet of Things (IoT), which connects individual physical objects for the purpose of interacting with other objects, people, and companies. The goal of this solution is to create value from a wide exchange of information.
Network	The network unites all components of a digital business model. Key actors playing different roles are identified in the network. The role of actors can change over the duration of the bond in the life cycle of the digital business model.

Source: Own study based on Blaschke, 2017, pp. 126–128.

References

Barney, J.B. (1991). "Firm Resources and Sustained Competitive Advantage", *Journal of Management*, 17, 99–120. DOI: 10.1177/014920639101700108.

Blaschke, M., Cigaina, M., Riss, U.V., and Shoshan, I. (2017). "Designing Business Models for the Digital Economy", in G. Oswald and M. Kleinemeier (eds.), *Shaping the Digital Enterprise*, Switzerland: Springer, pp. 126–136. DOI: 10.1007/978-3-319-40967-2_6.

Bomba, R. (2013). "*Narzędzia cyfrowe jako wyznacznik nowego paradygmatu badań humanistycznych*", in A. Radomski and R. Bomba (eds.), *Zwrot cyfrowy w humanistyce*, Lublin: E-naukowiec. Available at: http://e-naukowiec.eu/zwrot-cyfrowy-w-humanistyce/

Boschma, R. (2015). "Towards an Evolutionary Perspective on Regional Resilience", *Regional Studies*, 49, 733–751. DOI: 10.1080/00343404.2014.959481.

Briscoe, G. (2010). "Complex Adaptive Digital EcoSystems", in *Proceedings of the International Conference on Management of Emergent Digital EcoSystems, MEDES'10*, ACM, New York, pp. 39–46, DOI:10.1145/1936254.1936262.

Chaffey, D. (2009). *e-Business and e-Commerce Management* (4th ed.), Essex: Prentice Hall.

Chen, S. (2005). *Strategic Management of e-Business* (2nd ed.), Chichester: John Wiley & Sons.

Delfs, J., Neubauer, B., and Mueller, J. (1999). "E-Business: Aktivitäten im Mittelstand", in PriceWaterhouseCoopers, *Leitfaden E-Business: Erfolgreiches Management*, Frankfurt am Main.

Digital Economy Report (2019). *Value Creation and Capture: Implications for Developing Countries*, New York: United Nations Publications, p. 5.

El-Sawy, O. and Pereira, F. (2013). "Anticipating Game Changers for 'Enterprise 2020' in a Digitally-Intensive World", in *Business Modelling in the Dynamic Digital Space*, Berlin: Springer, pp. 1–12.

Gardener Glossary, Digitalization (2018). Available at: www.gartner.com/it-glossary/digitalization/ (accessed 14 November 2018).

Härting, R.Ch., Reichstein, Ch., and Schad, M. (2018). "Potentials of Digital Business Models: Empirical Investigation of Data Driven Impacts in Industry", *Procedia Computer Science*, 126, 1495–1506. DOI: 10.1016/j.procs.2018.08.121. Available at: https://poradnikprzedsiebiorcy.pl/-peer-to-peer-definicja-historia-powstania-i-wplyw-na-rozwoj-internetu-cz-1

IBM Global CEO Study (2008). "The Enterprise of the Future: New York", www.935.ibm.com/services/de/bcs/html/ceostudy.html (accessed 7 October 2009).

Jelassi, T. and Enders, A. (2005). *Strategies for e-Business: Creating Value through Electronic and Mobile Commerce. Concept and Cases*, Essex: Prentice Hall, p. 142.

Jung, B. (2017). "Ekonomiki wokół gospodarki cyfrowej", *Ekonomiczne Problemy Usług*, 1(126), 7–140. DOI: 10.18276/epu.2017.126/1-14.

Keen, P. and Williams, R. (2013). "Value Architectures for Digital Business: Beyond the Business Model", *MIS Quarterly*, 37(2), June, 643–648.

Koźmiński, A.K. and Latusek-Jurczak, D. (2017). *Rozwój teorii organizacji, Od systemu do sieci*, Warszawa: Poltext.

Kushida, K.E. and Zysman, J. (2009). "The Services Transformation and Network Policy: The New Logic of Value Creation", *Review of Policy Research*, 26(1–2), 173–194. DOI: 10.1111/j.1541-1338.2008.00374.x.

Kuhn, T.S. (1968). *Struktura rewolucji naukowych*, Warszawa: PWN.

Laudon, K.C. and Traver, C.G. (2014). *e-Commerce: Business, Technology, Society* (10th ed.), Harlow: Pearson.

Lenkenhoff, K., Wilkensa, U., Zheng, M., Süße, T., Kuhlenkötter, B., and Ming, X. (2018). "Key Challenges of Digital Business Ecosystem Development and How to Cope the Function with Them", *Procedia CIRP*, 73, 167–172. DOI: 10.1016/j.procir.2018.04.082.

Li, F. (2017). "The Digital Transformation of Business Models in the Creative Industries: A Holistic Framework and Emerging Trends", *Technovation*. DOI: 10.1016/j.technovation.2017.12.004.

Lisiński, M. (2018). "Prawa nauk o zarządzaniu", *Przegląd Organizacji*, 5, 5: 3–12.

Martín-Peña, M.L., Díaz-Garrido, E., and Sánchez-López, J.M. (2018). "The Digitalization and Servitization of Manufacturing: A Review on Digital Business Models", *Strategic Change*, 27(2), 91–99. DOI: 10.1002/jsc.2184.

Nachira, F. (2002). *Towards a Network of Digital Business Ecosystems Fostering the Local Development*, Bruxelles: European Commission Discussion Paper, pp. 1–23.

Ng, I.C.L. (2014). *Creating New Markets in the Digital Economy: Value and Worth*, Cambridge: Cambridge University Press.

Niemczyk, J. (2016). "Metodologia nauk o zarządzaniu", in Wojciech Czakon and Wydawnictwo Nieoczywiste (eds.), *Podstawy metodologii badań w naukach o zarządzaniu*, Piaseczno: Wydawnictwo Nieoczywiste.

Osterwalder, A. and Pigneur, Y. (2010). *Business Model Generation*, New Jersey: John Wiley & Sons.

Papazoglou, M. and Ribbers, P. (2006). *e-Business: Organizational and Technical Foundations* (1st ed.), New Jersey: Hoboken.

Quinn, R. E. and Rohrbaugh, J. (1983). "A spatial model of effectiveness criteria: Towards a competing values approach to organizational analysis", *Management Science*, 29(3), 363–377.

Quinn, R.E. (1988). *Beyond Rational Management: Mastering the Paradoxes and Competing Demands of High Performance*, San Francisco: Jossey-Bass.

Rachinger, M., Rauter, R., Müller, Ch., Vorraber, W., and Schirgi, E. (2018). "Digitalization and its Influence on Business Model Innovation", *Journal of Manufacturing Technology Management*, 30(8), 1143–1160. DOI: 10.1108/JMTM-01-2018-0020.

Rayport, J.F. and Jaworski, B.J. (2001). *Introduction to e-Commerce*, Boston: McGraw-Hill/Irwin.

Ritter, T. and Pedersen, C.L. (2019). "Digitization Capability and the Digitalization of Business Models in Business to-business Firms: Past, Present, and Future", *Industrial Marketing Management*, 86(4). DOI: 10.1016/j.indmarman.2019.11.019.

Ross, A. (2016). *The Industries of the Future*, New York: Simon & Schuster UK.

Schneider, G.P. (2017). *Electronic Commerce*, Australia: Cengage Learning.

Selander, L., Henfridsson, O., and Svahn, F. (2013). "Capability Search and Redeem Across Digital Ecosystems", *Journal of Information Technology*, 28, 183–197. DOI. 10.1057/jit.2013.14.

Senyo, P.K., Liu, K., and Effah, J. (2019). "Digital Business Ecosystem: Literature Review and a Framework for Future Research", *International Journal of Information Management*, 47, 52–64. DOI: 10.1016/j.ijinfomgt.2019.01.002.

Sułkowski, Ł. (2012). *Epistemologia i metodologia zarządzania*, Warszawa: Polskie Wydawnictwo Ekonomiczne.

Süße, T., Weber, P., Lasi, H., and Wilkens, U. (2017). "Enterprise Interoperabilität in Internetbasierten Ökosystemen", in N. Gronau (ed.), *Industrial Internet of Things in der Arbeits- und Betriebsorganisation*, Berlin: GITO-Verlag, pp. 25–46.

Szarucki, M. (2016). "Koncepcja doboru metod w rozwiązywaniu problemów zarządzania", *Wydawnictwo Uniwersytetu Ekonomicznego w Krakowie, Kraków*, 247.

Szpringer, W. (2019). *Blockchain jako innowacja systemowa, Od Internetu Informacji do Internetu Wartości, Wskazania dla Sectora finansowego*, Warszawa: Wydawnictwo Poltext.

Täuscher K. and Laudien S.M. (2018). "Understanding Platform Business Models: A Mixed Methods Study of Marketplaces", *European Management Journal*, 36(3), 319–329. DOI: 10.1016/j.emj.2017.06.005.

Teece, D.J. (2018). "Business Models and Dynamic Capabilities", *Long Range Planning*, 51(1), 40–49. DOI: 10.1016/j.lrp.2017.06.007.

Teece, D.J., Pisano, G., and Shuen, A. (1997). "Dynamic Capabilities and Strategic Management", *Strategic Management Journal*, 18(7), 509–533. DOI: 0143-2095/97/070509-25.

Weill, P. and Woerner, S. (2018). *What's Your Digital Business Model?: Six Questions to Help You Build the Next-Generation Enterprise*, Boston: Harvard Business Review Press.

Westerman, G, Bonnet, D., and McAfee, A. (2014). *Leading Digital: Turning Technology into Business Transformation*, Boston: Harvard Business Review Press.

Wirtz, B.W. (2000a). *Electronic Business* (1st ed.), Wiesbaden: Gabler.

Wirtz, B.W. (2000b). "Rekonfigurationsstrategien und multiple Kundenbindung in multimedialen Informations- und Kommunikationsmärkten", *Zeitschrift für betriebswirtschaftliche Forschung (ZfbF)*, 52(5), 290–306. DOI: 10.1007/BF03372619.

Wirtz, B.W. (2019). *Digital Business Models: Concepts, Models, and the Alphabet Case Study*, Switzerland: Springer Nature. DOI: 10.1007/978-3-030-13005-3.

Zakrzewska-Bielawska, A. (2018). "Modele badawcze w naukach o zarządzaniu", *Organizacja i Kierowanie*, 2(181), 11–26.

2 Digital business models in the new economy

Introduction

The digital economy is developing very dynamically, which is reflected in the conceptualisation and operationalisation of innovative business models. The key trends of the digital economy based on the ideological assumptions of modern consumerism include the Sharing Economy, the Circular Economy, Big Data, Sustainable Business Models, and Social Business Models. In the context of the dynamics of the development of these solutions, the number of business models designed is growing rapidly. They use both the technological and ideological potential of these concepts, shaping the new economic order in markets, destroying the existing order of things. This leads to change in the market position of traditional business models of enterprises, which makes them volatile and non-scalable. New solutions based on the digitalisation of the economy drive the existing players out of business and reduce their competitiveness. These changes, resulting from the widespread availability of mobile phones and the Internet, are building a new framework for developing entrepreneurial business solutions. Different sectors of the economy are susceptible to digital transformation to a different extent, and at the same time they are threatened by the development of digital technologies. According to the results of research conducted among senior managers in spring 2015 by the Global Centre for Digital Business Transformation, by 2020, digitalisation may drive about 40% of companies that currently have a strong position in their sectors out of business. The most radical changes may take place primarily in "data-driven industries" such as new technologies (including products and services), media and entertainment, financial services, telecommunications, as well as retail trade. According to the Fri Digital Vortex report, it is these sectors that rely most on the Internet of Everything, that is, networks linking residents, objects, data, and processes used for the digital exchange of values. On the other hand, sectors that are most "resistant" to digital transformation include the oil and gas sectors, the pharmaceutical sector, and the utilities sector (enterprises from the energy, gas, heating and plumbing sectors) (Gajewski, Paprocki, and Pieriegud, 2016, p. 14). The new and unique services of the digital economy include activities such as e-commerce, as was initiated by Alibaba, Amazon, and

Rakuten, which sell effectively, offering inexpensive services; search engines with online advertising such as Google and Yahoo, with lowered prices; free search engines, such as Wikipedia and Linux; social networks, such as Twitter, Facebook, LinkedIn, and YouTube; cloud computing platforms such as Amazon, Apple, Cisco, IBM, Google, and Microsoft provide services that convert fixed costs into marginal costs.[1] This has a key impact on the scalability of digital business models. The combination of systems within cyberspace, Big Data, Data Mining, data analytics, the Internet of Things (IoT), and new business models can provide great opportunities for creating the more sustainable production of industrial value, value capture, and the Circular Economy (Antikainen, Uusitalo, and Kivikyto-Reponen, 2018, p. 45).

The purpose of this chapter is to identify key perspectives for the development of digital business models in the context of the conditions of the new economy. The digital economy stimulates many concepts and solutions that, when properly adopted, allow for the creation of innovative solutions in the sphere of business.

Prospects for the development of business models in the digital economy

Digital business models differ in essence from the business models of traditional sectors of the economy. According to Timmers, a digital business model is a configuration of the architecture of a product, services, and information flow, including a description of various business entities and their roles and a description of potential benefits for various business entities, as well as a description of sources of income (Timmers, 1998, p. 4). Digital business models are characterised by a specific arrangement of features. El-Sawy and Pereira defined the framework for action in the digital economy, which consists of an interface-based business ecosystem, the role of digital service platforms, and the need to build a community – an ecosystem of many actors. In terms of their approach, digital business models are based on the identification of five key components which they called VISOR (2013): value proposition, interface (between a customer and a service platform), service platforms, an organising model, and a revenue model.

Attention should also be paid to classification in the context of multilateral markets: the value creation dimension (platform type, key activities, price presentation method, verification system); the value delivery dimension (key value proposition, transaction content, transaction type, industry scope, market participants, geographical coverage); the value capture dimension (key revenue stream, price mechanism); the type of price discrimination, if applicable (e.g. location, quantity, other); and the source of revenue (Täuscher and Laudien, 2018, pp. 319–329).

The design of digital business models clearly indicates their dependence on the technologies used, which results from the need to embed them in a specific technical ecosystem constituting the business ecosystem subsystem, as well as on the fact that they operate outside the organisation's boundaries, in a way. Digitalisation allows them to go beyond the organisational boundaries and achieve results in a space which is dependent on the availability and location of services rendered.

Digitalisation, as an idea with a practical attitude, is conceptualised and operationalised through business models. Automation plays a key role in this aspect, supporting digitalisation especially in technological business models. Companies like Amazon synergistically use a digital strategy through the use of automation, which refers to cases where a company uses digital technologies to automate or improve existing activities and processes. Companies use digital technologies to support new ways of doing business that complement, but do not completely replace, existing activities and processes (Li, 2017). In practice, digital business models include issues such as IT driving new business, the Internet of Things, cloud technology, Big Data, mobile technologies, Artificial Intelligence and robotics, and others (Sousa and Rocha, 2019, p. 258). These new trends of economic activity make entrepreneurial activities strongly dependent on the knowledge of technology and the ability to detect new user needs, as well as areas of life for which it is possible to conduct digital transformation processes.

New, digitally driven business models are changing the nature of competition as digital functionalities allow companies to provide customers with value in a completely new way.

Aiming to provide a broad, holistic overview of business model development perspectives, Adam Jabłoński and Marek Jabłoński compared the defined business model development perspectives with the concepts of the new economy. For this purpose, they defined 21 perspectives for the development of business models characterised by 17 concepts of the new economy. They indicated priority perspectives which are relevant to the defined concepts of the new economy. The results of these relationships are included in Table 2.1.

The presented approach to designing business models against the background of the so-called new economy shows how broad the scope of contemporary conditions for searching for innovative business solutions is. The concepts of the new economy create a great deal of opportunities to create a unique business model based on popular ideas and suitable technology. Innovations in digital business models are thus created in ecosystems stimulated by technical solutions. The key element in this aspect is the value system, called the ecosystem, which shapes the conditions that value proposition and delivery to recipients can be based on. (See Figure 2.1.)

In the case of manufacturing companies, a traditional value chain in the value system is transformed into a service model, in which business digitalisation is the foundation and the causative factor. The activities of suppliers play a key role in this respect. Therefore, service is the starting point for designing contemporary business formulas that are attractive to users.

The presented perspectives for business model development are included in the context of the concept of the new economy. The theoretical and practical

Table 2.1 Priority perspectives relevant to the defined concepts of the new economy

New economy concepts / *Business model development perspectives*	*Business model development systemic perspective*	*Business model development network perspective*	*Business model development process perspective*	*Business model development design perspective*	*Business model development traditional economy perspective*	*Business model development new digital economy perspective*	*Business development life cycle perspective – startup*	*Business model development life cycle perspective – business model of a mature company*	*Business model development sectoral perspective*	*Business model development perspective – a mono business model*	*Business model development perspective – a business model portfolio*	*Business model development perspective – social management goals and intentions*	*Business model development perspective – economic management goals and intentions*	*Business model development perspective – environmental orientation – sustainable business models*	*Business model development technological perspective*	*Enterprise size perspective – micro, small, and medium-sized*	*Enterprise size perspective – large*	*Business model development perspective related to company value management*	*Business model development financial accounting perspective*	*Business model development perspective – a hybrid approach*	*Solutions constituting a mix of different development perspectives*
Sharing Economy	X	X				X	X					X		X	X						
Circular Economy	X	X				X	X					X		X	X						
Big Data	X	X				X	X					X		X	X						
Gift Economy						X	X					X		X	X						
Barter Economy						X	X					X		X	X						
Industry 4.0	X	X				X	X								X						

Network Economy	X	X	X	X			X
Social Economy			X	X	X		
Artificial Intelligence			X	X			X
Cognitive Computing			X	X			X
Augmented Intelligence			X	X			X
Internet of Things			X	X			X
Remix Economy			X	X			X
Access Economy			X	X			X
Creative Economy			X	X	X	X	
Reputational Economy			X	X	X	X	
Experience Economy			X	X	X	X	
Trust Economy			X	X	X	X	
GIG Economy		X	X	X	X	X	
Platform Economy	X	X	X	X	X	X	
Sustainability (Triple Bottom Line) – 3P – People, Planet, Profit	X		X	X		X	

Source: Own study.

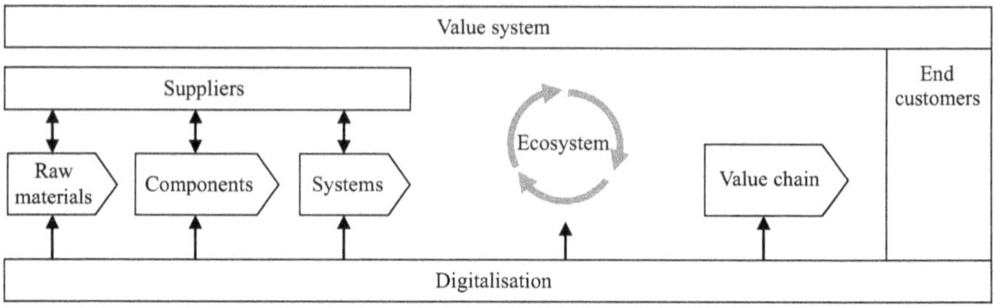

Figure 2.1 Digitalisation taking into account the value system/ecosystem.
Source: Own study based on Kohtamäki, 2019.

implications of the functioning of digital business models result from the transformation processes of the traditional economy towards the digital economy. The achievements of management theory and practice in this context should be redefined. The popularity of new concepts and trends in the functioning of world economies confirms this thesis.

Digital business models in the Sharing Economy

The concept of the Sharing Economy covers a very wide range of business and social activity. The term "Sharing Economy" has become an umbrella term defining a wide range of unconventional forms of consumer activities, such as exchange, barter trade, renting, and sharing (Habibi, Davidson, and Laroche, 2017, p. 113).

Because the Sharing Economy is an umbrella term with a very broad context of functioning, scientists will probably never agree on one definition. Nevertheless, as Acquier, Daudigeos, and Pinkse have written, its three cores can be distinguished as follows: the Access Economy, the Platform Economy, and the Community-based Economy (Acquier, Daudigeos, and Pinkse, 2017, p. 4). These three key areas, namely accessibility, cost-effectiveness, and the possibility of building communities, provide opportunities to shape innovative contemporary digital business models. Without this platform that combines technological and logical dimensions, there would be no opportunity to create such solutions. Business models of the Sharing Economy are characterised by the following features:

- A business model is based on access.
- The market is based on building an ecosystem as part of the use of online platforms.
- A service provider operates on demand (Barbu et al., 2018, p. 159).

The concept of sharing plays a special role in the construction and implementation of digital business models. This is due to the fact that many organisations which use digital business models use sharing mechanisms of assets and processes. Therefore, the principles of building company resources also change in economic and financial terms. To achieve business success and manage continuity, there is no need nowadays to build an extensive fixed assets system. It is sufficient to have an innovative digital business model and access to strategic resources that determine its monetisation. However, there is one threat in this case, primarily due to a specific mismatch between the digital management mechanisms and the rules for granting loans and receiving financing from financial institutions to meet investment needs. This is due to the failure of financial institutions to keep up with the modification of the rules for assessing creditworthiness and business credibility in relation to the construction of innovative digital business models by companies. An important factor which significantly affects the degree of use of sharing principles in digital business models is trust. This is primarily due to the fact that, in the Sharing Economy, social capital strongly affects the owners and temporary users of a given resource. Trust then becomes an attribute that links the ongoing relationship and affects further transactions.

The definitions of the concept of the Sharing Economy in broad and narrow terms are presented in Table 2.2.

The complex nature of the definition of the concept of the Sharing Economy means that the platform for its understanding and explanation is comprised of practical solutions that reflect the logic of the representatives of business models of specific companies belonging to this concept. The platform which combines technological and logical dimensions offers an opportunity to create such solutions. The potential of the Sharing Economy concept is very large, as evidenced by the number and degree of the monetisation of companies using business models based on this concept. Certainly, these solutions should be considered a phenomenon of the modern global economy.

Assumptions of Sharing Economy business models

The Sharing Economy is the result of several overlapping concepts, technologies and social solutions. Acquiera, Daudigeosb, and Pinksec pointed to the central position of the Sharing Economy against the background of the following concepts: the Access Economy, the Community-based Economy, the Platform Economy, the Access Platform, Community-based Access, and the Community-based Platform. The Access Economy includes a set of initiatives that share assets (material resources or skills) to optimise their use. The Platform Economy is the second core of the Sharing Economy. It is defined as a set of indirect initiatives for decentralised exchanges between users via digital platforms. The Community-based Economy is the third core of the Sharing Economy. It refers to coordinating initiatives through non-contractual, non-hierarchical or non-monetised forms of interaction to perform work, participate in a project, or create exchange relationships (Acquier, Daudigeos, and Pinkse, 2017, pp. 3–7).

Table 2.2 Examples of narrow and broad definitions of the Sharing Economy

Examples of definitions in the narrow sense	*Definition*
R. Belk	Distinguishes between "true sharing" and "pseudo-sharing". Sharing is an alternative to private property that is emphasised in both market exchange and gifts. Pseudo-sharing is a phenomenon in which the exchange of goods and the potential exploitation of consumer co-creators present themselves under the umbrella of sharing or business relationships subordinated to joint sharing.
D.G. Cockayne	The "on demand" or "sharing" economy is a term that describes digital platforms that connect consumers to a service or good by means of a mobile application or website.
G.M. Eckhardt and F. Bardhi	The access economy, ... also known as the sharing or peer-to-peer economy, provides ... temporary access to consumer resources for a fee or for free without any transfer of ownership.
K. Frenken and J. Schor	Defining the Sharing Economy as consumers granting each other temporary access to underused physical assets (idle resources), perhaps for money.
A. Stephany	The Sharing Economy is the value of using underused resources and making them available to the community, which reduces the need for these assets.
Examples of definitions in the broad sense	*Definition*
M.R. Habibi, A. Davidson, and M. Laroche	They suggest a sharing exchange that helps distinguish the extent to which current sharing is offered.
L. Lessig	Defining the hybrid economy as a commercial entity that aims to gain value from activities in the Sharing Economy.
P. Muñoz and B. Cohen	A socio-economic system enabling an indirect set of the exchange of goods and services between individuals and organisations, which aims to increase efficiency and optimise the resources used in society.
J. Schor, C. Fitzmaurice, L.B. Carfagna, W. Attwood-Charles, and E.D. Poteat	The Sharing Economy falls into four broad categories: recirculation of goods, greater use of fixed assets, exchange of services and sharing of production assets.
R. Botsman	An economic model based on sharing unused resources from the skill space for monetary or non-monetary benefits (e.g. an online article).

Examples of definitions in the broad sense	*Definition*
H. Heinrichs	Refers to economic and social systems that enable shared access to goods, services, data and talent. These systems take a variety of forms but all leverage information technology to empower individuals, corporations, non-profits and government with information that enables distribution, sharing and reuse of excess capacity in terms of goods and services.

Source: Own study based on Belk, 2014, pp. 7–23; Cockayne, 2016, pp. 73–82; Eckhardt and Bardhi, 2016, pp. 210–225; Frenken and Schor, 2017, pp. 3–10; Stephany, 2015; Lessig, 2008; Muñoz and Cohen, 2017; Schor et al., 2016, pp. 66–81; Botsman, 2013; Heinrichs, 2013.

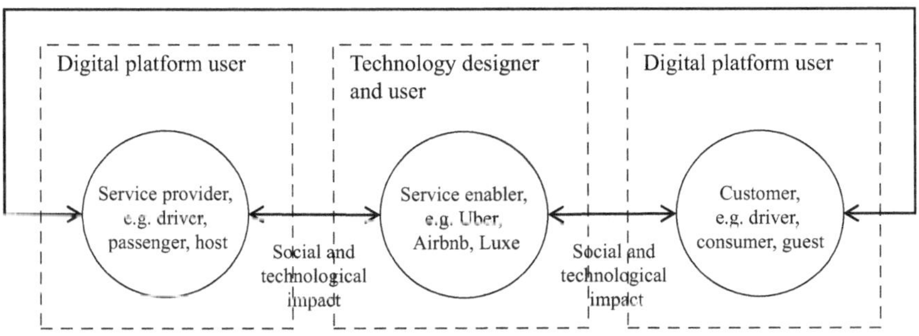

Figure 2.2 Conceptual framework for the Sharing Economy business model.
Source: Own study based on Kumar, Lahiri, and Bahadir Dogan, 2018, p. 148.

In the Sharing Economy, roles are assigned to three entities which form a triadic B2B platform relationship: service enablers (such as Uber, Airbnb, Luxe), service providers (such as drivers, apartment hosts), and customers (such as passengers, guests, and users). Here, a customer can be a company (B2B) or a person (B2C) (Kumar et al., 2018, p. 147). Figure 2.2 shows the relationship between actors constituting the structure of the Sharing Economy business model.

In the context of the Sharing Economy, attention should be paid to technological and social impact. Technical devices interact via interfaces, while each relationship creates social impact (e.g., new acquaintances) that can create a community. In turn, the community can be focused around various ideas, for example involvement in intentional movements (pro-ecological), or self-contained movements (shared passions and interests).

There are many representatives of the Sharing Economy business models, although not all meet theoretical assumptions. While BlaBlaCar shares space in

Table 2.3 Sharing Economy companies, divided into various categories or sectors of the economy

Companies, start-ups or applications – examples by type of sector/industry

Mobility and transport	Services, tourist, leisure, other	Services	Finance	Use	Goods	Food	Education
• Sharing driving • Car sharing • Other vehicle sharing	• Accommodation • Workplace • Storage	• Personal services • Professional services	• Money lending • Crowdfunding • Payments • Insurance	• Telecommunications • Energy	• Buy and sell • Product lending	• Common food	• Peer-to-peer education • Open courses
• Uber, Hailo, Grab, Sidecar, Blablacar • RealyRides, Getaround, Zipcar, Autoshare, car2go • Liquid, spinlister, Sailo, Boaubound, Jetsharter	• Airbnb, Couchsurfing, Homeaway, VRBO • Wework, Pivotdesk, ShareDesk, Liquidspace • MakeSpace, Roost, Spacer, SpaceOut	• Taskrabbit, Handy, DogVacay, Zaarly, fiverr • Upwork, Crowdspring, Hourtynerd, BidWilly	• LendingClub, Zopa, Borrowell, Prosper • Indigogo, Kickstarter, GoFundMe, CircleUp • TransferWise, M-pesa • Friendsurance, Wesura, Inspeer, metromile	• Fon, OpenGardem • Grindmates, Vandebron	• Poshmark, Wallapop, eBay, Craiglist, Etsy • NeighborGoods, peerby, Renttherunway, Streetbank, OpenShed	• Eatwith, Mealsharing, VizEat, LeftoverSwap	• P2PU, Skillshare, SharingAcademy • Coursera, KhanAcademy, Udemy

Source: Own study based on Conference materials: Prof. Joan Enric Ricart, Professor of Strategic Management, Carl Schroeder Chair of Strategic Management, Presentation at the 2nd Business Model Conference, 2018, University of Florence.

a car and Airbnb shares a place in a private home, doubts arise in the case of Uber as to whether a private car lift is tantamount to sharing resources. Table 2.3 shows examples of companies included in the group of entities representing Sharing Economy assumptions.

The examples of companies presented above confirm how many areas of the economy have already been appropriated by new solutions based on the concept of the Sharing Economy.

Digital business models and Big Data

The concept of Big Data has been developed thanks to technological solutions that enable the processing of very large amounts of data and the creation of targeted information sets from them in many areas of business and life. It turned out that using them provides the possibility of monetising value, which is used to create innovative business models based on the use of these information resources. Big Data covers a wide range of areas and use, including Big Data management, Big Data cleaning, Big Data aggregation, Big Data analytics, Big Data machine learning, and others. New trends in Big Data also include various analysis techniques such as Data Mining, Web Mining, Visualisation Methods, Machine learning, Optimisation Methods, and Social Network Analysis (Yaqoob et al., 2016, pp. 8–9). The term Big Data is usually used to describe large, unstructured and dynamically changing data sets. The specificity of Big Data is often described in the 3V or 4V models. The 3V Model (Volume, Velocity, Variety) was developed in 2001 by the analytical company Gartner (formerly Meta Group) to show the main characteristics of Big Data – their size, diversity and variability. Combining data from multiple sources helps streamline decision and management processes in many sectors and thus enables the better operationalisation of digital business models, especially in telecommunications, tourism, banking, insurance and marketing.

The concept of Big Data has developed thanks to technological solutions that enable the processing of vast amounts of data and, as a result, the construction of purposeful information sets. It turned out that their use makes it possible to monetise value, which helps create innovative business models based on the use of these information resources. The attributes of the Big Data concept are specific, determining the principles of conducting business and social activities based on the use of Big Data sets. Key attributes include data variety, velocity, volume, veracity, and value (Brock and Khan, 2017, pp. 1–7), and they determine the assumptions for shaping business models based on access and the way data is used. The logic of generating value for the recipient is then embedded in the strategic resource that is data access. New trends in Big Data sets also include various analysis techniques. They include Data Mining, Web Mining, Visualisation Methods, Machine Learning, Optimisation Methods, and Social Network Analysis (Yaqoob et al., 2016, pp. 8–9). These methods build a set of strategic and operational functionalities of tools based on the Big Data concept and allow for the development of new possibilities of using such data. They can be commercialised, but can also be used to analyse voter preferences, consumer preferences and behaviours, social analyses and diagnoses, and so on. These tools help build strategies for mass customers as well as those focused on individual customer-specific needs.

Big Data is a set of data which, unlike ordered databases, is unstructured, unorganised, and even inconvenient to use in simple analytical devices. However, there are a huge number of signals in the informational noise waiting to be discovered (McAfee and Brynjolfsson, 2012, pp. 60–68).

Big Data is becoming the most valuable – even strategic – resource that companies can monetise: personalise, monitor, measure, optimise, and use to predict future events. It is important to understand the mechanisms of using Big Data. This can be done by answering some key questions.

- How to control the avalanche of data growth?
- How to use the full potential of data?
- How to secure, archive, process, and analyse data?
- What methods should be implemented to improve the quality of data work?

Big Data sets have different applications. Their wide possibilities of use open up new potential, not only for designing innovative digital business models, but also for advanced business analytics for the purposes of creating competitive advantages and new spaces for creating value for customers/users. Figure 2.3 shows the wide range of applications of Big Data sets for building value arrays in digital business models.

Key data and data supporting business models have been presented. The variety of applications of Big Data sets results from the possibility of data archiving and their multiple use for many different purposes. This makes them an essential element of the functionality of digital business models.

It is worth noting that the concept of Big Data-based business models uses the various principles of advanced analytics. Advanced analytics (AA) currently focuses on performance improvement in the industry considering the context of smart manufacturing (SM) in the information age (IA). Although overlapping in the definitions of AA may occur, the types of AA and their descriptions are:

- Descriptive analytics: accounting and analysis of historical data. Used in backcasting practices and forecasting of seasonal demands.
- Predictive analytics: considers recent data to predict coming future trends, biases, tendencies, behaviour, etc., through causation and correlation.
- Prescriptive analytics: finds or prescribes the best mode, route, manner, or moves to operate (outputs) based on given data and models (inputs).

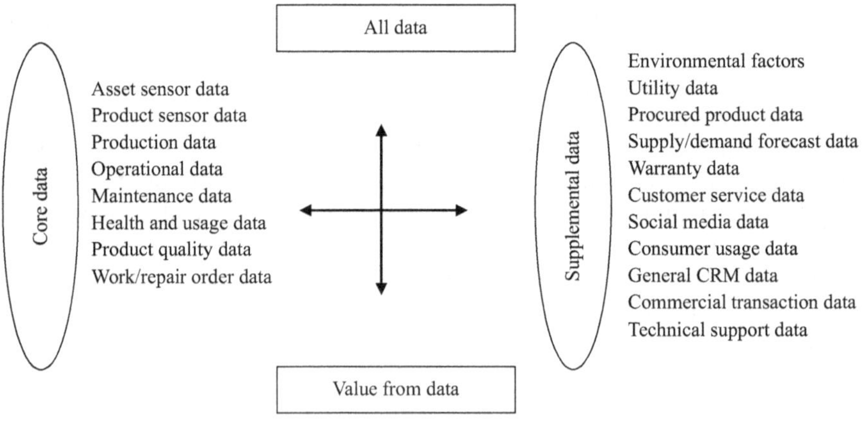

Figure 2.3 Ranges of Big Data application in creating value arrays in digital business models.

Source: Own study based on Liozu and Ulaga, 2018, p. 75.

- Detective analytics: undertakes diagnostics of collected data to eliminate and rectify inappropriate values used in predictive analytics as well as infeasibilities to achieve optimal results in prescriptive analytics.
- Cognitive analytics: automated predictions, prescriptions, and detections for smarter decisions over time considering adaptative and learning processes (Menezes et al., 2019, pp. 568–573).

Predictive analytics aims to determine future market development scenarios, and customer and company behaviours, among others. Prescriptive analytics provides a source of knowledge of how to model these behaviours and influence the formation of expected attitudes, among other things.

The presented set of methods of predictive and prescriptive analytics is very broad. Prescriptive analytics covers the area of data analysis, which is focused on searching for the best course of action in terms of the optimal scenario, taking into account the analysis of available data. Predictive analytics is focused on assessing performance in terms of imagining future events by means of analysing historical (past) data. Through event repetition analysis, attempts are made to identify future event scenarios.

Table 2.4 presents the methods to be used for predictive analytics.

Table 2.4 Classification of methods of predictive analytics

Predictive Analytics	Probabilistic Models	Bayesian Network Markov Chain Monte Carlo Hidden Markov Model
	Machine Learning/Data Mining	Pattern recognition Random Forest Gaussian process Conditional inference tree Support Vector Machine Ensemble learning Artificial Neural Network Random search Decision tree Clustering-based heuristics k-nearest neighbours algorithm Kernel methods Multiplayer perceptron Gradient Boosted Tree
	Statistical Analysis	Linear regression Multiple linear regression Rank regression ARIMA Logistic regression Multinomial logistic regression Density estimation Support vector regression

Source: Own study based on Lepenioti et al., 2020, pp. 57–70.

Table 2.5 Classification of methods of prescriptive analytics

Prescriptive Analytics	Probabilistic Models	Markov Decision Process Hidden Markov Model Markov Chain
	Machine Learning/Data Mining	k-means clustering Reinforcement Learning Privacy preservation Boltzmann Machine Nadaraya-Watson estimator Artificial Neural Networks
	Mathematical Programming	Mixed Integer Programme Linear Programme Binary Quadratic Programme Non-Linear Programme Binary Linear Integer Programme Stochastic Optim Conditional Stochastic Optim Constrained Bayesian Optim Fuzzy Linear Optim Robust and Adaptive Optim Dynamic Programme Optimal searcher path
	Evolutionary Computation	Genetic algorithm Evolutionary Optim Greedy algorithm Particle Swarm Optim
	Simulation	Simulation over Random Forest Risk Assessment Stochastic simulation What-if scenarios
	Logic-based Models	Association rules Decision rules Criteria-based rules Fuzzy rules Distributed rules Benchmark rules Desirability function Graph-based recommendation 5W1H

Source: Own study based on Lepenioti et al., 2020, pp. 57–70.

Table 2.5 presents the methods to be used for prescriptive analytics. The concept of Big Data can be based on the popular and accepted Seven V's model, among others. The Seven V's can be defined as:

- Volume: refers to the ever-growing magnitude and size of data generated. Big Data sizes easily reach multiple terabytes, even petabytes.

- Variety: represents the heterogeneity, diversity and unevenness of data types in a dataset. Advanced ICTs in today's companies generate various types of structured, semi-structured, and unstructured data of various types such as text, sensor data, audio, video, log files and so on.
- Velocity: is the frequency of data generation and the high-speed at which it should be processed, analysed and acted upon.
- Veracity: introduced by IBM as a defining attribute of Big Data. Veracity refers to the degree of truthfulness and uncertainty related to most sources of data. Big Data proposes the use of specific tools and analytics to deal with imprecise and unreliable data.
- Variability: pioneered by SAS as an additional attribute of Big Data. The variability and complexity in the process of data generation implies a significant need to connect, match, cleanse and transform data received from different sources.
- Volatility: refers to the capacity of storage and retention of data. With the huge volume and velocity of data, the issue of storage retention along with data security becomes significant for Big Data.
- Value: coined by Oracle as the seventh V. The value of data generated is insignificant in its raw form compared to a huge volume thereof. This value can be significantly increased by processing and analysing large volumes of such data (Tewari and Dwivedi, 2019, pp. 937–947).

The concept of a Big Data Business Model is strongly used in social media in terms of the degree of the assessment of their effectiveness.

Figure 2.4 shows how to apply the Big Data concept to the principles of Social Media.

When undertaking a critical analysis of the concept of Big Data in constructing digital business models, attention should be paid to the fact that the concept of Big Data is constantly changing; it is important to refer to it not only through the prism of the huge amount of processed data, but above all the process of creating value for the organisation. It should also be noted that the processing of Big Data sets requires new knowledge which business analysts, who have the knowledge and competence of the Data Scientist profile, must possess. It is critical that these data are processed very quickly and contain a lot of often unstructured content. At the same time, it should be remembered that these data may come from various unstructured sources, such as:

- the number of clicks on websites,
- the number of likes on social networks (Twitter, blogs, Facebook, and others),
- the number of video recordings from various facilities,
- recording of calls in a call centre, etc.,
- information received in real time from various types of detector sensors, sensors, RFID, GPS devices, cell phones and other identifying and monitoring devices.

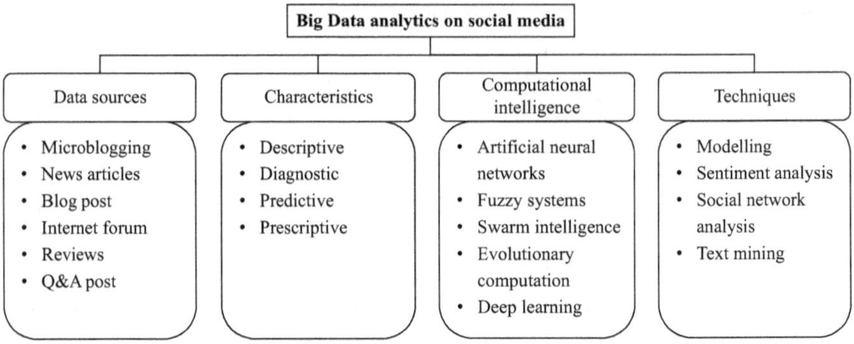

Figure 2.4 Classification of Big Data analytics on social media.
Source: Own study based on Ghani et al., 2019, pp. 417–428.

The problem in this case is the different arrangement of the data and information received, which complicates the process of proper selection and interpretation.

Internet platforms and their business models

Currently, digital Internet platforms are one of the key tools for monetising digital business models. It is through them that various rules for communicating with users – who, in turn, often become their customers – are built. The interpretative aspect of defining and using various Internet platforms is complex, as creators, users, customers, and suppliers can perform many functions therein while also creating replaceable forms. Figure 2.5 shows a holistic view of a digital platform covering its most important components.

On the basis of digital platforms, unique, innovative digital business models are built based on the modern concepts of the so-called new economy. The digital platform is a central node which brings together all the components that build a complex technical and organisational system with technical and social impact. This ecosystem shapes economic and social relationships:

1. Foundation: Cloud services
2. Digital Glue: API strategy and architecture
3. Accelerator: Open source and reusable software
4. Digital Treasure Chest: Mobile development platforms
5. Real-time Business Models: Driven by the Internet of Things
6. Containers: Independence and portability of software (Accenture).

An important aspect of building online platforms is the business model based thereon. According to Ali, Wang, and Ming, the structure of the Internet platform-based business model can consist of the following components: value

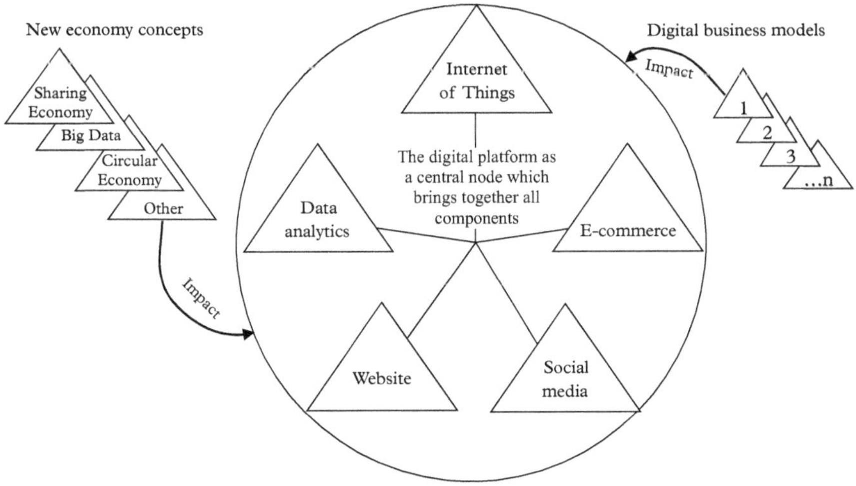

Figure 2.5 A holistic view of a digital platform.
Source: Own study based on Liozu and Ulaga, 2018, p. 7.

module (value creation, value delivery, value allocation, value capture), service module (information service, transaction service), transaction module (transaction roles, transaction contents, transaction mode), and the basic module (platform resources, platform capability) (Ali, Wang, and Ming, 2018, pp. 1882–1890). An interesting typology of platform business models was presented by Anurag Tewari and Paarth Sareen, as described in Table 2.6:

This approach to building business models gave rise to the concept of the Platform Economy. The Platform Economy is that portion of the economy which is composed of digital platforms enabling users to share, lend, rent, or purchase goods and services. Highly profitable ventures such as Uber and Airbnb are examples of the phenomenon, as are non-profit "pure sharing" platforms as well. The platform economy has been found to give rise to several unresolved theoretical and regulatory questions, for which there is a paucity of relevant literature (Kilhoffer, Lenaerts, and Beblavý, 2017).

Platforms are big news and big business – and, some would say, the focus of overblown and unwarranted hype. Books by business scholars and tech-economy pundits tout the efficiency and generativity of platform-based business models, even though new platform ventures often struggle to turn a profit after moving out of the startup phase. Tech journalists, activists, and scholars in a variety of academic fields argue that platforms are seemingly reshaping every area of human endeavour, from innovation to commerce to cultural production to social organisation, but disagree on how to assess the effects of platforms (Cohen, 2017, pp. 133–204). The emerging Platform Economy gives rise to new regulatory issues that make it necessary to adjust EU contract law to the changing

Table 2.6 Types of Platform Business Models with descriptions and examples

No	*Type of Platform Business Model*	*Business model description*	*Example*
1.	Telco-Centric platform Model	In this model, the user accesses services via a portal screen. The portal provider is incorporated in the network and platform operator, creating a single entity that plays a mediating role. The network operator grants access to the network, while the platform operator provides the necessary technical tools to facilitate this access and provides an environment in which the portal provider can operate. The portal provider also aggregates services making them more easily available to the end user. The business entity comprising these different actors, which in real life is usually a telecom company, establishes relationships with select service providers who can offer their services via the portal. Service providers can be exclusive partners of the network operator, or third parties. Revenue streams can be identified between the user and the telecom company, and between the latter and the service provider. Services flow from the service providers to the user via the telecom company (Ballon et al., 2008, pp. 72–79).	Vodafone Live! Platform
2.	Device Centric Platform Model	In this model, several services are offered as an integral part of the device. The user gets access to a number of services embedded in the device, which can be operated in an intuitive way. In this model, the device manufacturer functions as portal provider, choosing and controlling which services are made available to consumers. This actor also defines what specific platform is used to provide services to the user. Most of the platform operator activity is performed by the device manufacturer, as almost all information and tools needed to develop services and applications for the device are internal to this actor. The manufacturer can also provide tools and resources in the form of a Service Development Kit (SDK) to service providers for the development of new services. Profile information can be managed by the device manufacturer or by the service provider, depending on the type of service. The device manufacturer already integrates a large set of services into the device. One of the selling points may be that these are mobile versions of services which the manufacturer already offers for other devices (i.e. laptop and desktop computers). The device may be offered to the user in various ways. It can be	Apple

No	*Type of Platform Business Model*	*Business model description*	*Example*
		linked to a specific network operator's subscription through a system of contracts and for example SIM cards. In another model, the device is offered in an operator-agnostic way. The network operator may also strike a deal with the manufacturer to subsidise part of the device towards the customer, locking the latter in to the network operator for a specific amount of time, for example. Services are presented to the user on the home screen of the device. There is another aspect to this model that provides a role for a mediator, be it online or offline. This refers to the fact that the user can access certain services without the need for a mobile network operator; he or she can connect his or her mobile device directly to his personal computer in order to be provided with offline and online services, with access being provided by another actor than the mobile network operator (i.e. an ISP). For instance, an important service is the possibility for the user to buy music online through his fixed computer and place it on his mobile device, without the brokerage of the mobile network provider (Ballon et al., 2008, pp. 72–79).	
3	Aggregator-Centric platform Model	In this model, the service aggregator takes on the role of portal provider. It serves as the portal to the user, who can choose to install several smaller applications that coincide with personal interests and preferences. The user pays the network operator for access to the network and gains access to the portal. However, the service aggregator is not bound to a specific network operator, and so the portal can be accessed by any supported device. Herein also lies the main difference with the telco-centric model. Service providers can develop a slew of smaller applications that can run in the portal. This means service providers are confined to the platform which the portal uses to deliver the services. However, in some cases users can access services without the mediation of the portal. A service provider can choose to provide service access via the portal provider and/or provide the service to the user directly, that is, via a webpage. In this model, the role of the platform operator is performed by the portal provider/service aggregator. This actor defines the language in which applications have to be developed, hosts	Facebook

(continued)

Table 2.6 Continued

No	*Type of Platform Business Model*	*Business model description*	*Example*
		the services, facilitates the assembly and creation of services and manages profile information. Indirect revenues are expected to be crucial in this model, either from advertisers or from revenue-sharing deals with device manufacturers or network operators (Ballon et al., 2008, pp. 72–79).	
4.	Service Centric Platform Model	The meta-platform operator offers a container API, which allows developers to link different services together and exchange profile information, for example. At the moment, this system is mainly a theoretical model, but it can be argued that Google has laid the foundations for such a system with its Open Social initiative. Right now it offers no more than the option to develop widgets that exchange information, but if expanded in the announced direction, such an initiative could mean true "social network portability". Both Facebook and Google have recently joined the Data Portability Workgroup (Kirkpatrick, 2008), which strives for total data portability, allowing users to take their personal data from one website to reuse it on another. This may be interpreted as an illustration of the fact that fierce competition among platform providers to attract the largest numbers of users as well as developers is forcing them progressively to take down barriers to service development and use (Ballon et al., 2008, pp. 72–79).	Google

Source: Own study based on Tewari and Sareen, 2014.

market structure. In particular, adequate solutions have to be developed for the "triangular" contractual relationships that are a characteristic feature of the platform business model (Busch et al., 2016, pp. 1–72). Will the platform replace the firm? Beyond the controversy, the remarkable feature of today's platforms is that algorithms have taken over the functions of a traditional company: they coordinate production, match supply and demand, organise, control and appraise the workforce, and even make them "redundant" by disconnecting them where necessary (Daugareilh, Degryse, and Pochet, 2019). With reference to the statements described, it is worth paying attention to many legal and social controversies linked to the functioning of digital platforms and their business models. This is related to both the mechanisms for applying and complying with intellectual property and the rules for the functioning of the labour market.

Algorithm-based business models

One of the key perspectives for the development of digital business models is algorithm-based business models, understood as a finite series of clearly defined activities which are necessary to perform certain types of tasks, as a way of dealing with the problem. Digital business models can be implemented based on algorithms. This applies, inter alia, to digital advertising mechanisms and the definition of customer preferences using Big Data. This includes, but is not limited to, studying customer behaviour and identifying target groups of users first, followed by customers. Algorithms also fulfil a prognostic function which can be used for the entire business model or in every component of the business model. Algorithms are also used to build business process models. To evaluate the clustering algorithm, Ordoñez, and colleagues use the following algorithms:

- Algorithms for clustering of web documents: STC (Suffix Tree Clustering) and Lingo
- Algorithms used for data clustering: K-means
- Algorithms based on graph theory: Stars, Cliques, and FullStart
- An algorithm for hierarchical clustering of business processes: HC.

These algorithms were adapted for BP grouping based on results obtained from the previously defined multimodal search model (Ordoñez et al., 2017, pp. 163–177). Genetic Algorithms are often used in the digital economy. Genetic algorithms are metaheuristic optimisation algorithms resembling natural evolution. By relying on the evolutionary theory of the survival of the fittest and on the ideas of selection and mutation, genetic algorithms aim to simulate the evolution of solutions over different generations so as to eventually identify an optimal or near-optimal solution for an optimisation problem (Mitchell, 1995, pp. 31–39).

The approach provides a back-propagation neural networks and genetic algorithm (GA)-based approach, that is, ISB2C-NNGA (ISB2C controls design using neural networks and genetic algorithms), a hybrid optimisation model using neural networks, and genetic algorithms for the design of ISB2C controls, which uses a back-propagation neural networks (BPN) model as a prediction of controls using system environments, and GA as a pattern-directed search mechanism to estimate the exponent of independent variables (i.e., ISB2C controls) in non-linear regression analysis of power models (Lee and Ahn, 2011, pp. 4326–4338). Algorithms can also be used in the digital sector to build a function architecture between companies and content producers for video advertising. It is interesting to combine the canvas of the business model with the principles of using algorithms based on cluster analysis in order to make it possible for the organisation to achieve a high level of efficiency. Interesting research in this area was conducted for airlines by Urban and colleagues (2018, pp. 175–192). It reflects the business specificity in the context of monitoring the effectiveness of the algorithms used. These types of solutions combine the traditional approach to business model design using the potential of algorithms.

Cognitive business models in the digital economy

Because cognitive computing is somehow a computer simulation of human thought processes, a theory which is relevant to an assessment of the dynamics of business models based on this concept is the System Dynamics method described above.

Generally speaking, the term means a set of technologies that are largely the result of studies of the operation of the human brain. It is a kind of combination of artificial intelligence and Signal Processing – two crucial elements for the development of machine technology awareness. They combine a set of modern tools such as self-learning machines, reasoning and inferring, natural language processing, speech, computer-human interactions, and many more (www.forbes.pl/opinie/cognitive-computing-jak-action-artificial-intelligence/hfg65d6 [accessed: 15 December 2019]). The key trends in the concept of cognitive computing include contextual analytics, sensor-generated data, cognitive visualisation, and influential SAAS models. Cognitive computing is the use of artificial intelligence and machine learning to enable computers to understand data, generate insights, and use them as a future educational experience. With the help of cognitive computing, it is easier to introduce artificial intelligence in computers because it reduces the emphasis on making computers intelligent in terms of one type of task and scaling the scope of tasks in many phases. The use of cognitive computing involves entering data into an intelligent algorithm that can analyse them, understand correlations, and learn from data to automatically improve its intellect. Modern technologies are driven by algorithms that fit into the assumptions of the theory of complexity (Sejnowski, 2019, pp. 235–236).

An algorithm can be treated as an abbreviated name of a social engineering assemblage containing: an algorithm (in technical terms), a model, a target group, data, applications, and hardware – all related to the social environment (Kreft, 2019, p. 31).

To implement the assumptions of the concept of cognitive computing, the interdependent use of Big Data, Machine Learning, and Cloud Computing is necessary. These are the three main technologies behind each level of cognitive processing (www.newgenapps.com/blog/what-is-cognitive-computing-applications-companies-artificial-intelligence [accessed: 14 December 2019]). Examples of applications of this solution are described in Table 2.7.

Examples of the use of artificial intelligence, on the basis of which these business models are operationalised in the context of marketing needs, include:

- Voice processing technologies (placing orders via Amazon's Alexa device or applications, virtual assistants which support the performance of tasks (Siri, Google Home, Cortana)).
- Text processing technologies (using a virtual assistant as a guide to the shopping centre (Alpine.Al)).

Table 2.7 Suitable solutions for designing cognitive business models

Chatbots	*Sentiment analysis*	*Face detection*	*Risk assessment*	*Fraud detection*
Chatbots are programmes that can simulate human conversation by understanding communication in a contextual sense. To enable this, a machine learning technique called natural language processing is used. Natural language processing allows programmes to receive input from people (voice or text), analyse it, and then give logical answers. Cognitive computers allow chatbots to communicate with a certain level of intelligence, such as understanding the user's needs based on previous communication, giving suggestions, and so on.	Sentiment analysis is the science of understanding emotions conveyed in communication. Although people can easily understand the tone, intentions and so on in a conversation, they are much more complicated for machines. To enable machines to understand interpersonal communication, it is necessary to provide training data on human conversations, and then to analyse the accuracy of the analysis. Sentiment analysis is commonly used to analyse communication on social media, such as tweets, comments, reviews, complaints, and so on.	Face detection is an advanced level of image analysis. The cognitive system uses data such as structure, outlines, eye colour, and so on to distinguish it from others. After generating a face image, you can use it to identify faces based on an image or a movie. Although this was traditionally done using 2D images, it can now also be done using 3D sensors that provide greater accuracy. This can be used in security systems such as for cabs and even mobile phones.	Risk management in financial services involves analysing market trends, historical data, and so on to predict uncertainty associated with investments. However, this analysis is not only related to data, but also to trends, intuition, behaviour, and so on. Therefore, it is both art and science. The analysis of Big Data sets (i.e. the analysis of previous trends) is not sufficient to assess risk. Due to the intuition and experience in predicting the future of markets, intelligent algorithms are necessary. Cognitive computers help to combine behavioural data and market trends for analysis. They can subsequently be verified by experienced analysts for further analysis and forecasts.	Fraud detection is another application of cognitive computing in finance. It is basically a type of anomaly detection. The purpose of fraud detection is to identify transactions that do not appear to be normal (anomalies). It also requires past data analysis programmes to understand the parameters that should be used to evaluate transactions. A number of data analysis techniques can be used to detect anomalies, such as logistic regression, decision tree, random forest, clustering, and so on.

Source: Own study based on NewGenApps (2017).

- Image recognition and processing technologies (face recognition as a way of making payment (KFC)).
- Decision making (individual matching of a travel destination based on the style of music listened to (Spotify, Emirates)).
- Autonomous robots and vehicles, unattended stores (Ford & Alibaba, Amazon Go, Zaitt Brasil) (Mazurek, 2019, pp. 164–165).

These types of business models are characterised by natural dynamics resulting from direct contact with objects interested in the designed functionalities. The key aspect of the effectiveness of this type of business model is the monetisation process.

The dynamics of business models are manifested in their ability to change as well as a multi-variant method of monetisation. The faster the model's ability to change, the greater its ability to constantly create value. The more monetisation scenarios built into business model logic, the greater the chances of achieving the expected economic result. The dynamics assessed in the course of analysing modern business models are a crucial attribute which is responsible for ensuring the company's ability to survive in the context of the application of a specific business model and its monetisation method.

Based on the conducted literature review and the conceptualisation of the issue of the dynamics of business models of digital economy companies in terms of monetisation, several key final conclusions can be formulated:

1. The System Dynamics method enables the construction of continuous simulation models, which is part of the business model functioning in interaction with users, improving the relational processes used for monetisation.
2. A good example of the use of dynamics in business models is the experience of designing cognitive business models, the assumption of which is the use of a set of technologies that are largely the result of studies on the operation of the human brain. They are a kind of combination of artificial intelligence and Signal Processing – two key elements for the development of technology machine awareness.

The presented explanations of the application of the Deep Learning concept in the field of cognitive business models use the concept of machine learning, the use of artificial intelligence, the use of neural networks and broadly natural sciences, and direct business in areas that were previously the domain of scientists. Nowadays they have become an opportunity to create new spaces of value propositions for business.

Servitisation of business models

The starting point for the identification of servitisation assumptions is the concept of Product-Service Systems (PSS). Most product and service system classifications distinguish three main categories, namely:

- Product-related services.
- Product-oriented services.
- Result-oriented services (Tukker, 2004).

Traditionally, products and services were considered to be separate areas of the economy. Enriching products with additional services and combining services with the product offer creates a new business model (Janczewski, 2014). Servitisation is a phenomenon in which companies that have worked in the classic "make & sell" model to date (e.g. production companies), change their business model, and begin to add services to their offer or even completely switch to the service model, that is, "make and maintain" (https://fuzers.com/pl/serwityzacja-czy-wszystko-stanie-sie-usluga/ [accessed: 21 June 2019]). The concepts that accompany this issue are just emerging and are the subject of numerous research papers. They refer to terms such as: "Product-Service System", "PSS", "Servicisation", "Servitisation", "Servicification", "Productisation", "Product-Service Offer", "Integrated Product-Service", "Industrial Product-Service System", "IPSS", "Sustainable Product-Service Systems", "Functional Economy", and "Dematerалisation" (Mahut et al., 2017, p. 2104). Such a multitude of terms confirms that the issue is interdisciplinary and requires extensive theoretical studies and empirical research. In the context of the digital economy, mainly in terms of the Sharing Economy, the greatest importance and usefulness is observed in the case of usability-oriented product and service systems, which are divided into three subcategories:

1. Leasing of products: the supplier retains ownership of the product and is often responsible for its maintenance, repair and condition control. The lessor pays regular fees for using the product. In this case, a customer usually has unlimited and individual access to the rented product.
2. Leasing of the product or sharing it with another user: this time the product is the property of the supplier, who is also responsible for its maintenance, repair and condition control. The user pays for the use of the product. The main difference from renting a product is that the user does not have unlimited and individual access; other users may also use the product at other times. The same product is sequentially used by different users.
3. Combining products – this is similar to renting or sharing a product. However, in this case, the product is simultaneously used by different users (Santarek and Salwin, 2017, pp. 678–688).

Thus, the issue of transforming the economy from product orientation to service orientation is operationalised through the attributes of the designed business models. With the blurring of boundaries, companies emerge that no longer define themselves as producers of goods, but as suppliers of solutions, functions, or sensations. In response, new theoretical research perspectives began to appear, including:

- Functional economy, according to which companies do not sell products to their customers, but rather functions instead.
- The economy of experiences that grew out of the economy of services.
- Service-dominant (SD) logic – according to SD logic, goods are perceived as mechanisms used in the process of providing services to distribute value (Matusek, 2018).

From the perspective of the digital economy, in the context of the presented assumptions of the phenomenon of servitisation, companies need dynamic tools to support them in managing digital innovations. To this end, the established framework identifies five key areas that need to be measured and assessed while managing digital products and service innovation:

1. First, digital products and services must not only be efficient and easy to learn, but also offer rich service. Such user experience can be measured based on its usability, aesthetics and commitment.
2. Second, companies must clearly present the value offer of each digital product and service, and how they create value for users. The quality of such value propositions is assessed based on the dynamics of customer segmentation, combining products and services, and commissions for channel owners.
3. Third, digital evolution scanning requires gathering intelligence on new devices, digital channels such as web services, mobile operating systems and social media, and application stores, as well as API standards and interfaces, to identify and take advantage of innovation opportunities in the context of new applications and behaviour of new users.
4. Fourth, digital innovation requires new skills; therefore companies need to evaluate their mechanisms to support the continuous learning of the unique qualities of digital technologies in order to create dynamic innovation teams.
5. Fifth – and finally – digital innovation processes are often triggered when members of an organisation introduce digital technologies into the learning process by acting within the time needed for improvisation (Nyle´n and Holmstrom, 2015).

In light of the above analyses, the services provide space for shaping innovative solutions in the sphere of designing innovative ways of reaching potential and real users of digital business models, the attributes of which should consequently favour the effective monetisation of sales based on the level of the business model's ability to create value and capture the expected value from the market.

Servitisation as a new direction of improving business effectiveness

The effectiveness of companies can be achieved by the servitisation of their business models. Blurring the boundaries between products and services is the result of focusing on business models which constitute a platform for implementing product and service business systems. Product and service systems are a combination of products and services that are systematised to provide the desired usability or functions that meet customer needs. They represent an approach to a specific solution that provides the opportunity to fulfil the individual needs of customers and increase the competitiveness of companies (Long et al., 2016). The concept of servitisation emerges from the definition of production and service systems, which stimulates the creation of innovative business models. As early as 1988, this concept was defined in the scientific literature by Vandermerwe and Rada (1988). However, servitisation is a phenomenon observed especially in recent years due to the dynamically growing role of services in the global economy, the focus on the use of services within households, as well as the extension of supply chains by offering additional value which integrates product delivery with after-sales service. Globalisation, the mobility of production factors, decreased transaction costs, and diffusion of technological progress play an important role among the factors which influence the development of the service sector. All these determinants stimulate the internationalisation and fragmentation of production, and contribute to increased relationships between economy sectors. Services determine the course of production processes, and create added value and a competitive advantage for a given industry or company (this phenomenon is referred to as servitisation) (Ulbrych, 2016, p. 262). The boom in service civilisation is determined by the process of servitisation (Szymańska, 2015, p. 98). The manufacturer's servitisation effect means that, in addition to the key role of information flow, services provided are becoming more important in the lower part of the supply chain (Matusek, 2018, p. 329). Thus, servitisation is defined as the transition from a "clean" product to a "clean" service (Smith, Maull, and Ng, 2014). In traditional terms, this concept determines the transformation of supply chains into service chains, while in the case of innovative business models, servitisation is already embedded in the core idea of shaping these business models. In this context, new areas of creating business models developed from the perspective of services rendered emerge, namely the functional economy – companies do not sell products but their functions, the experience economy, as well as service-dominant logic (SD), are factors that stimulate increased interest in systems production and services (Matusek, 2018, p. 346). Servitisation is an innovation of the organisation's ability and processes to change from focusing on selling products to selling integrated products and services that provide value-in-use (Baines et al., 2009, p. 547) In particular, the concept of Vargo and Lusch's service-dominant logic (Vargo and Lusch, 2006, pp. 43–56) stimulates new formulas for defining value – Value Dominant Logic (Mahajan, 2017, pp. 217 235), which is a factor that determines the effectiveness and efficiency of designed business models based on functioning in the service ecosystem. The ecosystem is part of the business context. Chandler and Vargo define the context as a set of unique actors in the unique interrelationship between them. The heterogeneity of the context thus affects the way resources are used for service

(Chandler and Vargo, 2011, pp. 35–49). In this approach, the designed systems are configurational, combining exogenous and endogenous factors into one common system. Configuration systems are increasingly being used as a means to effectively design customised service systems to meet the diverse needs of customers (Shen et al., 2017, p. 6120). The business model is the embodiment of the configuration due to the component arrangement of shaping its form. In the servitisation process, the orientation of business models changes from product to service orientation (Palo, Åkesson, and Löfberg, 2018, pp. 1–11). This transposition of the features of designing modern business models provides much wider possibilities of value creation and delivery. A classic portfolio based on value for money does not matter in this situation, because the attributes of choice are not the value itself, but the method of its delivery. Business models of enterprises that do not have built-in service formulas may lose their market position in favour of such models where these functionalities determine their essence. It is therefore crucial to transform the product-oriented business model into a service-oriented business model.

Conclusions

The content presented in Chapter 2 clearly indicates the complexity of the process of configuring digital business models. The assumptions of the new economy create opportunities for creating innovative business models that break existing competition rules on global markets. The concepts of the Sharing Economy, the Circular Economy and Big Data generate opportunities for creating new value propositions for digital platform users. An algorithm-based approach, cognitive business models, and servitisation prove that the number of potential business solutions based on innovative technology is infinite. The new directions of development of digital business models are based on intelligent solutions which use the assumptions of artificial intelligence. These business formulas function in specific business ecosystems based on the networks of integrated relationships between people and machines.

Note

1 Marginal cost (MC): the cost incurred by the producer due to increasing the production volume of a given good by one unit. It is an increase in total costs associated with the production of an additional unit of a good. The difference is the amount of costs previously incurred by the producer and the costs incurred after increasing production is the marginal cost.

References

Accenture (2016). *Trend 3 Platform Economy: Technology-driven Business Model Innovation from the Outside in High Performance. Delivered. Technology Vision.*

Acquier, A., Daudigeos, T., and Pinkse, J. (2017). "Promises and Paradoxes of the Sharing Economy: An Organizing Framework", *Technological Forecasting & Social Change*, 125, 3–7. DOI: 10.1016/j.techfore.2017.07.006.

Ali, S.A., Wang, S., and Ming, X. (2018). "Platform Enterprise Business Model: Their Essence and Particularity", *Journal of Research in Business, Economics and Management*, 10(2), 1882–1890.

Antikainen, M., Uusitalo, T., and Kivikyto-Reponen, P. (2018). "Digitalisation as an Enabler of Circular Economy", *Procedia, CIRP*, 73, 45. DOI: 10.1016/j.procir.2018.04.027.

Baines, T.S., Lightfoot, H.W., Benedettini, O., and Kay, J.M. (2009). "The Servitization of Manufacturing: A Review of Literature and Reflection on Future Challenges", *Journal of Manufacturing Technology Management*, 20(5), 547–567. DOI: 10.1108/17410380910960984.

Ballon, P., Walravens, N., Spedalieri, A., and Venezia, C. (2008). *The Reconfiguration of Mobile Service Provision: Towards Platform Business Models*, pp. 72–79. DOI: 10.2139/ssrn.1331549.

Barbu, C.M., Bratu, R.Ş., and Sirbu E.M. (2018). "Business Models of the Sharing Economy", *Review of International Comparative Management*, 19(2), 154–166. DOI: 10.24818/RMCI.2018.2.154.

Belk, R. (2014). "Sharing versus Pseudo-sharing in Web 2.0", *Anthropologist*, 18(1), 7–23.

Botsman, R. (2013). "The Sharing Economy Lacks a Shared Definition", Fast Company. Available at: www.fastcompany.com/3022028/the-sharing-economy-lacks-a-shared-definition

Brock, V. and Khan, H.U. (2017). "Big Data Analytics: Does Organizational Factor Matters Impact Technology Acceptance?", *Journal of Big Data*, 4(21), 1–7. DOI: 10.1186/s40537-017-0081-8.

Busch, Ch., Schulte-Nölke, H., Wiewiórowska-Domagalska, A., and Zoll, F. (2016). "The Rise of the Platform Economy: A New Challenge for EU Consumer Law?", *Journal of European Consumer and Market Law*, 5, 1–72.

Chandler, J.D. and Vargo, S.L. (2011). "Contextualization and Value-in-context: How Context Frames Exchange", *Marketing Theory*, 11(1), 35–49. DOI: 10.1177/1470593110393713.

Cockayne, D.G. (2016). "Sharing and Neoliberal Discourse: The Economic Function of Sharing in the Digital On-demand Economy", *Geoforum*, 77, 73–82. DOI: 10.1016/j.geoforum.2016. 10.005.

Cohen, J.E. (2017). "Law for the Platform Economy", *University of California Davis Law Review*, 51, 133–204.

Daugareilh, I., Degryse, Ch., and Pochet, P. (eds.) (2019). *The Platform Economy and Social Law: Key Issues in Comparative Perspective*, Working Paper 2019.10, European Trade Union Institute.

Eckhardt, G.M. and Bardhi, F. (2016). "The Relationship between Access Practices and Economic Systems", *Journal of the Association for Consumer Research*, 1(2), 210–225. DOI: 10.1086/684684.

Forbes (2017). "Cognitive Computing, czyli jak naprawdę działa sztuczna inteligencja". Available at: www.forbes.pl/opinie/cognitive-computing-jak-dziala-sztuczna-inteligencja/hfg65d6 (accessed 15 December 2019).

Frenken, K. and Schor, J. (2017). "Putting the Sharing Economy into Perspective", *Environmental Innovation and Societal Transitions*, 23, 3–10. DOI: 10.1016/j.eist.2017.01.003.

FUZERS (2018). "Serwityzacja. Czy wszystko stanie się usługą?" Available at: https://fuzers.com/pl/serwityzacja-czy-wszystko-stanie-sie-usluga/ (accessed 21 June 2019).

Gajewski, J., Paprocki, W., and Pieriegud, J. (2016). *Cyfryzacja gospodarki i społeczeństwa, Szanse i wyzwania dla Sectorów infrastrukturalnych, Instytut Badań nad Gospodarką Rynkową*, Gdańska: Akademia Bankowa, pp. 11–14.

Ghani, N.A., Hamid, S., Hashem, I.A.T., and Ahmed, E. (2019). "Social Media Big Data Analytics: A Survey", *Computers in Human Behavior*, 101, 417–428. DOI: 10.1016/j.chb.2018.08.039.

Habibi, M.R., Davidson, A., and Laroche, M. (2017). "What Managers Should Know About the Sharing Economy", *Business Horizons*, 60, 113–121. DOI: 10.1016/j.bushor.2016.09.007.

Heinrichs, H. (2013). "Sharing Economy: A Potential New Pathway to Sustainability", *Gaia*, 22(4), 228–231. DOI:10.14512/gaia.22.4.5.

Jabłoński, A. and Jabłoński, M. (2019). *Modele biznesu przedsiębiorstw, perspektywy rozwoju – ujęcie koncepcyjne*, Warszawa: CeDeWu, pp. 173–175.

Janczewski, J. (2014). "Systemy produktowo-usługowe w transporcie – wybrane przykłady", *Zarządzanie innowacyjne w gospodarce i biznesie*, 1(18), 60.

Kilhoffer, Z., Lenaerts, K., and Beblavý, M. (2017). "The Platform Economy and Industrial Relations Applying the Old Framework to the New Reality", Research Report No. 2017/12, DOI: 978-94-6138-631-1.

Kirkpatrick, B. and Galderisi, S. (2008). "Deficit schizophrenia: an update", *World Psychiatry*, 7(3), 143–147.

Kohtamäki, M., Parida, V., Oghazi, P., Gebauer, H., and Baines, T. (2019). "Digital Servitization Business Models in Ecosystems: A Theory of the Firm", *Journal of Business Research*, 104, 380–392.

Kreft, J. (2019). *Władza algorytmów, U źródeł potęgi Google i Facebooka*, Kraków: Wydawnictwo Uniwersytetu Jagiellońskiego.

Kumar, V., Lahiri, A., and Bahadir Dogan, O. (2018). "A Strategic Framework for a Profitable Business Model in the Sharing Economy", *Industrial Marketing Management*, 69, 147–148. DOI: 10.1016/j.indmarman.2017.08.021.

Lee, S. and Ahn, H. (2011). "The Hybrid Model of neural networks and Genetic Algorithms for the Design of Controls for Internet-based Systems for Business-to-consumer Electronic Commerce", *Expert Systems with Applications*, 38, 4326–4338. DOI:10.1016/j.eswa.2010.09.102.

Lepenioti, K., Bousdekis, A., Apostolou, D., and Mentzas, G. (2020). "Prescriptive Analytics: Literature Review and Research Challenges", *International Journal of Information Management*, 50, 57–70. DOI: 10.1016/j.ijinfomgt.2019.04.003.

Lessig, L. (2008). *Remix: Making Art and Commerce Thrive in the Hybrid Economy*, London: Penguin.

Li, F. (2017). "The Digital Transformation of Business Models in the Creative Industries: A Holistic Framework and Emerging Trends", *Technovation*, 92–93. DOI: 10.1016/j.technovation.2017.12.004.

Liozu, S.M. and Ulaga, W. (2018). *Monetizing Data: A Practical Roadmap for Framing, Pricing and Seeling your B2B Digital Offers*, Value Innoruption Advisors Publishing.

Long, H.J., Wang, L.Y., Zhao, S.X., and Jiang Z.B. (2016). "An Approach to Rule Extraction for Product Service System Configuration that Considers Customer Perception", *International Journal of Production Research*, 54(18), 5337–5360. DOI: 10.1080/00207543.2015.1078012.

Mahajan, G. (2017). "Value Dominant Logic", *Journal of Creating Value*, 3(2), 217–235. DOI: 10.1177/2394964317730655.

Mahut, F., Daaboul, J., Bricogne, M., and Eynard B. (2017). "Product-Service Systems for Servitization of the Automotive Industry: A Literature Review", *International Journal of Production Research*, 55(7), 1–19. DOI: 10.1080/00207543.2016.1252864.

Materiały Konferencyjne: Prof. Joan Enric Ricart, Professor of Strategic Management, Carl Schroeder Chair of Strategic Management, Prezentacja na 2nd Business Model Conference, 6–7 June 2018, University of Florence.

Matusek, M. (2018). "Zjawisko serwicyzacji przedsiębiorstw produkcyjnych – dwoistość usług w dostarczaniu zintegrowanych rozwiązań produktowo-usługowych", *Zeszyty Naukowe Politechniki Śląskiej. Organizacja i Zarządzanie*, 121, 333–355. DOI: 10.29119/1641-3466.2018.121.24.

Mazurek, G. (2019). *Transformacja cyfrowa, Perspektywa marketingu*, PWN,

McAfee, A. and Brynjolfsson, E. (2012). "Big Data: The Management Revolution", *Harvard Business Review*, 90(10), 60–68.

Menezes, B.C., Kelly, J.D., Leal, A.G., and Le Roux, G.C. (2019). "Predictive, Prescriptive and Detective Analytics for Smart Manufacturing in the Information Age", *IFAC PapersOnLine*, 52(1), 568–573. DOI: 10.1016/j.ifacol.2019.06.123.

Mitchell, M. (1995). "Genetic Algorithms: An Overview", *Complexity*, 1(1), 31–39. DOI: 10.1002/cplx.6130010108.

Muñoz, P. and Cohen, B. (2017). "Mapping Out the Sharing Economy: A Configurational Approach to Sharing Business Modeling", *Technological Forecasting and Social Change*. DOI: 10.1016/j.techfore.2017.03.035.

NewGenApps (2017). "What is Cognitive Computing? 5 Ways to Make Your Business More Intelligent". Available at: www.newgenapps.com/blog/what-is-cognitive-computing-applications-companies-artificial-intelligence (accessed 14 December 2019).

Nyle´n, D. and Holmstrom, J. (2015). "Digital Innovation Strategy: A Framework for Diagnosing and Improving Digital Product and Service Innovation", *Business Horizons*, 58(1), 57–67. DOI: 10.1016/j.bushor.2014.09.001.

Ordoñez, A., Ordoñez, H., Corrales, J.C., Cobos, C., Wives, L.K., and Thom, L.H. (2017). "Grouping of Business Processes Models Based on an Incremental Clustering Algorithm Using Fuzzy Similarity and Multimodal Search", *Expert Systems With Applications*, 67, 163–177. DOI: 10.1016/j.eswa.2016.08.061.

Palo, T., Åkesson, M., and Löfberg, N. (2018). "Servitization as Business Model Contestation: A Practice Approach", *Journal of Business Research*, 104, 1–11. DOI: 10.1016/j.jbusres.2018.10.037.

Santarek, K. and Salwin, M. (2017). *Systemy produktowo-usługowe*, Warsaw: Politechnika Warszawska, pp. 678–688.

Schor, J., Fitzmaurice, C., Carfagna, L.B., Attwood-Charles, W., and Poteat E.D. (2016). "Paradoxes of Openness and Distinction in the Sharing Economy", *Poetics*, 54, 66–81. DOI: 10.1016/j.poetic.2015.11.001.

Sejnowski, T.J. (2019). *Deep Learning, Głęboka Rewolucja, Kiedy sztuczna inteligencja spotyka się z ludzką*, Warszawa. Wydawnictwo Poltext, pp. 235–236

Shen, J., Ahmet Erkoyuncu, J., Roy, R., and Wu, B. (2017). "A Framework for Cost Evaluation in Product Service System Configuration", *International Journal of Production Research*, 55(20), 6120–6144. DOI: 10.1080/00207543.2017.1325528.

Smith, L., Maull, R., and Ng, I.C.L. (2014). "Servitization and Operations Management: A Service Dominant-logic Approach", *International Journal of Operations & Production Management*, 34(2). DOI: 10.1108/IJOPM-02-2011-0053.

Sousa M.J. and Rocha Á. (2019). "Skills for Disruptive Digital Business", *Journal of Business Research*, 94, 257–263. DOI: 10.1016/j.jbusres.2017.12.051.

Stephany, A. (2015). *The Business of Sharing: Making it in the New Sharing Economy*, New York: Palgrave MacMillan.

Szymańska, E. (2015). "Serwicyzacja gospodarki jako źródło jej transformacji", *Optimum. Studia Ekonomiczne*, 1(73), 97–109. DOI: 10.15290/ose.2015.01.73.09.

Täuscher, K. and Laudien, S.M. (2018). "Understanding Platform Business Models: A Mixed Methods Study of Marketplaces", *European Management Journal*, 36(3), 319–329. DOI: 10.1016/j.emj.2017.06.005.

Tewari, A. and Sareen, P. (2014). *Platform Business Models and Mobile Ecosystem*, Conference Paper, April 2014. DOI: 10.13140/2.1.1371.9367. (All content following this page was uploaded by Anurag Tewari on 08 January 2015.)

Tewari, S. and Dwivedi, U. (2019). "Ensemble-based Big Data Analytics of Lithofacies for Automatic Development of Petroleum Reservoirs", *Computers & Industrial Engineering*, 128, 937–947. DOI: 10.1016/j.cie.2018.08.018.

Timmers, P. (1998). "Business Models for Electronic Markets", *Electronic Markets*, 8(2), 3–8. DOI: 10.1080/10196789800000016.

Tukker, A. (2004). "Eight Types of Product-Service System: Eight Ways to Sustainability? Experiences from Suspronet", *Business Strategy and the Environment*, 13(4), 246–260. DOI: 10.1002/bse.414.

Ulbrych, M. (2016). "Serwicyzacja produkcji przemysłowej. Wnioski dla Polski", *Finanse, Rynki Finansowe, Ubezpieczenia*, 3(81), 253–264. DOI: 10.18276/frfu.2016.81-22.

Urban, M., Klemm, M., Ploetner, K.O., and Hornung, M. (2018). "Airline Categorisation by Applying the Business Model Canvas and Clustering Algorithms", *Journal of Air Transport Management*, 71, 175–192. DOI: 10.1016/j.jairtraman.2018.04.005.

Vandermerwe, S. and Rada, J. (1988). "Servitization of Business: Adding Value by Adding Services", *European Management Journal*, 6(4), 314–324. DOI: 10.1016/0263-2373(88)90033-3.

Vargo, S.L. and Lusch, R. (2006). "Service-dominant Logic: What It Is, What It Is Not, What It Might Be", in R. Lusch and S.L. Vargo (eds.), *The Service-dominant Logic of Marketing, Dialog, Debate, and Directions*, Armonk: M.E. Sharpe, pp. 43–56.

Yaqoob, I., Abaker Targio Hashem, I., Gani, A., Mokhtar, S., Ahmed, E., Badrul Anuar, N., and Vasilakos, A.V. (2016). "Big Data: From Beginning to Future", *International Journal of Information Management*, 36(6), 8–9. DOI: 10.1016/j.ijinfomgt.2016.07.009.

3 Social aspects in digital business models

Introduction

The digital economy is developing a social dimension. Social issues are reflected both in building the community and the very idea of the optimal use of resources. Sharing these resources using Big Data as well as the waste-oriented Circular Economy creates new opportunities to build sustainable organisational strategies aimed at building a balance of economic, ethical, and ecological issues. They enable the next stage of development of the concept of the triple bottom line (TBL), which underlies the idea of sustainable development, the equivalence of the sphere of the economy, environment and society (Elkington, 1999). In this spirit, the foundations for designing sustainable business models are created. They are applied particularly in the digital economy because they are no longer forced, as was previously the case in corporate social responsibility strategies, but are built into genotypes – the DNA of digital economy business models. A social aspect is the main driver of the success of digital economy business models, which is reflected in the reversal of management intentions, where the main goal is to build a community treated as a key capital, which can translate into expected business model monetisation after gaining critical mass in the number of community participants – if such an assumption is accepted by the creators of innovative solutions. The social business model of companies operating in the digital economy can be understood as a business model where factors that stimulate development are social aspects expressed in balancing economic, ecological and social issues with community involvement and dynamic communication focused on the selected attributes of business models based on digital platforms that stimulate growth and are favourable to achieving success. To sum up, holistic thinking is important in the business model; it involves expanding the field of results and not referring them to those who are employed in a social enterprise, but showing how and what actions taken improve the quality of life of the local community where the organisation operates. The proper planning of activity in the area related to customer relationships contributes to choosing the methods of acquiring, increasing, and retaining the value of customers for a longer period of time. The main activities which managers in social enterprises indicate as those that significantly affect the building of the image of their organisation include activities related to building prestige and trust, which contributed to networking and cooperation in the local community and among the representatives of the authorities. This is supported by correctly identified channels that can be used to provide customers with products or services provided by social enterprises (Frączkiewicz-Wronka and Cziura, 2017).

The aim of the chapter is to show how important the social factors of business model design and the creation of social value are in modern business.

Theoretical framework of the social aspects of business models in the digital economy

A social factor is crucial for the existence of digital business models. Through the use of technological solutions, contemporary business models significantly increase the availability of services, which has a positive effect on the development of social factors of the modern economy. For example, the development of Tourism 2.0 based on better accessibility of tourist services through digitalisation has shaken up the current traditional tourist services market (2019 saw the collapse of one of the largest and oldest travel agencies in the world, Thomas Cook). The availability of services through the use of digital applications therefore affects the social aspect in the sense that economic barriers to the use of goods and services are reduced. This availability, supported by attractiveness, can be a useful source of value for many recipients. The number of users of a given digital business model increases the chance of monetising business models. Therefore, the functionality of the proposed solutions can result in the migration of communities to attractive business models. A large community centred around the digital business model is the largest source of capital for its creators. Therefore, there is no doubt that the social aspect is a key bearer of value in business models (Spieth et al., 2019, pp. 427–444). It is not easy to build large communities around the business model. This model must be distinguished by specific attributes, which will create the opportunity to capture market value when compared to competing propositions. Thus, community building is more effective when aspects that positively affect business ethics, the environment, and economic results are included in the business model. Goods can be divided in a sustainable manner only if the economic factor allows it. The managerial intentions of managers determine how (whether honestly and pro-environmentally) goods will be produced and how they will affect their perception by society. In this context, social factors have a dual nature. On the one hand, they constitute an element of building intellectual (relational) capital – a community of supporters of the proposed solution. On the other hand, value should be created with respect for the natural environment and in a fair manner (the examples of Circular Economy business models). The socialisation of business models can be a distinguishing feature of competing digital business models which struggle to capture the volume of the community (Jabłoński and Jabłoński, 2020). Value will always migrate to more attractive business models.

Social business models go beyond traditional economics, pointing to the intangible nature of values. Business models that create effective social value factors have a chance to be successful on the market. Social business models generate strategic value that in some cases turns into valuable items or services, and sometimes creates a higher level of social value. These are values that refer to human desires, dreams and expectations. Modern business models create value for shareholders, but serve society from a broader perspective. The effectiveness of these business models should be sought not only in terms of business, but also in the context of the social economy. The digital economy is shaping a new perspective on business model design processes. The digital economy also draws attention to the social benefits of modern business models. So far, the impact of the value economy on shaping business models has been covered in the literature to a negligible extent. Modern business models based on the concepts of the Sharing Economy, Big Data, and the Circular Economy are based on technological solutions. Easy access to information on their use results from the widespread use of mobile telephones and the Internet. Business models in the digital economy lead to a situation in which these models change the priorities of people's choice and their attitude towards goods, which is revealed by transforming decisions with the desire for access. In this respect, business is socialised with an emphasis on improving the quality of life of business model users, and these models serve this purpose. At the same time, the strategic transformation of market behaviour from the assumptions of the classical economy based on maximising shareholder value to the Sharing Economy is evident. In this economy, not only economic profit matters, but social profit as well. The strategic intentions of the creators of modern business models play a crucial role. An economic factor is not always the main stimulus for their creation. It seems important to note that the social aspect occurs in two areas. The first is the positive intentions of business model creators, and the second is the generation of social value through the use of their functionality. The key in this respect is the conceptualisation and operationalisation of the assumptions of creating social business models in terms of management intentions and the impact of these models on society and people's quality of life through the availability of resources. The analysis of the place and role of social aspects in the design of business models is developmental, as evidenced by the emerging number of scientific articles on business models which use social aspects (Daunoriene et al., 2015; Hyup Roh, 2016; Mauri et al., 2018). The area of this knowledge is developmental and multidimensional. The first attempts to conceptualise and operationalise social aspects in business models have been made, for example as part of defining the archetypes for sustainable business models (Bocken et al., 2014; Calvo and Villarreal, 2018, p. 27; Yip and Bocken, 2018, p. 150).

The issue of the impact of digital business models on the achievement of social benefits not only in the context of business effectiveness, but the social economy as well, is also poorly recognised. Attempts should be made to explain this knowledge gap in terms of the social approach to the design and application of innovative business models in the digital economy. The interpretation and observation of social phenomena that affect the creation of modern business models will be important in this respect. One should also be aware of the new interpretation in this respect, which makes a change in the current understanding of economics. As Brożek argues, every fragment of our knowledge – at least potentially – can change in the interpretation process. This does not mean, of course, that these changes can take place in any way, nor that theories can be changed or alternative interpretative paraphrases rejected easily. Some of the elements of background knowledge, especially the "central" ones, that is, the fundamental concepts or the most general theories, are relatively stable: we can modify them, but it is usually a long process. You cannot change the framework of the conceptual grid in one go because it would result in the structural instability of the language and, consequently, the inability to understand each other. Similarly, it is impossible to replace all theories explaining the world with alternative concepts at one time, because a new Tower of Babel would emerge. Our conceptualisations of reality, entangled in the theories proclaimed, change evolutionally, not through a revolution (Brożek, 2014, p. 280).

We deal with such a new interpretation in the area of changes caused by technological progress. The Sharing Economy model can provide social enterprises with the opportunity to overcome their market problems because social value can be fully embedded in the sharing process in the economic cycle. Using innovative and proactive platforms as part of the concept of the Sharing Economy based on ICT technologies can be a new idea for shaping social entrepreneurship. Furthermore, the activities of social enterprises which are able to create both social and economic value, considered to be organisations with a so-called "double bottom line", prove the development of new opportunities to shape social values. These findings have practical and strategic implications for the development and transfer of social values. The Sharing Economy is a new economic model that goes beyond the mass production and consumption paradigm. This means that sharing things instead of possessing them is becoming increasingly popular, creating a new paradigm of capitalism (Hyup Roh, 2016).

The potential of the digital economy to develop socially oriented activities

The operationalisation of the digital economy in terms of building social ties has a specific character. As a rule, it is based on technological solutions implemented in practice. Generally, this approach is in the field of social interaction technology, or Social Identity Theory (SIT). This is a very wide-ranging field that includes a large list of topics: interactive and network data processing, mobile social services and social networks, social software and social media, marketing and advertising, the various aspects and uses of blogs and podcasts, corporate value and online collaboration, e-administration and online democracy, virtual volunteering, various aspects and applications of the community, tagging and a social semantic cloud of tags, blog-based knowledge management systems, online learning systems, their ePortfolio, blogs and wiki in education and journalism, legal issues and social interaction technologies, data monitoring and online fraud, neogeography, social software usability, social software in libraries and non-profit organisations, and broadband visual communication technology to strengthen social interaction [Redondo]. Several tools are associated with social software:

1. The tools facilitate participation in the creation, publication, and dissemination of content such as video, photos, music, and texts via the Internet.
2. Social software allows people with similar interests to find each other and connect through social networking sites such as Facebook.
3. People can coordinate their activities and cooperate by acquiring petitions and funds as well as planning and conducting mobile campaigns and social programmes.
4. People can create reliable and complex products such as open source software, for example Linux (the largest example of community development). There are three features commonly attributed to social software:
   - Interactions in conversations between individuals or groups.
   - Social opinions that allow the group to assess the contribution of others.
   - Social networks to explicitly create and manage the digital expression of personal relationships.

Social software serves many purposes:

- Ensuring communication between groups;
- Enabling communication between many people;
- Ensuring the collection and sharing of resources;
- Providing the collection and indexing of information;
- Providing new tools to aggregate knowledge and create new knowledge;
- Delivering data to various platforms depending on the creator, recipient and context [Redondo].

Such a wide range of services offered creates a set of multiple activities that develop the social potential of the functioning of the modern market economy, which increases the chances of creating social values, as reflected in the specific formulas of business models.

The digital economy is developing a social dimension. Social issues are both reflected in community building and the optimisation of resources. Sharing these resources, the use of large data sets, as well as the Circular Economy focused on the elimination of waste, creates new opportunities for building sustainable strategies of organisations focused on a balance of economic, ethical, and ecological issues. Through them, the concept of the triple bottom line (TBL) experiences the next stage of development: a concept that underlies the idea of sustainable development, the equivalence of economic, environmental, and social spheres (Elkington, 1999). In this spirit, the foundations are created for the design of sustainable business models. They are applicable in the digital economy in particular because they are no longer forced, as was previously the case in corporate social responsibility strategies, but are built into genotypes – the DNA of digital economy business models of innovative concepts indicated in this monograph. A social aspect is the main success driver of digital economy business models, which is reflected in the inversion of the priorities of managerial intentions, where the main goal is to build a community treated as key capital. Only after obtaining a critical mass in terms of the volume of community participants can this translate into the effect of the expected monetisation of a business model, provided that such an assumption is adopted by the creators of innovative solutions. The social business model of digital economy companies can be understood as a business model, of which the factors that stimulate development are social aspects expressed in balancing economic, environmental, and social issues with the involvement of communities and dynamic communication focused on the selected attributes of business models based on digital platforms stimulating growth and facilitating success, the expression of which can be economic and/or social profit. The satisfaction of the stakeholders with such a solution is another condition for embedding this solution in the sphere of the social economy.

Parida, Sjödin, and Reim undertook an interesting literature review in terms of the place and role of digitalisation in building innovative business models and sustainable industry (2019, p. 391). (See Figure 3.1.)

Sustainability aspects have been added to the base model presented by Parida, Sjödin, and Reim (2019). Digitalisation should affect sustainability, and social commitment should improve the quality of dialogue with stakeholders. Thus, it should be possible to create, deliver, and capture value from the market and to shape innovative business models focused on the assumptions of sustainability.

This is a very interesting approach because it justifies the inclusion of digitalisation principles focused on the degree of the use of digital technologies,

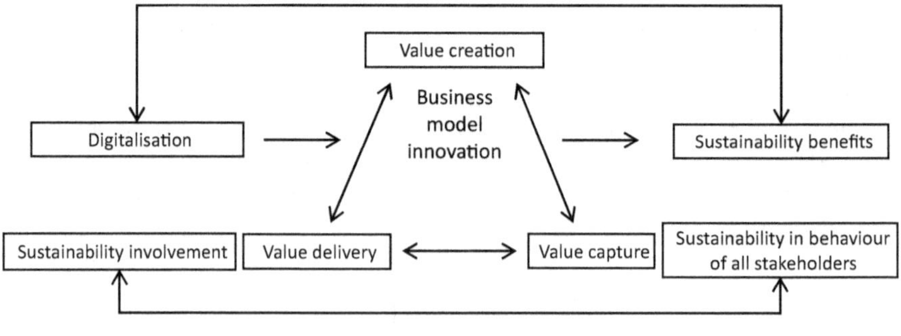

Figure 3.1 Construction of innovative business models focused on the assumptions of the sustainability concept.

Source: Own study based on Parida, Sjödin, and Reim, 2019, p. 391.

the function of digitalisation in business and the principles of business analytics based on the logic of digitalisation in the mechanisms of value creation of sustainable business models.

The architecture of the digital world generates a new dimension of market and social realities. Areas such as social media, cloud computing, Big Data, mobile technology, real-time computing, digital communications, and the Internet of Things not only create new development spaces, but also generate specific threats, which, inter alia, are associated with two opposing problems – on the one hand, the emergent digital dependence of young people, and on the other hand, the digital exclusion of elderly people. It is interesting that, for example, digital exclusion no longer applies only to elderly people, but can also include younger people who are not able to keep up with dynamically progressing technological changes. Finally, digital exclusion may also result from a lack of basic competences in this area. With regard to digital addiction, it may primarily relate to the so-called generation of "native users" (who have known the Internet since they were born). These people cannot imagine life without a smartphone and access to the internet. The ecosystem of new digital technologies creates many related threats, including those related to cyber security. Another common threat is public misinformation through false information and data on the web; hence, the implementation of cybersecurity principles in business is simply a requirement and a necessity. In the context of social aspects, it is important for network users to be aware of leaving so-called digital footprints.

Social issues have a significant dimension in the context of building new companies and enterprises. In the context of assessing the activity of companies focused on achieving profitability, how income is generated and what types of value enterprises can create is important. A balanced approach results from a different route to defining company goals. Currently, the goals of creating business models focus in many cases on building communities and relationships with business stakeholders and their monetisation is postponed for the future. The priority is to build a digital corporate brand that has an impact on communities, their lifestyles, understanding the world and perception of values. Contemporary trends operationalised by means of business models help build social attitudes by means of participation in enterprises and creating communities which share the same values, interests, and priorities. A review of the literature and observation of economic phenomena appearing in the business space confirm the significant impact of new business solutions based on technological solutions on building social bonds, creating social values and building a sustainable model of business activity in the digital economy.

Modern technological solutions create conditions for shaping social attitudes and undermine the existing principles of classical economics. Markets parallel to existing ones are emerging that are increasingly ontological in nature. The virtual world creates new markets, sets new rules for cooperation between people and creates new communication formulas. The old model of action based on a conventional approach is changing into a relational approach. Social and personal interactions are important factors that motivate companies to carry out transactions (Mauri et al., 2018, p. 42).

The technological revolution generates solutions in the social sphere, establishing new rules for market creation and people's behaviour. The impact of digital technology on these aspects is visible. New concepts and ideological trends are operationalised through innovative technological solutions, which enable the implementation of global solutions, the potential of which is not yet fully utilised. This is due not only to technological problems but also sociological ones, whereby new generations use these solutions to a greater extent than older ones. Quality of life is currently strongly correlated with access to digital technologies. Countries with higher levels of digitalisation have more potential, which allows them to implement new social ideas faster and improve people's quality of life. The potential of the Sharing Economy, the Circular Economy, and Big Data is very high. It allows for the creation of business solutions, also related to the so-called new concept of public management. The Sharing Economy is a plan for a future business idea that explains how to link economic, environmental, and social issues (Daunoriene et al., 2015, p. 837).

The digital economy creates new opportunities for building entrepreneurial initiatives. New entrepreneurship offers a chance to create social values in which the priority of the company is not profit, but rather social value. Social business models are satisfactory not only to their creators, but, above all, to their users and recipients. There are different approaches to defining social enterprises. Contemporary trends in creating social values are operationalised by means of business models. Features that distinguish classical entrepreneurial activities in the context of classical economics from contemporary, modern entrepreneurial activities focused on the use of social values in a network economy are important. The assumptions formulated in this way refer to how to create, capture, and preserve social value in the company and among groups of stakeholders. It is crucial to identify key determinants that build entrepreneurial attitudes focused on designing social business models in digital ecosystems.

The value economy is a holistic view of creating value for various stakeholder groups. It explores and deals with fields of knowledge such as economics, philosophy, sociology, cultural anthropology, business ethics, and corporate social responsibility. As Hausner observes, the dispute about value is constantly present at the centre of the discussion on scientific cognition and on the different nature of exact and social sciences. It is impossible to formulate the correct economic theory of values without recognising that values have a social nature and that existential, rather than instrumental, values give sense to our existence (Hausner, 2017, p. 71).

The value economy is an important trend that should be considered in the design process of modern business models. The value economy plays an important role in the process of shaping social business models in the digital economy. The criteria for qualifying business and life values are significant. An attempt to combine business aspects of the classical economy with a new approach to value, namely sharing resources according to the concept of the Sharing Economy, seems interesting. The social nature of value is widely revealed in these solutions. As part of the identification of features describing the modern business environment, the attributes of building social bonds within the network economy and network organisations are critical. The value economy in the context of social business models should be considered in ontological, epistemological, and methodological categories.

The social perspective of running business activity in the modern economy

Due to the dynamic development of the relational nature of market participants entering into multilateral interactions, the social aspects of conducting business and public activity have created opportunities to develop new forms of building social business models. Technology has created opportunities for the development of this form of conducting business. In addition to the classical forms of achieving organisational goals, in many cases, broadly understood social values are generated directly or indirectly. Enterprises are usually classified according to two criteria: ownership (public or private) and goals (profit-oriented or non-profit-oriented). According to traditional two-dimensional typologies of enterprises based on ownership and goals, social enterprises are defined as private, not directly profit-oriented enterprises. Over the past three decades, the concept of a social enterprise has grown in many regions of the world. A social enterprise refers to organisations that conduct business activity, both to increase income and to further improve social missions (Hyup Roh, 2016, p. 503). A social enterprise is embedded between the needs of private companies and households.

To develop the social aspects of conducting business activity, it is necessary to define social drivers for business models. The essence presented in the model is the integration of social value, the economic value of the company and value creation. While the company ensures the delivery of an offer that meets customers' needs, it also creates social aspects. This may include the creation of direct values by a social enterprise within its value chain, intermediation services by means of which it provides transactions related to social benefits, the indirect generation of social values through the company's impact on the environment or through social projects financed by the economic profits generated. Moreover, social enterprises focus on making their offer affordable and actively shaping the value chain in line with their overall values and mission, thereby strengthening their partners and contributing to community development. Thus, the factors driving social business models are innovative ways of integrating social impact on the offer and creating company value (Spieth et al., 2019, pp. 427–444).

The presented models clearly show that it is possible to generate economic values without harming social values, which in many cases strengthen the configuration and ensure the integrity of these business models. Social aspects are an indispensable element of creating a multidimensional and interdisciplinary construct of value creation.

Sustainable business models and hybridisation and the development of social issues

Sustainable business models as a concept are dynamically developing not only in terms of balancing environmental, ethical, and economic aspects, but they are also used to support operations in the long term. This is the basis for building cooperation between various groups of stakeholders in a networked environment and creating conditions for the effective reception of social business activity. The issue of sustainable business models has not been widely studied in terms of the digital economy. It is important to identify key issues related to shaping sustainable business models in the digital economy and their impact on social development. The modern approach goes significantly beyond the classical approach based on the principles of the "triple bottom line" (Elkington, 1999). The social character is evident in the configurations of modern business models and the hybrid combination of economic and social aspects.

The concept of hybridisation has been analysed in recent years in a broad context. Business models based on the joint implementation of the Big Data and the Sharing Economy concepts are one such example of a hybrid business model. The combination of both concepts at the level of business models offers a chance to create pioneering solutions. New ideas can transform the current approach based on the classical value chain into one which suits the network economy (Jabłoński, 2018).

Hybridisation is often associated with a combination of management practices in corporate management and public management. Public management is subject to dynamic changes aimed at improving the efficiency of managing public funds and shaping social values. Hybridisation can be an effective way of shaping social business models. In particular, it can be used in the digital economy. A multidimensional approach to using the concept of hybridisation can be useful for building social business models. The concept of hybridisation can be used to develop the core features of social business models by combining solutions used in public administration in terms of the analysis of Big Data with a commercial approach. The operationalisation of data will enable social effects from access to Big Data sets.

Taking into account technological, social, and organisational aspects, assumptions for the archetypes of sustainable business models can be built (Bocken et al., 2014).

The identification of the archetypes of sustainable business models shapes a suitable approach to value-based management, including value proposition, value creation, value delivery, and value capture.

Value proposition includes the development of products and services which require less resource consumption, waste, and emissions into the environment with the delivery of similar functionalities. Value creation and delivery includes activities and partnerships that aim to apply resource savings and generate fewer losses, emissions and less waste, as well as to focus on production and innovation processes and to build new forms of partnership and value networks by reconfiguring and improving value chain effectiveness. On the other hand, value capture includes costs reduced by optimising material consumption and losses due to emissions, leading to increased profitability and price competitiveness as well as a positive impact on society and the environment (Bocken et al., 2014).

The archetypes of sustainable business models can be shaped by innovative solutions through technological, social, and organisational aspects. Technical grouping includes activities that use technology to maximise materials and energy efficiency to create value from waste and replace traditional processes with renewable energy sources and natural processes (Calvo and Villarreal, 2018). Sustainable innovation in the business model is increasingly seen as leverage for changing systems of sustainable development in various companies and industries (Yip and Bocken, 2018). The social integration of a sustainable company can be accomplished by actively supporting the creation of two-way links between stakeholder networks, which takes place in the digital economy by building interactions between the social structure of entrepreneurial ecosystems and emerging sustainable business models. Sustainability is thus a way to achieve success and ensure the efficiency and effectiveness of the business model. It also influences the behaviour of investors towards business models based on the principles of sustainability, and, most importantly, the factors responsible for the migration of values (Neumeyer and Santos, 2018). In addition, it is a condition for achieving success by using it with the embedded subject functionalities.

The principles on the basis of which social business models can be built have not been clearly developed. Based on the theoretical approach and practical implications, it is possible to identify assumptions about the design of social business models. It is important to look for solutions in concept development and the operationalisation of social business models in the digital economy. Different approaches to the notation of business models can be used to identify and select such components of business models that affect the development of social issues, and at the same time can ensure better consistency of the business model. Solutions such as the business model canvas by Osterwalder and Pigneur can be very useful. In particular, authors' approaches to the operationalisation of social business models of the digital economy seem to be worth developing.

Many good practices occur in social business models throughout the world. It should be noted that the understanding of social aspects is different in different geographical areas around the world. Therefore, the features of social business models will also be different. However, it is worth looking for good practices in the field of designing social business models and their assessment in terms of a wide range of selected criteria. The Sharing Economy goes hand in hand with the process of strengthening the attitudes of active action, aiming to fulfil their income aspirations, and the ability to share property with others in the name of the common good. It will have to be shifted to shaping a new dimension of social relations (Poniatowska Jaksh and Sobiecki, 2016, p. 18). As part of identifying such aspects of the digital economy business models that are social in nature, the following dimensions can be defined:

1. The leading role played by the community in value creation.
2. Active and conscious participation of people in value creation.
3. Bidirectional or multidirectional communication system between business model participants.
4. Building communities involved in a given topic, often with visible passion.
5. Designing business models with a focus on social values.
6. Changing priorities, redefining the purpose of the company from generating profit to building a community.
7. Co-creation of business models with communities.
8. Changes in business model configurations as a result of consultations with communities.
9. Breaking the current order of things and creating social innovations.
10. Overtaking the existing legal order many times, as it cannot keep up with dynamic changes.
11. Improving the quality of life and participation of people excluded so far in communities.

In the context of the research problem posed, it is important to explain the place and role of social aspects in the design of contemporary business models operating in the digital economy. Social aspects are a prerequisite for the success of digital economy companies. They are an important component of these business models and are a condition for their consistency. The management intentions of their creators very often expose social aspects as those that determine the existence of a given business model, while the monetisation of the business model is postponed until social aspects have proven the validity of the adopted, initial design assumptions. Thus, the social aspect is very often embedded in the DNA of the business model and is a condition for achieving the adopted assumptions even when the economic results are distant in time due to the development of these social factors. Social aspects are a condition for achieving the efficiency and effectiveness of digital business models.

Social and economic strategic value in digital business models

The concept of value is crucial to understanding the logic of the concept of business models. Value is the core element on the basis of which complex constructs of innovative business models are built. Value-in-use, expected and experienced, is dominant in business models. The terms "value creation" and "value creation process" are only used to create customer value-in-use. The reason is that in the contemporary marketing and management literature, as in the axiology literature, customers are perceived as those who create value from the resources they have obtained (Grönroos, 2011, pp. 240–247). Therefore, value in business models is defined by the concepts of value creation, value capture, value retention, and value delivery. The interactive, interdependent, and dynamic nature of value creation has led theorists and practitioners to seek a better understanding of value-based management processes in business relationships (Corsaro, 2019, pp. 99–116). Value, being a combination of product and service features and other variables, is a complex structure of attributes which is important in the customer's choice. In this way, the term strategic value appears, that is, one that is equally important for the organisation and the customer and is the result of a unique configuration of the business model. This is what the designers of innovative, winning business models expect to receive. In the digital economy, strategic value is of fundamental importance in the process of building a community, in the process of achieving the expected monetisation and in the process of building corporate reputation. In this approach, strategic value is the sum of all values strengthening the ideas contained in a given business model. By increasing strategic value, understood as a synergistic and complementary sum of all values that are a core feature of the business model, companies have the chance to achieve success on a difficult global market.

The management of social and economic value – the perspective of trying to find balance in the context of the attributes of digital business models – is an interdisciplinary issue. Attempts to balance social and economic aspects, especially in terms of the specificity of the functioning of the digital economy, seem to be an important aspect that requires both theoretical and application solutions. The reality of modern business sets out the need for a better understanding of the reasons for the success and failure of those business models whose success factors are asset components that include social aspects.

The social aspect in digital business models has two dimensions. The first is embedded in the idea of building a community by using multilateral technology platforms that stand out compared to other business models, while the second relates to the social impact of the value delivered by the business model. Both shape a pro-social approach, which is reflected in delivering social value to business model stakeholders. Both of these approaches are complementary and create the image of socially acceptable business models, where this social aspect is a condition for the adaptability of such designed business models to the expectations of the modern global market. Noticeable uncertainty, and even in a way chaos, on global markets requires neutralisation through the implementation of sustainable strategies focused on broadening the acceptance of business designed and conducted by societies. Building a community that supports a business solution due to its economic and social values increases trust in such solutions and mitigates the risk of the project being rejected by the market. It is therefore profitable for its creators, in particular in terms of market activity in the longer term. Another aspect that is part of the social nature of digital business models is the idea of sustainability, the assumptions of which are based on the concept of the triple bottom line (TBL) (Elkington, 1999). This concept underlies the idea of sustainable development; it is the concept of the equivalence of economy, environment, and society. The goal of the TBL is that company activities in relation to the environment and the social sphere are treated in the same way as financial results, and that the results in these areas are assessed, in accordance with the assumption that only what (a company, an organisation, or a person ...) supervises and accounts for is what he/she/it pays attention to. It is worth realising that the term "bottom line", which the concept of TBL derives from, refers to the company's net earnings, that is, the sphere of economics. The inclusion of social and environmental spheres means that we are left with a triple bottom line (http://odpowiedzialnybiznes.pl/artykuly/garsc-refleksji-na-temat-koncepcji-potrojnej-linii-ałuniu/ [accessed 13 December 2018]). In the digital economy, this approach applies and is revealed through the assumptions of business models based, for example, on the concept of the Circular Economy. The social aspects of digital business models play a significant role in the creation of value drivers for these business models, which are responsible for the efficiency of these solutions in the business ecosystem which takes the community into account.

Based on the review of the relevant literature, the authors' observations and experience, and the resulting analyses, a scientific problem was identified, which is to indicate the key problem of displaying social value as part of an inverted model for setting priority goals for modern digital business models, where it is crucial to build a community centred around new socio-economic ideas. At the same time, value for shareholders (Rappaport, 1999) is important, but requires the implementation of long-term strategies based on these ideas. In other words, the social acceptance of business models and social value drivers is a condition for creating shareholder value.

The business model as a management concept has already established a place in the space of science and practice. It has particular significance in the global economy supported by the development of information technologies and the ideological concepts of modern economics resulting from their possibilities. A new approach to competitiveness is emerging. The next generation of competition is changing the way business is conducted. Contemporary business activity is based not only on this competition, but in particular on cooperation and collaboration. Acceleration in the area of competition is based on a bonus for rapid implementation (and continuous updating) of the new business model (Teece and Linden, 2017, p. 3). In the context of the core features of the business model, the concept of values plays a leading role. Value that can be created with the help of a business model determines the strength, efficiency, and effectiveness of the business model. Value and its flow in the business ecosystem is crucial. The paradox of value includes value-in-use ("utility", contribution to someone else's goals) and value-in-exchange ("purchasing power of other goods" reflected in the market price) (Eggert et al., 2018, p. 82).

According to the theory of economics, the word value should be seen as having two different meanings. Sometimes it expresses the utility of a particular object, and sometimes the power to buy other goods. In this way, the terms "value-in-use" and "value-in-exchange" can be used. Things that have the greatest value-in-use often have little or no value-in-exchange, and on the

Table 3.1 Different approaches to value in the context of the assumptions of the concept of business models

Approach to value	*Description*
Value Creation	Value creation is usually analysed in terms of the Resource-based View, where development or taking over dynamic capabilities in relation to high effectiveness play an important role. Cf. Dyduch and Bratnicki, 2018, p. 7.
Value Capture	Value Capture is the process of retaining a certain percentage of the value earned in each transaction. There are two main approaches to capturing value: - Maximisation. An organisation should try to capture the greatest value. - Minimalisation. An organisation should gain the least value as long as it is sufficient. As long as one manages to collect enough to cover one's needs, not every money driver should be captured. It is necessary to create as much value as possible to make the captured value worth it. Cf. https://personalmba.com/value-capture/
Value Retention, Value Appropriation	It answers the following question: if value is captured by a company, how is this value distributed among a company's internal stakeholders? Cf. Di Gregorio, 2013, p. 42.

Source: Own study based on Dyduch and Bratnicki, 2018, p. 7; Di Gregorio, 2013, p. 42, https://personalmba.com/value-capture/).

contrary, those that have the greatest value-in-exchange often have little or no value-in-use. Nothing is more useful than water. On the contrary, a diamond has no value-in-use, but a very large number of other goods can be exchanged for that value (Eggert et al., 2018, p. 81). In terms of business models, the following approaches to value are created in Table 3.1.

In the context of digital business, value is exposed through multilateral digital platforms which ensure multilateral communication between various groups of stakeholders, thereby creating a network of values. Figure 3.2 presents the interpretation of value in the context of the digital economy.

Value is completely a function of choice. Digital business focuses on using interference forces that open up the space of choice. Therefore, it is necessary to build value architectures that are suitable for constant value change (Keen and Williams, 2013, p. 646). Value creation and value destruction are crucial in the context of explaining the concept of value (see Table 3.2).

Value co-creation and value co-destruction is of particular importance as regards business models based on the network paradigm where a value network plays a leading role in the flow of this value between actors. In this context, a social factor also develops, which creates a new perspective on the assumptions of the traditional economy, and in particular the identification of the primary goal of the company's existence, which is generating profit.

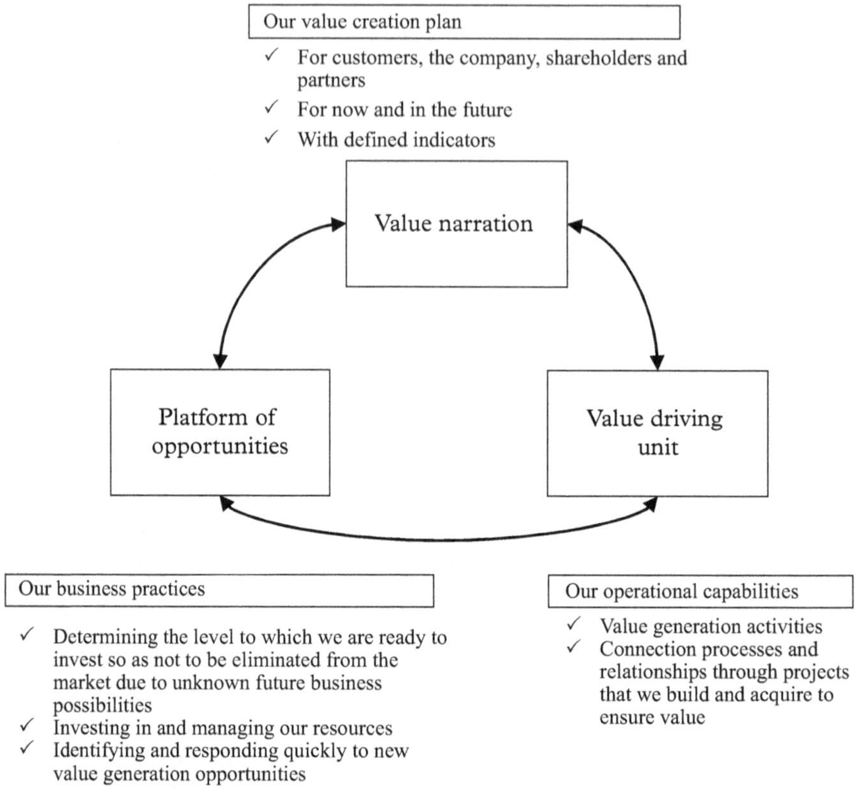

Figure 3.2 Value architecture.
Source: Own study based on Keen and Williams, 2013, p. 645.

Social aspects are a condition for achieving the efficiency and effectiveness of digital business models. They condition problems relevant to this research space. The following assumptions of social value creation can be indicated in the scope of the verification of the concept of business models.

1. Social aspects are a core component of digital business models, and are responsible for building a business ecosystem based on community activities.
2. Sustainable business models functioning as part of the concept of the Sharing Economy, the Circular Economy, and Big Data sets management strongly expose social issues based generally on their potential.
3. The change in the perception of the classical economy in the context of the collaborative economy changes the priorities from a contractual approach to a relational model.

Table 3.2 Value co-creation and value co-destruction in various types of relationships

	B2C interaction	*B2B interaction*	*Actors' interaction in terms of public services*
Value co-creation	Value co-creation can be revealed in the following forms: dialogue, customer engagement, self-service, customer experience, problem solving, code marking and joint development.	Value co-creation appears in the following forms: closeness, trust, transparency, relationships, information and ongoing problem solving.	Value co-creation arises in the context of volunteer activities or involuntary involvement of service users in any form, such as design, management, delivery or evaluation of a public service.
Value co-destruction	Value co-destruction occurs due to improper customer behaviour, which can lead to decreased well-being of company employees.	Value co-destruction occurs, for example, when actors face mistrust, communication is insufficient, there is inadequate coordination, insufficient human capital and a strength or imbalance thereof.	Value co-destruction occurs when public commitment reduces value by generating bad or negative results because of mistakes in providing services in accordance with established standards and the misuse of the resource provider or user.

Source: Own study based on Järvi, Kähkönen, and Torvinen, 2018, p. 66.

4. Business and public activities overlap in many matters and social issues bind them.
5. Technology and access to it improves the quality of life and increases the chances of eliminating social exclusion.
6. The increased digitalisation of the economy and society has a positive impact on the adaptability of new, innovative business models.
7. The condition of using the potential of innovative business models and their positive impact on social issues shapes legal regulations which are relevant to technical progress (Jabłoński, quoted in Hausner, manuscript in press).

In practice, a number of modern business solutions are hybrid, combining economic and social factors in a coherent manner, which, integrated into the configuration of resources supported by positive management intention, focus not only on maximising profit but, to a large extent, on creating social profit. Hybrid organisational forms which combine commercial and welfare institutional logic play an increasingly important role in facing great social challenges. As Spieth and colleagues point out, it is crucial to understand the specificity and value drivers of the hybrid social goal as opposed to purely commercial business models. The authors followed a well-grounded theoretical approach in their inference, basing the conclusions on the results of intelligence data from 17 social enterprises. Based on the specific features of social enterprises, they proposed four factors that drive social business models: responsible efficiency, impact complementarities, shared values, and integration novelties (Spieth et al., 2019, pp. 427–444).

The presented models clearly show that it is possible to generate economic values without harming the production of social values, which in many cases cement the configuration and ensure the integrity of these business models. Social aspects are an indispensable element of creating a multidimensional and interdisciplinary construct of value creation. In order to better understand how social value is created by selected entrepreneurs, a reference framework should first be provided on how social value can exist at a moderate level. In the discussion about what constitutes social value, financial, reputational, ethical values, consumer surplus, positive externalities, and strengthening of human capabilities as dimensions of creating social value are mentioned. Achieving financial value not only allows the company to survive, but also provides opportunities for reinvestment, which can be used by individuals directly involved in the original transactions. In addition, the reputation and ethical values achieved through the interaction of the company with the environment can also be conducive to increasing the scale of activities related to the creation of social values and bring benefits to people who are not directly involved in the original transactions. These dimensions of social value creation and positive externalities can be seen as indirect social value creation. Consumer surplus and strengthening human capacities are direct forms of creating social values. It is important to create social innovations treated as "an innovative solution to the social problem. … The main criterion for innovation qualifying as social innovation is the ability to benefit" by society or society as a whole – instead of private profits for entrepreneurs, investors, and ordinary consumers (not at a disadvantage) (Sinkovics, Sinkovics, and Yamin, 2014, p. 696).

Based on the literature on institutional complexity and social movements and the theory of paradoxes, Cherrier, Goswami, and Ray explored the possibility of institutional complexity providing opportunities for social entrepreneurship. Their ethnographic case study based on a social undertaking in India shows that institutional complexity manifests itself in forms of overlap and/or conflicting institutional logic and provokes paradoxical tension. They identify four strategic responses to institutional complexity: appropriation, integration, differentiation, and working-through. These strategies allow a company to reach a wider group of stakeholders. In conclusion, they claim that institutional complexity can be resourceful in the dynamic process of social value creation (Cherrier, Goswami, and Ray, 2018, p. 245).

Social aspects related to the concept of business models also have a place in the context of so-called positive marketing. Positive marketing is defined as any marketing activity that creates value for the company, its customers, and society (Gopaldas, 2015, p. 2446).

Monetary value is expanded to include social value and the value of the visitor creates total value for the customer. In this way, value is embedded in the aspect of applying business solutions which are suitable for the digital economy.

Social media technologies have revolutionised the way businesses interact with consumers. Customers who expect interactions between these networks also expect a similar level of interaction in their activity. This concept is also an important aspect of social value in terms of online relations (Kukkonen, 2018, p. 71). In the context of the digital economy, social value is a significant link which underlies the assumptions of digital business models. Three concepts of value on the Internet, that is, monetary, social, and visitor relationships, form the online customer value-based management framework. (See Figure 3.3.)

The approach presented in this way, resulting from the principles of the functioning of digital economy business models, prompts researchers to take a slightly different view of value.

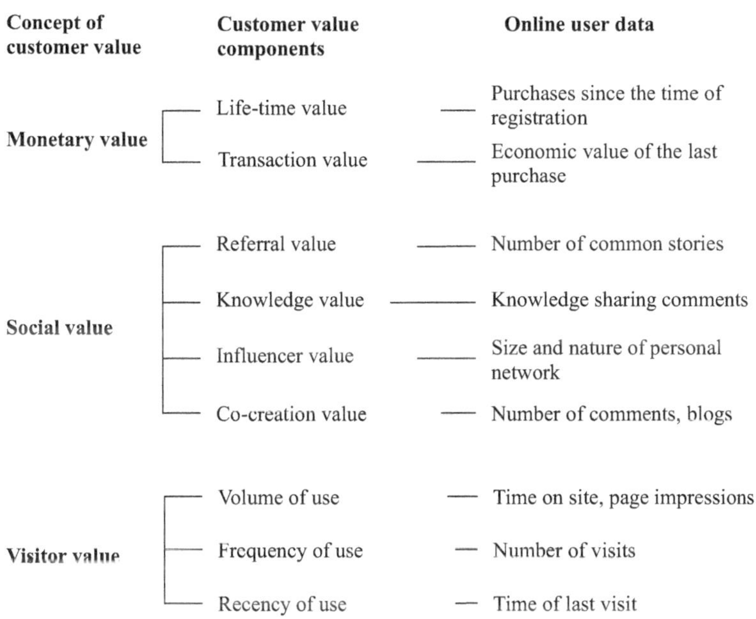

Figure 3.3 Framework for managing customer value in the online system.
Source: Own study based on Kukkonen, 2018, p. 71.

Sustainable value-based management and the perspective of business models

Sustainable value-based management reveals a new space for studying business models. The traditional approach is based on the assumption that the goal of any business is to make money. All decisions regarding supply and production should be made to maximise profit. The discrepancy in creating non-economic value is sometimes the result of separating ownership from control over a company. Although shareholders are interested in maximising profit, company managers who actually make decisions may also pursue other goals (Begg, Fisher, and Dornbusch, 2003, p. 175). In addition to economic aspects, the management intentions of modern managers are also influenced by factors arising from the organisational culture built and co-created within the organisation, and sometimes with the participation of external actors, such as suppliers and customers. The sources of social value creation will be the management intentions of top management, in many cases initiated by the adopted values and rules on the basis of which resources are bonded within the structure of the business model. In modern companies, there is a noticeable culture of corporate management based on the assumptions of turquoise organisation management, which is based on a new approach to shaping the model of work organisation, making work productive, sensible, and fulfilling (Laloux, 2015, 2016). By using self-organising teams, the radical simplification of project management processes and building a community are part of the socialisation of business in the sense that it adds value not only to selected stakeholders but to the wider public. The sources of financial and social value creation for creating sustainable value are shown in Figure 3.4.

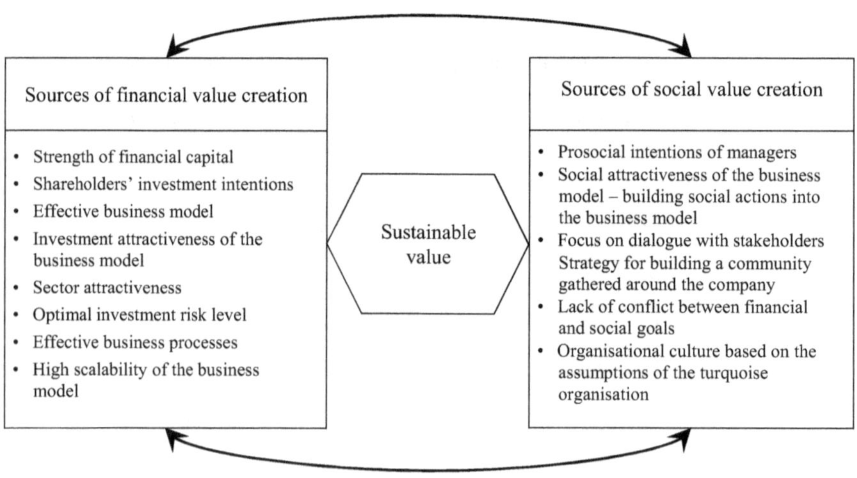

Figure 3.4 Sources of financial and social value creation for creating sustainable value.
Source: Own study.

Sustainable value is based on the identification of sources of creation that refer to economic and social value. Economic value is created through social value and vice versa. This allows the complementarity of the created value to be mutually supportive. The business model that is integrated from both of these values should be more resistant to crises than one that focuses only on generating economic value. The contemporary successes of digital economy business models confirm this hypothesis. The concurrent implementation of economic and social goals increases robustness and affects the success of contemporary business models. This results from the specificity of the business ecosystem built as part of the business model, which in essence is based on the use of social factors used to merge a business model into a complex ecosystem capable of producing value.

The essence of digital business models is that they are based on the functionality of IT platforms which use new technological trends based on Big Data sets, the Sharing Economy, the Circular Economy, and other spaces of contemporary business, which, in the context of their attributes, strongly exposes social factors. The social nature of these models means that they are perceived – in spite of legal doubts – as those that create new pro-social attitudes, which are part of the general principles of sustainable business. Public goods are produced within the adopted assumptions of business models. A public good is a good that, when consumed by one person, can be consumed by others at the same time – for example, clean air, and public safety. These are goods that we can all use at the same time (Begg et al., 2003, p. 100).

This aspect of microeconomics is strongly exposed in their case. The concept of public goods is widely recognised in terms of economic sciences, while the dynamic processes of operationalisation of these solutions can be noticed in terms of applying the concept of business models. They are revealed from the perspective of balancing economic and social factors, which affects the development of sustainable business models embedded in the realities of the concept of a new economy. This fosters building socially attractive business models commonly accepted by stakeholder groups. The subject is not easy in terms of scientific exploration due to its interdisciplinary nature. It certainly requires further empirical research to confirm the validity of such assumptions, bearing in mind that technologies stimulate new trends that should be considered through the prism of the current paradigms of economics and management as well as new emerging assumptions which are ahead of the achievements of the science of management and quality as well as economics and finance. This is a challenge for researchers of modern business ecosystems.

The following final conclusions can be drawn:

1. Social aspects are a crucial component of digital business models responsible for building a business ecosystem based on community activities.
2. Sustainable business models functioning as part of the concept of the Sharing Economy, the Circular Economy, and management of Big Data sets strongly expose social issues based generally on their potential.

3. The change in the perception of the classical economy in the context of the Sharing Economy changes the priorities from a contractual approach to a relational model.
4. Business and public activities overlap in many matters and social issues are a bond between them.
5. Technology and access to it increase the quality of life and the chances of eliminating social exclusion.
6. The increased digitalisation of the economy and society has a positive impact on the adaptability of new, innovative business models.
7. The condition of using the potential of innovative business models and their positive impact on social issues shapes legal regulations which are relevant to technical progress.

Defined based on the literature review and the authors' own reflections, the conclusions clearly show that social factors are an inherent feature of digital business models which use social relationships to disseminate knowledge about them and access to a large number of users. The added value is social profit from the exploitation of these business models.

Digital business models in the Circular Economy

Globalisation challenges set new market and social needs. Society is increasingly becoming a key stakeholder in a value-based economy. The environmental factor has been aspiring to be a strategic factor within these values for many years. It is even becoming a determinant of creating new markets and innovation challenges. At the same time, environmental changes in the world open new directions for creating social, environmental, and economic behaviour. From this perspective, the so-called Circular Economy business models emerge. The Circular Economy is currently one of the core areas of social and market development. Due to feedback occurring therein, the Circular Economy should be considered in terms of the system. A systematic approach is used not only to achieve goals focused on the efficient use of resources, but also their skilful rotation. This systematic approach should take into account an assessment of the organisation's life cycle and its business model. Life cycle assessment is a

> tool for analysing the environmental burden of products at all stages of their life cycle – from resource extraction, through the production of materials, parts of products and the product itself, as well as the use of the product for post-reject management, through reuse, recycling or final disposal (in effect "from cradle to grave").
>
> (Guinée, 2002, pp. 311–313)

A systemic approach allows the Circular Economy to integrate social, economic, and environmental aspects at every level of management:

- Micro level – by creating eco-projects, eco-products, minimising waste, introducing an environmental management system, etc.
- Meso level – by creating industrial eco-parks.
- Macro level – the creation of eco-cities, eco-municipalities, and eco-regions (Geng and Doberstein, 2008, pp. 231–239).

The Circular Economy aims to separate prosperity from resource consumption, that is, how to consume goods and services, and thus provide closed loops that prevent the possible storage of used goods in landfills. Production and consumption also involve "transferring pollutants" to the environment at every stage. In this sense, the Circular Economy is a movement towards sustainability. It proposes a system in which reuse and recycling ensure substitutes for the use of primary raw materials. By reducing dependence on such resources, it improves our ability and the ability of future generations to meet their needs. The Circular Economy increases the likelihood of sustainable development (Sauvé, Bernard, and Sloan, 2016, p. 53). Accenture has defined five types of circular business models:

- Input circular models – focused on the possibilities of reusing energy and input material for the process of goods production.
- Waste value models – consist of recovering the resources used in recycling processes, as a result of which waste generated in one production process becomes useful as input material in another production process.
- Life expectancy models – aimed at extending the life of products as well as components through actions such as repair, modernisation or resale.
- Platform models – based on the efficiency of using products by making them available to a wider group of users (e.g. Sharing products).
- Product in the service model – focused on offering services instead of selling goods (thus the company remains the owner of the product it is responsible for) (Lacy et al., 2014).

It can be assumed that circular business models are a specific variation of sustainable business models, whereby the resource approach plays a crucial role not only as a source of competitive advantage, but also as a source of repeated technological and innovative renewal. Circular business models supply the market, creating a counterbalance to other business models by functioning virtually in every sector where emissions to the environment occur. Based on the environmental and social responsibility of business, they generate new values that have not been noticed before. These values materialise, creating new layers of social and environmental effect without harming the economic effect. In this interpretation, Circular Economy business models have reversed this polarisation by adopting such logic. So far, the economic effect has been created without detriment to the social and environmental effect. In these models, it is just the opposite. Circular Economy business models answer the following questions, among others:

- How long can the quality of resources be maintained over their long life cycle?
- How to maximise value through circulating resources?
- How to extend the life cycle of resources while creating their strategic renewal?

From this perspective, circular business models create new spaces for achieving business and social effects while maintaining strategic balance at the level of the economy, sector, and companies themselves.

Digitalisation can boost the transformation towards a more sustainable Circular Economy. It can help to close the material loops by providing accurate information on the availability, location, and condition of products. Digitalisation also enables more efficient processes in companies, helps minimise waste, promotes longer life for products, and minimises the transaction costs. Thus, digitalisation boosts the Circular Economy business models by helping to close the loop, slow the material loop, and narrow the loop with increased resource efficiency. However, there are still many challenges to be solved in order to gain the desired benefits and gaps hindering the implementation of digital technology-aided circular business models (Antikainen, Uusitalo, and Kivikyto-Reponen, 2018, pp. 45–49).

Circular business models can be implemented in conjunction with solutions relevant to the Industry 4.0 concept, especially in the context of business digitalisation. Factors enabling the connection of CE and Industry 4.0 identified through literature review and experts' opinions are presented in tabular form in Table 3.3 with their citing references (Rajput and Prakash Singh, 2019, pp. 98–113).

From literature review and experts' opinions, 15 challenging factors in the links between CE and Industry 4.0 are identified and presented in tabular form in Table 3.4 with their citing references (Rajput and Prakash Singh, 2019, pp. 98–113).

Schroeder and colleagues believe technology and digitalisation affects these issues in contrasting ways. On the one hand, the diffusion of digital technologies may enable us to address the obstacles to the improvement, expansion, and replication of Circular Economy models in new ways and transform resource-intensive linear value chains into circular ones. The diffusion of digital technologies may motivate entrepreneurial activity among individuals in lower income countries, facilitating access to resources and relations and supporting new opportunity-based ventures. On the other hand, the diffusion may itself create obstacles and unintended consequences such as mismanaged e-waste, the fastest growing waste stream worldwide. In addition, the wide uptake of digital technologies exacerbates the resource constraints described above: digitalisation is underpinned by a number of critical materials and metals for which recovery and recycling rates need to be significantly increased if they are to achieve their huge development potential (Schroeder et al., 2018, pp. 77–78). Figure 3.5 illustrates the grouping of the technologies that were discussed in

Table 3.3 List of factors

No.	Factors	Description	Authors
1.	Reliability	It is the system's ability to work together with heterogeneous devices/components and it will not fail for a specified operating period under stated conditions.	Borgia (2014, pp. 1–31); Monostori (2014, pp. 9–13); Tan and Wang (2010)
2.	Scalability	Scalability of the system means the capability to manage an increased load of large data and applications in an extreme environment.	Tan and Wang (2010)
3.	Modularity	It emphasises the system's components for interchangeability. It indicates that components are capable of serving the technical or production functions independently.	Tan and Wang (2010)
4.	Quality of Service (QoS)	It has the capability to provide better service over a congested network (bandwidth delay). It is involved in managing network resources by setting priorities for different data types.	Ahmed et al. (2017, pp. 459–471); Tan and Wang (2010); Zhong et al. (2016, pp. 572–591)
5.	Integration and interoperability	It integrates low power communication technologies to enhance system robustness as well as to develop semantics among devices connected in a network to provide data in standardised formats for efficient communication.	Tan and Wang (2010)
6.	Self-organisation and adaptation	This feature enables the system to retrieve data from heterogeneous devices in the required format and to monitor the functioning of the system.	Athreya and Tague (2013, pp. 25–33); Miorandi et al. (2012, pp. 1497–1516); Xu (2012, pp. 75–86)
7.	Predictive Maintenance and recovery	It detects the changes in the condition of the system, that is, down time, service reliability, updating, detecting errors, and addresses failure to carry out maintenance services.	Pozza et al. (2015, pp. 1101–1131); Wortmann and Flüchter (2015, pp. 221–224)
8.	Flexibility	It ensures the system responds when internal or external changes occur. When any reprogrammable device or plug-in is integrated into the system, it responds dynamically and increases the efficiency of the system.	Beigne et al. (2015, pp. 164–167)

(*continued*)

Table 3.3 Continued

No.	Factors	Description	Authors
9.	Visual Computing	It acquires, analyses, and synthesises visual data by means of computers that provide automation and flexibility to the production process.	Posada et al. (2015, pp. 26–40)
10.	CIoT	It lies in the types of applications/devices and the technologies which drives consumers and their purpose. This enables consumers to be more responsive, creates shorter feedback loops, and makes it possible to take decentralised decisions among consumers.	Datta, Bonnet, and Haerri (2015, pp. 1–2); Hsu and Lin (2016, pp. 516–527); Williams et al. (2017, pp. 179–181)
11.	Self-configure and routable	It co-ordinates with other networked heterogeneous devices for information sharing between source and destination.	Arora et al. (2006, pp. 304–319); Fiorini and Jabbour (2017, pp. 241–249)
12.	Self-optimisation	It acquires the current state of the system as well as the system's environment and adapts its behaviour accordingly.	Arora et al. (2006); Brettel et al. (2016, pp. 93–98); Fiorini and Jabbour (2017)
13.	Value networks	It is a collaborative relationship that develops tangible and intangible values through potential networks between two or more entities.	Blunck and Werthmann (2017, pp. 12–14)
14.	Block chain	It maintains immutable information about products and processes throughout the supply chain, and regulates financial flow within the supply chain.	Kshetri (2018, pp. 80–89); Sandner (2018); Queiroz and Wamba (2019, pp. 70–82); Weyns, Ramachandran, and Singh (2018, pp. 67–84)
15.	Laws and Policy	It is required for plastics, chemical waste and product legislation. It aims to focus on the eco-design, eco-innovation, and quality standard of products.	Govindan and Hasanagic (2018, pp. 278–311)

No.	Factors	Description	Authors
16.	Infrastructure building	It is required for implementation of technical equipment and facilities and is required to develop an agile and automated supply chain.	Govindan and Hasangic (2018); Kalmykova et al. (2018, pp. 190–201)
17.	Product Service System	It has the ability to reduce environmental impacts of both production and consumption. It focuses more on the consumer stage of the product life cycle.	Somers et al. (2018, pp. 173–178); Kalmykova et al. (2018)
18.	Functional Service Economy	It optimises the use of goods and services while consuming less energy or resources to increase the usage value to a maximum limit for the longest period.	Jesus et al. (2018, pp. 2999–3018)
19.	Industrial System Integration	It enables the network to exchange resources or by-products, and allows the sharing of utilities, and ensures minimum usage of resources, cost reduction and creates economic and environmental benefits.	Muina et al. (2018, p. 255)
20.	EIoT	It can monitor soil, water, humidity, wind, temperature etc. providing on-line and real-time environment information.	Kalmykova et al. (2018)
21.	Energy recovery	It is an alternative to those waste products which cannot be sustainably recycled in an eco-efficient manner.	Frank et al. (2019, pp. 15–26); Kalmykova, Sadagopan, and Rosado (2018)
22.	Waste recovery	It is helpful in aggregating waste into meaningful volumes and facilitating the re-use of waste products to enhance environmental and social effectiveness.	Kalmykova, Sadagopan, and Rosado (2018)
23.	Cloud manufacturing	It assists in full sharing, high usage, and on-demand use of distributed manufacturing resources in a centralised way	Alacer and Machado (2019); Charro and Scahefer (2018, pp. 1018–1033); Lu and Xu (2019, pp. 92–102); Tao et al. (2014, pp. 1547–1557); Wang and Ji (2018, pp. 265–292)

(continued)

Table 3.3 Continued

No.	*Factors*	*Description*	*Authors*
24.	Big data	It has the capability to store, manage, and analyse high variety, high volume, and high velocity sets of data. It has the ability to enhance supply chain visibility, and adapt to the dynamic environment.	Alacer and Machado (2019); Frank, Dalenogare, and Ayala (2019); Gupta et al. (2018, pp. 112–129); Lamba and Singh (2017, pp. 877–890; 2018, pp. 629–658); Luthra et al. (2018); Mangla et al. (2018, pp. 551–569); Witkowski (2017, pp. 763–769
25.	Cyber-physical production system (CPPS)	It involves autonomous and coordinating sub-systems which are dependently connected to each other across all levels of manufacturing processes. It provides the communication link among humans, machines and products and interacts with the physical world via interfaces.	Cardin (2019, pp. 11–21); Lu et al. (2019, pp. 56–66)
26.	Collaborative robotics	It is intended to develop physical interaction between robots and humans in collaborative workspace. It provides an added incentive in achieving quality production, accuracy and precision in manufacturing process.	Alacer and Machado (2019); Frank, Dalenogare, and Ayala (2019)

Source: Rajput and Prakash Singh, 2019, pp. 98–113.

literature, according to the three architectural layers (Pagoropoulos, Pigosso, and McAloone, 2017, pp. 19–24).

A crucial condition for designing an effective business model that fulfils the assumptions of the concept of the digital economy is the use of data to optimise resource consumption. This creates a social impact focused on the internal areas of the business model and its environment.

The authors have defined two types of impact within the modified model of the description of the concept architecture of the Circular Economy. Internal impacts ensure data exchange in the life cycle. They are collected, integrated, and analysed. External impacts are actions aimed at neutralising the adverse impact on the natural environment or seeking ideas for remedial actions of the natural environment. The data-based management system should generate a

Table 3.4 List of challenging factors

No.	*Factors*	*Description*	*Authors*
1.	Data analysis	As a large amount of data is captured in different formats, it means analysing data and making informed decisions using analytics.	Tan, Vuran, and Goddard (2009, pp. 44–50)
2.	Collaborative model	It is required for direct interaction with humans and also designed robots; offers safe work to humans within a defined workspace.	Tan, Vuran, and Goddard (2009)
3.	CPS standards and specifications	It is required for validation purposes to ensure that the system is capable of handling the specific requirements.	Tan, Vuran, and Goddard (2009)
4.	CPS modelling and modelling integration	The CPS model interacts between the physical and virtual world and also involves the physical and computing components. Therefore, CPS requires different computing models with a unified framework.	Tan, Vuran, and Goddard (2009)
5.	Smart devices development	Different advanced and smart devices are required to communicate in an Industry 4.0 environment to reduce human intervention.	Tan, Vuran, and Goddard (2009)
6.	Investment cost	It is required to standardise the infrastructure and develop smart devices.	Tan, Vuran, and Goddard (2009)
7.	Design	It is required to design models and to include CPS-enabled landscapes.	Leitao, Colombo, and Karnouskos (2016, pp. 11–25)
8.	Compatibility	It keeps the system's components working together in a functioning environment without implementing any changes to the system.	Leitao, Colombo, and Karnouskos (2016); Elkhodr, Shahrestani, and Cheung (2016, pp. 85–102)
9.	Infrastructure standardisation	Infrastructure is required to equip the advance technologies. It is required to integrate the heterogeneous devices/components in automation systems.	Leitao, Colombo, and Karnouskos (2016)
10.	Interfacing and networking	It enables underlying wireless technologies and sensor technology to interface with the physical world.	Elkhodr, Shahrestani, and Cheung (2016)

(*continued*)

Table 3.4 Continued

No.	*Factors*	*Description*	*Authors*
11.	Semantic interoperability	To execute the transaction of data between the two or more machines, a protocol is required for different devices for efficient and effective communication.	Elkhodr, Shahrestani, and Cheung (2016)
12.	Process digitisation and automation	Industry 4.0 induces mobility in the processes and reduces the cost, computerises the production processes, and implements new disruptive technologies.	Schumacher et al. (2016, pp. 161–166)
13.	Automation system virtualisation	It maximises the real-time visibility of the operation processes which offers reliable and efficient solutions.	Babiceanu and Seker (2016)
14.	Fog computation	It provides data storage and processing services locally to fog devices rather than storing them in the cloud.	Atlam, Walters, and Wills (2018)
15.	Sensor technology	Industry 4.0 requires sensor-based technology such as RFID to capture a large amount of information to communicate smartly with other devices.	Schutze et al. (2018)

Source: Rajput and Prakash Singh, 2019, pp. 98–113.

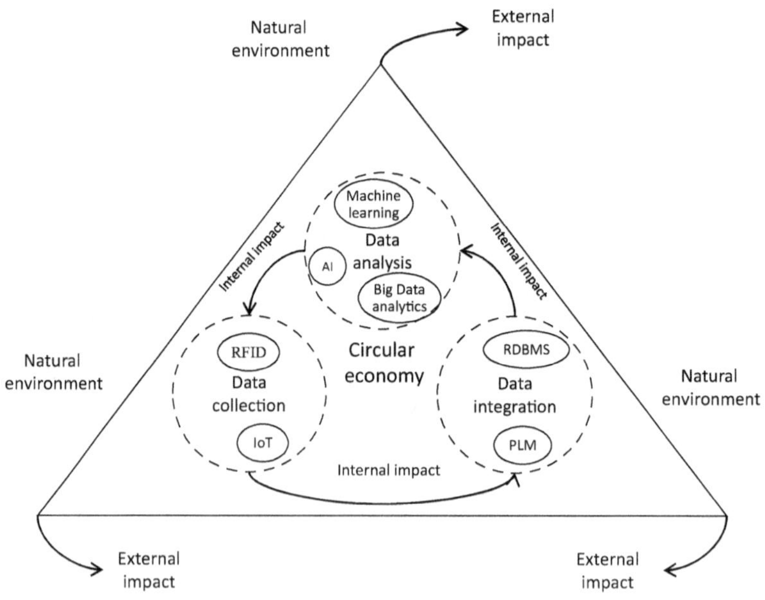

Figure 3.5 Grouping of digital technologies according to three architectural layers.
Source: Own study based on Pagoropoulos, Pigosso, and McAloone, 2017, pp. 19–24.

significant external impact on the environment. This impact should be a factor in reducing global climate change, for example a grain-to-grain principle, and the impact will be noticeable for present and future generations.

When undertaking a critical analysis of the concept of digitalisation in the Circular Economy, it should be noted that the main task that the Circular Economy faces is to continuously improve the economy's ability to grow without the corresponding increase in energy and resource consumption (source boundaries) and environmental impact (absorption boundaries). The main assumption of this concept concerns the creation of economic systems that will not only be efficient, but above all waste-free. The Circular Economy as a concept assumes the full recycling and reuse of products, including product life cycle management. Therefore, it is not easy to link the digital economy with the Circular Economy in such a direct way, in particular due to the fact that the Circular Economy should be considered multidimensionally within the entire, complete logistics cycles rather than from the perspective of one company. From the point of view of the labour market, the combination of these two areas will generate strong robotisation, which may result in a social problem related to, inter alia, a potential increase in unemployment by replacing simple work with activities which make the industry mechanised. Thus, social inclusion at the centre of digital and ecological transformation is an important factor, as digitalisation and the introduction of intelligent solutions are of great importance when it comes to accelerating sustainable development at the local and regional levels.

Conclusions

The discussion in Chapter 3 highlights the vital role of social aspects in shaping digital business models. Social factors are an important element of the DNA of digital business models. In addition to economic profits, these models largely enable the creation of social profits. The effect of the implementation of the business socialisation strategy in the digital economy is the ability to meet ethical, economic, and environmental assumptions. In this way, the assumptions for the functioning of sustainable digital business models can be defined. These are business models that are based on the assumptions of sustainable development, in line with the contemporary expectations of various stakeholder groups – environmental organisations, associations which develop new directions in the development of social policy, equality and freedom, and the citizens of the world for whom concern for the protection of nature is important in terms of the survival of planet earth and improvement of people's quality of life.

References

Ahmed, E., Yaqoob, I., Abaker, I., Khan, I., Ibrahim, A., and Imran, M. (2017). "The Role of Big Data Analytics in Internet of Things", *Computer Networks*, 129, 459–471. DOI: 10.1016/j.comnet.2017.06.013.

Alacer, V. and Machado, V.C. (2019). "Scanning the Industry 4.0: A Literature Review on Technologies for Manufacturing Systems", *Engineering Science and Technology an International Journal*, 22(3), 899–919. DOI: 10.1016/j.jestch.2019.01.006.

Antikainen, M., Uusitalo, T., and Kivikyto-Reponen, P. (2018). "Digitalisation as an Enabler of Circular Economy", *Procedia CIRP* , 73, 45–49. DOI: 10.1016/j.procir.2018.04.027.

Arora, H., Raghu, T.S., Vinze, A., and Brittenham, P. (2006). *Collaborative Self-configuration and Learning in Autonomic Computing Systems: Applications to Supply Chain*, ICAC 2006 in Dublin, Ireland Paper Presented in IEEE International Conference on Autonomic Computing, pp. 304–319.

Atlam, H.F., Walters R.J., and Wills, G.B. (2018). "Fog computing and the internet of things: A review", *Big Data and Cognitive Computing*, 2(10), 1–18.

Athreya A. and Tague, P. (2013). *Network Self-organization in the Internet of Things*, IoT-NC Paper Presented in IEEE International Workshop of Internet-of-Things Networking and Control, pp. 25–33. DOI: 10.1109/IoT-NC.2013.6694050.

Babiceanu, R.F. and Seker, R. (2016). "Big data and virtualization for manufacturing cyber-physical systems: A survey of the current status and future outlook", *Computers in Industry*, 81, 128–137.

Begg, D., Fisher, S., and Dornbusch, R. (2003). *Mikroekonomia*. Warszawa: PWE.

Beigne, E., Christmann, J., Valentian, A., Billoint, O., Amat, E., and Morche, D. (2015). *UTBB FDSOI Technology Flexibility for Ultra Low Power Internet-of-Things Applications*, Paper Presented in European Solid-State Device Research Conference, pp. 164–167. DOI:10.1109/ESSDERC.2015.7324739.

Blunck, E. and Werthmann, H. (2017). *Industry 4.0: An Opportunity to Realize Sustainable Manufacturing and its Potential for a Circular Economy*, Croatia Paper Presented in Proceedings of the DIEM: Dubrovnik International Economic Meeting in Dubrovnik (accessed 23 August 2018).

Bocken, N.M.P., Short, S.W., Rana, P., and Evans, S. (2014). "A Literature and Practice Review to Develop Sustainable Business Model Archetypes", *Journal of Cleaner Production*, 65, 42–56. DOI: 10.1016/j.jclepro.2013.11.039.

Borgia, E. (2014). "The Internet of Things Vision: Key Features, Applications and Open Issues", *Computer Communications*, 54, 1–31. DOI: 10.1016/j.comcom.2014.09.008.

Brettel, M., Fisher, F.G., Bendig, D., Weber, A.R., and Wolff, B. (2016). *Enablers for Self-optimizing Production Systems in the Context of Industrie 4.0*, Italy, 41 Paper Presented in 48th CIRP Conference on Manufacturing Systems – CIRP CMS 2015 in Ischia, pp. 93–98.

Brożek, B. (2014). *Granice Interpretacji*, Kraków: Copernicus Center Press.

Calvo, N. and Villarreal, O. (2018). "Analysis of the Growth of the e-Learning Industry through Sustainable Business Model Archetypes: A Case Study", *Journal of Cleaner Production*, 191, 26–39. DOI 10.1016/j.jclepro.2018.04.211.

Cardin, O. (2019). "Classification of Cyber-physical Production Systems Application: Proposition of an Analysis Framework", *Computers in Industry*, 104, 11–21. DOI: 10.1016/j.compind.2018.10.002.

Charro, A. and Scahefer, D. (2018). "Cloud Manufacturing as a New Type of Product-Service System", *International Journal of Computer Integrated Manufacturing*, 31(10), 1018–1033. DOI: 10.1080/0951192X.2018.

Cherrier, H., Goswami, P., and Ray, S. (2018). "Social Entrepreneurship: Creating Value in the Context of Institutional Complexity", *Journal of Business Research*, 86, 245–258. DOI: 10.1016/j.jbusres.2017.10.056.

Corsaro, D. (2019). "Capturing the Broader Picture of Value Co-creation Management", *European Management Journal*, 37, 99–116. DOI: 10.1016/j.emj.2018.07.007.

Datta, S.K., Bonnet, C., and Haerri, J. (2015). *Fog Computing Architecture to Enable Consumer Centric Internet of Things Services*, ISCE 2015 in Madrid Paper Presented in International Symposium on Consumer Electronics, pp. 1–2. DOI:10.1109/ISCE.2015.7177778.

Daunoriene, A., Draksaite, A., Snieska, V., and Valodkiene, G. (2015). "Evaluating Sustainability of Sharing Economy Business Models", 20th International Scientific Conference Economics and Management – 2015 (ICEM-2015), *Procedia – Social and Behavioral Sciences*, 213, 836–841. DOI: 10.1016/j.sbspro.2015.11.486.

Di Gregorio, D. (2013). "Value Creation and Value Appropriation: An Integrative, Multi-Level Framework", *Journal of Applied Business and Economics*, 15(1), 39–53.

Dyduch, W. and Bratnicki, M. (2018). "Strategizing Corporate Entrepreneurship for Value Creation and Value Capture", *International Journal of Contemporary Management*, 17(1), 7–26. DOI: 10.4467/24498939IJCM.18.001.8380.

Eggert, A., Ulaga, W., Frow, P., Payne, A. (2018). "Conceptualizing and Communicating Value in Business Markets: From Value in Exchange to Value in Use", *Industrial Marketing Management*, 69, 80–90. DOI: 10.1016/j.indmarman.2018.01.018.

Elkhodr, M., Shahrestani, S., and Cheung, H. (2016). "The Internet of Things: New Interoperability, Management and Security Challenges", *International Journal of Network Security and& Its Applications*, 8(2), 85–102. DOI: 10.5121/ijnsa.2016.8206.

Elkington, J. (1999). *Cannibals with Forks: The Triple Bottom Line of 21st Century Business*, Oxford: Capstone.

Fiorini, P.C. and Jabbour, C.J.C. (2017). "Information Systems and Supply Chain Management towards a More Sustainable Society: Where We Are and Where We Are Going", *International Journal of Information Management*, 37, 241–249. DOI: 10.1016/j.ijinfomgt.2016.12.004.

Frączkiewicz-Wronka, A. and Cziura, P. (2017). "Możliwość wykorzystania modeli biznesu do kształtowania wizerunku przedsiębiorstw społecznych", *Studia Ekonomiczne, Zeszyty Naukowe Uniwersytetu Ekonomicznego w Katowicach*, 313, 61–73.

Frank, A.G., Dalenogare, L.S., and Ayala, N.F. (2019). "Industry 4.0 Technologies: Implementation Patterns in Manufacturing Companies", *International Journal of Production Economics*, 210, 15–26. DOI: 10.1016/j.ijpe.2019.01.004.

Geng, Y. and Doberstein, B. (2008). "Developing the Circular Economy in China: Challenges and Opportunities for Achieving 'Leapfrog Development'", *International Journal of Sustainable Development & World Ecology*, 15(3), 231–239. DOI: 10.3843/SusDev.15.3:6.

Gopaldas, A. (2015). "Creating Firm, Customer, and Societal Value: Toward a Theory of Positive Marketing", *Journal of Business Research*, 68(12), 2446–2451. DOI: 10.1016/j.jbusres.2015.06.031.

Govindan, K. and Hasanagic, M. (2018). "A Systematic Review on Drivers, Barriers, and Practices towards Circular Economy: A Supply Chain Perspective", *International Journal of Production Research*, 56(1–2), 278–311. DOI: 10.1080/00207543.2017.1402141.

Grönroos, C. (2011). "A Service Perspective on Business Relationships: The Value Creation, Interaction and Marketing Interface", *Industrial Marketing Management*, 40(2), 240–247. DOI: 10.1016/j.indmarman.2010.06.036.

Guinée, J.B. (2002). *Handbook on Life Cycle Assessment: Operational Guide to the ISO Standards*, Dordrecht: Springer. DOI: 10.1007/0 306 48055-7.

Gupta, S., Kar, A.K., Baabdullah, A., and Al-Khowaiter, W.A. (2018). "Big Data with Cognitive Computing: A Review for the Future", *International Journal of Information Management*, 42, 78–89. DOI: 10.1016/j.ijinfomgt.2018.06.005.

Hausner, J. (2017). "Ekonomia wartości a wartość ekonomiczna", in B. Bartłomiej Biga , H. Izdebski , J. Hausner , M. Kudłacz , K. Obłój , W. Paprocki , P. Sztompka , and M. Zmyślony (eds.), *Open Eyes Book 2*, Kraków: Fundacja Gospodarki i Administracji Publicznej.

Hsu, C.L. and Lin, J.C. (2016). "An Empirical Examination of Consumer Adoption of Internet of Things Services: Network Externalities and Concern for Information Privacy Perspectives", *Computers in Human Behavior*, 62, 516–527. DOI:10.1016/j.chb.2016.04.023.

Hyup Roh, T. (2016). "The Sharing Economy: Business Cases of Social Enterprises Using Collaborative Networks", Information Technology and Quantitative Management (ITQM 2016), *Procedia Computer Science*, 91, 502-511.

Jabłoński, A. and Jabłoński, M. (2020). *Social Business Models in the Digital Economy, New Concepts and Contemporary Challenges*, London: Palgrave Macmillan. DOI: 10.1007/978-3-030-29732-9.

Jabłoński, M. (2018). "The Assumptions of Hybrid Business Models Based on the Concepts of Big Data and the Sharing Economy", in A. Jabłoński (ed.), *Hybridization in Network Management*, New York: Nova Publishers.

Järvi, H., Kähkönen, A-K., Torvinen, H. (2018). "When Value Co-creation Fails: Reasons That Lead to Value Co-destruction", *Scandinavian Journal of Management*, 34(1), 63–77. DOI: 10.1016/j.scaman.2018.01.002.

Jesus, A.D., Antunes, P., Santos, R., and Mendonca, S. (2018). "Eco-innovation in the Transition to a Circular Economy: An Analytical Literature Review", *Journal of Cleaner Production*, 172, 2999–3018. DOI: 10.1016/j.jclepro.2017.11.111.

Kalmykova, Y., Sadagopan, M., and Rosado, L. (2018). "Circular Economy: From Review of Theories and Practices to Development of Implementation Tools", *Resources, Conservation, and Recycling*, 135, 190–201. DOI: 10.1016/j.resconrec.2017.10.034.

Kaufman, J. (2012). *What Is "Value Capture"? The Personal MBA, Master the Art of Business*, London: Penguin Books.

Keen, P. and Williams, R. (2013). "Value Architectures for Digital Business: Beyond the Business Model", *MIS Quarterly*, 37(2), June, 643–647.

Kshetri, N. (2018). "Blockchain's Roles in Meeting Key Supply Chain Management Objectives", *International Journal of Information Management*, 39, 80–89. DOI: 10.1016/j.ijinfomgt.2017.12.005.

Kukkonen, E. (2018). "Organizing a Framework for Customer Value Management in Online Media Relationships", *The Marketing Management Journal*, 28(1).

Lacy, P., Keeble, J., McNamara, R., Rutqvist, J., Haglund, T., Cui, M., and Buddemeier, P. (2014). *Circular Advantage: Innovative Business Models and Technologies to Create Value in a World Without Limits to Growth*, Chicago: Accenture.

Laloux, F. (2015, 2016). *Pracować inaczej. Nowatorski model organizacji inspirowany kolejnym etapem rozwoju ludzkiej świadomości*, Warszawa: Wydawnictwo Studio Emka.

Lamba, K. and Singh, S.P. (2017). "Big Data in Operations and Supply Chain Management: Current Trends and Future Perspectives", *Production Planning and Control*, 28(11–12), 877–890. DOI: 10.1080/09537287.2017.1336787.

Lamba, K. and Singh, S.P. (2018). "Modelling Big Data Enablers for Operations and Supply Chain Management", *The International Journal of Logistics Management*, 29(2), 629–658. DOI: 10.1108/IJLM-07-2017-0183.

Leitao, P., Colombo, A.W., and Karnouskos, S. (2016). "Industrial Automation Based on Cyber-physical Systems Technologies: Prototype Implementations and Challenges", *Computers in Industry*, 81, 1–25. DOI: 10.1016/j.compind.2015.08.004.

Lu, Y. and Xu, X. (2019). "Cloud-based Manufacturing Equipment and Big Data Analytics to Enable On-demand Manufacturing Services", *Robotics and Computer-integrated Manufacturing*, 57, 92–102. DOI: 10.1016/j.rcim.2018.11.006.

Lu, Y., Peng, T., and Xu, X. (2019). "Energy-efficient Cyber-physical Production Network: Architecture and Technologies", *Computers & Industrial Engineering*, 129, 56–66.

Luthra, S., Mangla, S.K., Shankar, R., Garg, C.P., and Jakhar, S. (2018). "Modelling Critical Success Factors for Sustainability Initiatives in Supply Chains in Indian Context Using Grey-DEMATEL", *Production Planning and Control*, 29(9), 705–728. DOI: 10.1080/09537287.2018.1448126.

Mangla, S.K., Luthra, S., Mishra, N., Singh, A., Rana, N.P., and Dora, M. (2018). "Barriers to Effective Circular Supply Chain Management in a Developing Country Context", *Production Planning and Control*, 29(6), 551–569.

Mauri, A.G., Minazzi, R., Nieto-García, M., and Viglia, G. (2018). "Humanize Your Business: The Role of Personal Reputation in the Sharing Economy", *International Journal of Hospitality Management*, 73, 36–43. DOI: 10.1016/j.ijhm.2018.01.017.

Miorandi, D., Sicari, S., Pellegrini, F., and Chlamtac, I. (2012). "Internet of Things: Vision, Applications and Research Challenges", *Ad Hoc Networks*, 10(7), 1497–1516. DOI: 10.1016/j.adhoc.2012.02.016.

Monostori, L. (2014). *Cyber-physical Production Systems: Roots, Expectations and R&D Challenges*, Canada Paper Presented in Proceedings of the 47th CIRP Conference on Manufacturing Systems, Ontario, Vol. 17, pp. 9–13. DOI: 10.1016/j.procir.2014.03.115.

Muina, F.E.G., Sanchez, R.G., Ferrari, A.M., and Blundo, D.S. (2018). "The Paradigms of Industry 4.0 and Circular Economy as Enabling Drivers for the Competitiveness of Businesses and Territories: The Case of an Italian Ceramic Tiles Manufacturing Company", *Social Sciences*, 7(12), 255. DOI: 10.3390/socsci7120255.

Neumeyer, X. and Santos, S. C. (2018). "Sustainable Business Models, Venture Typologies, and Entrepreneurial Ecosystems: A Social Network Perspective", *Journal of Cleaner Production*, 172, 4565–4579. DOI: 10.1016/j.jclepro.2017.08.216.

Pagoropoulos, A., Pigosso, D.C.A., and McAloone, T.C. (2017). "The Emergent Role of Digital Technologies in the Circular Economy: A Review", *Procedia CIRP*, 64, 19–24. DOI: 10.1016/j.procir.2017.02.047.

Parida, V., Sjödin, D., and Reim, W. (2019). "Reviewing Literature on Digitalization, Business Model Innovation, and Sustainable Industry: Past Achievements and Future Promises", *Sustainability*, 11, 391. DOI:10.3390/su11020391.

Poniatowska-Jaksh, M. and Sobiecki, R. (2016). *Sharing Economy (Gospodarka Współdzielenia)*, Warszawa: Oficyna wydawnicza SGH Szkoła Główna Handlowa w Warszawie.

Posada, J., Toro, C., Barandiaran, I., Oyarzun, D., Stricker, D., de Amicis, R., Pinto, E.B., Eistert, P., Dollner, J., and Vallarino, I. (2015). "Visual Computing as a Key Enabling Technology for Industrie 4.0 and Industrial Internet", *IEEE Computer Graphics and Applications*, 35(2), 26–40. DOI: 10.1109/MCG.2015.45.

Pozza, R., Nati, M., Georgoulas, S., Moessner, K., and Gluhak, A. (2015). "Neighbor Discovery for Opportunistic Networking in Internet of Things Scenarios: A Survey", *IEEE Access: Practical Innovations, Open Solutions*, 3, 1101–1131. DOI: 10.1109/ACCESS.2015.2457031.

Queiroz, M.M. and Wamba, S.F. (2019). "Blockchain Adoption Challenges in Supply Chain: An Empirical Investigation of the Main Drivers in India and the USA", *International Journal of Information Management*, 46, 70–82. DOI: 10.1016/j.ijinfomgt.2018.11.021.

Rajput, S. and Prakash Singh, S. (2019). "Connecting Circular Economy and Industry 4.0", *International Journal of Information Management*, 49, 98–113. DOI: 10.1016/j.ijinfomgt.2019.03.002.

Rappaport, A. (1999). *Wartość dla akcjonariuszy. Poradnik menedżera i inwestora*, Warszawa: WIG-Press.

Romaniuk, P. (2018). "Garść refleksji na temat koncepcji Potrójnej Linii Przewodniej", Fundacja Sendzimira, Website Forum Odpowiedzialnego Biznesu. Available at: http://odpowiedzialnybiznes.pl/artykuly/garsc-refleksji-na-temat-koncepcji-potrojnej-linii-przewodniej (accessed 13 December 2018).

Sandner, P. (2018). *Blockchain: Proposition of a New and Sustainable Macroeconomic System.* Available at: https://medium.com/@philippsandner/blockchain-proposition-of-a-new-and-sustainable-macroeconomic-system-d9c628bd56b7 (accessed June 6 2018).

Sauvé, S., Bernard, S., and Sloan, P. (2016). "Environmental Sciences, Sustainable Development and Circular Economy: Alternative Concepts for Trans-disciplinary Research", *Environmental Development*, 17, 48–56. DOI: 10.1016/j.envdev.2015.09.002.

Schroeder, P., Dewick, P., Kusi-Sarpong, S., and Hofstetter, J.S. (2018). "Circular Economy and Power Relations in Global Value Chains: Tensions and Trade-offs for Lower Income Countries", *Resources, Conservation & Recycling*, 136, 77–78. DOI: 10.1016/j.resconrec.2018.04.003.

Schumacher, A., Selim E., and Wilfried, S. (2016). "A Maturity Model for Assessing Industry 4.0 Readiness and Maturity of Manufacturing Enterprises", *Procedia CIRP*, 52, 161–166. DOI: 10.1016/j.procir.2016.07.040.

Schutze, A., Helwig, N., and Schneider, T. (2018). "Sensors 4.0: Smart Sensors and Measurement Technology Enable Industry 4.0", *Journal of Sensors and Sensor Systems*, 7, 359–371.

Sinkovics, N., Sinkovics, R.R., and Yamin, M. (2014). "The Role of Social Value Creation in Business Model Formulation at the Bottom of the Pyramid – Implications for MNEs?", *International Business Review*, 23(4), 692–707. DOI: 10.1016/j.ibusrev.2013.12.004.

Somers, L., Dewit, I., and Baelus, C. (2018). *Understanding Product-service Systems in a Sharing Economy Context: A Literature Review*, Sweden Paper Presented in 10th CIRP Conference on Industrial Product- Service Systems, IPS2 in Linkoping, Vol. 41, pp. 173–178.

Spieth, P., Schneider, S., Clauß T., and Eichenberg, D. (2019). "Value Drivers of Social Businesses: A Business Model Perspective", *Long Range Planning*, 52(3), 427–444. DOI: 10.1016/j.lrp.2018.04.004.

Tan, L. and Wang, N. (2010). *Future Internet: Internet of Things*, China Paper Presented in 3rd International Conference on Advanced Computer Theory and Engineering (ICACTE), Chengdu.

Tan, Y., Vuran, M., and Goddard S. (2009). *Spatio-temporal Event Model for Cyber-physical Systems*, CSE Conference and Workshop Papers. Paper 147, 44–50. DOI: 10.1109/ICDCSW.2009.82.

Tao, F., Zuo, Y, Xu, L.D., and Zhang, L. (2014). "IoT-based Intelligent Perception and Access of Manufacturing Resource toward Cloud Manufacturing", *IEEE Transactions on Industrial Informatics*, 10(2), 1547–1557. DOI: 10.1109/TII.2014.2306397.

Teece, D.J. and Linden, G. (2017). "Business Models, Value Capture, and the Digital Enterprise", *Journal of Organization Design*, 6(8). DOI: 10.1186/s41469-017-0018-x.

Wang, L. and Ji, W. (2018). *Cloud Enabled CPS and Big Data Environment in Manufacturing*, Serbia Paper Presented in 3rd International Conference on the Industry 4.0 Model for Advanced Manufacturing, Belgrade, pp. 265–292. DOI: 10.1007/978-3-319-89563-5_20.

Weyns, D., Ramachandran, G.S., and Singh, R.K. (2018). "Self-managing Internet of Things", in A. Tjoa, L. Bellatreche, S. Biffl, J. van Leeuwen, and J. Wiedermann (eds.), *SOFSEM 2018: Theory and Practice of Computer Science*, SOFSEM 2018. Lecture Notes in Computer Science, Vol. 10706. Cham: Edizioni della Normale, pp. 67–84. DOI: 10.1007/978-3-319-73117-9_5.

Williams, R., McMahon, E., Samtani, S., Patton, M., and Chen, H. (2017). *Identifying Vulnerabilities of Consumer Internet of Things (IoT) Devices: A Scalable Approach*, ISI, Beijing Paper Presented in IEEE International Conference on Intelligence and Security Informatics, pp. 179–181. DOI: 10.1109/ISI.2017.8004904.

Witkowski, K. (2017). *Internet of Things, Big Data, Industry 4.0- Innovative Solutions in Logistics and Supply Chain Management*, Paper Presented in 7th International Conference on Engineering, Project, and Production Management, Vol. 182, pp. 763–769. DOI:10.1016/j.proeng.2017.03.197.

Wortmann, F. and Flüchter, K. (2015). "Internet of Things: Technology and Added", *Business & Information Systems Engineering*, 57(3), 221 224. DOI: 10.1007/s12599-015-0383-3.

Xu, X. (2012). "From Cloud Computing to Cloud Manufacturing", *Robotics and Computer-Integrated Manufacturing*, 28(1), 75–86, DOI: 10.1016/j.rcim.2011.07.002.

Yip, A.W.H. and Bocken, N.M.P. (2018). "Sustainable Business Model Archetypes for the Banking Industry", *Journal of Cleaner Production*, 174, 150–169. DOI: 10.1016/j.jclepro.2017.10.190.

Zhong, R.Y., Newman, S.T., Huang, G.Q., and Lan, S. (2016). "Big Data for Supply Chain Management in the Service and Manufacturing Sectors: Challenges, Opportunities, and Future Perspectives", *Computers & Industrial Engineering*, 101, 572–591. DOI: 10.1016/j.cie.2016.07.013.

4 Monetisation in digital business models

Introduction

A problem posed in the context of the title of the chapter is the analysis of profitability using the monetisation of digital economy business models. In many cases, the achievement of the expected ability to monetise a business model is the primary goal of today's business solution designers. Monetisation is a process of converting something into money. It is the conversion of assets such as a business model, data sets, and so on into money. It is important to show the difference between a revenue model and a monetisation model. The revenue model is just one aspect of the business model – and it is simply a method or process in which the company intends to extract (not attract) money from the "market" for the value created. The revenue model is the way money flows from the paying customer to the company. The basic revenue model is, for example, a single price (simple product sale at a fixed price). The general monetisation model is a continuous method based on the logic of a unique business model consisting of the processing of the product delivered or its users into permanent sales. The fundamental condition for obtaining the monetisation effect of the business model is attracting a large number of recipients of the business solution proposed. The business model should attract them by using service formulas and a specific value proposition that is unique compared to other market proposals. Often in business practice there are so-called opposite monetisation models, for example, offering software for free or cheaply and making money (monetisation) by selling non-standard programming services, consultations, or updates (see: www.quora.com/What-is-the-difference-between-a-revenue-model-and-a-monetisation-model). Monetisation is therefore a way in which the company earns by means of a business model and is not direct proof of the sale transaction.

The Centre for Information Systems Research (CISR) defines monetisation as "an act of exchanging information-based offerings for legal tender or something of perceived equivalent value". To put it simply, it is about converting digital currency, which is Big Data accumulated by the company, into analogue capital, which can be used in the market or which will help optimise business operations. Data monetisation is therefore the possibility of direct and indirect financing of knowledge of digital behaviours and the profiles of interest of the company's customers or Internet users (Portal BiznesTuba, 2016). Monetisation methods can include solutions such as freemium, premium, trial, subscriptions, and so on. Monetisation is included in the intention of business model designers, and it is not always possible for it to be effective from the very beginning. Efforts to create the possibility of monetising the business model are often required, even over a period of a few years, especially in the case of Start-Ups, and are not always successful. This way, monetisation becomes a fundamental object that the efforts of innovative business model designers are focused on. The financial aspect is of fundamental importance in this context. It seems right to say that new digital economy business models have a strategic problem, namely the monetisation of the business model and making profits, despite a number of positive social aspects of this form of activity. In the context of solving the scientific problem, this is a key challenge for searching for theoretical and practical methods of resolving this deadlock. Then perhaps it will be reasonable to talk about a real revolution in the area of sharing resources and digitalisation and their impact on the contemporary paradigms of economics and management.

The issue of monetisation of digital business models is complex. This results from the different logic of understanding and perceiving a company's financial mechanisms, among other things. Typical cash flow based on the so-called income model is of lesser importance in this case. The concentration of monetisation management logic is focused on the methods of monetisation of the value offered in any space, both in terms of location and time. At the same time, a very important attribute of monetisation is its unpredictability, which makes forecasting difficult. Economic conditions related to the monetisation of digital business models are therefore a crucial problem in terms of shaping them and assessing their effectiveness.

The first problem area in this case is the market itself, which is in fact a full-area virtual market or a virtual platform for its impact on users and online customers. Another very important issue is the virtual and/or real good itself delivered via the Internet, resulting from the exploration and exploitation of the digital business model. This good, and therefore the value offered, can be public, private, or shared, and the effect achieved from the value offered may be individual or network-based, focused mainly on economies of scale. It is also worth noting that observers, users, and customers are located in the space of the digital business model offering value. In such a virtual market, transaction costs are low and they significantly generate the high scalability of digital business models. Despite low transaction costs, cash flow asymmetry is a significant threat to companies using digital business models.

The aim of the chapter is to present the conditions, methods, and techniques of the monetisation of business models in the digital economy. The value of this chapter is the presentation of the joint implementation of the theoretical aspects of monetisation as well as the presentation of practical business solutions in this field. The scope of the chapter includes the relationship between the monetisation and degree of scalability of the business model.

Dynamics of business models and monetisation aspects

Business models as a scientific concept cover a wide range of impacts on the contemporary definition of theories in the field of management and quality science. Business models are considered from the dynamic perspective, especially in the context of dynamic capabilities (Teece, 2018). To a large extent, they constitute product or service architecture and information flows, including a description of various business entities and their roles. They indicate potential benefits for various business entities along with a description of revenue sources (Timmers, 1998, p. 4). The business model should at least answer the following questions: What value propositions are offered? Who are the customers? How do operations work? Why is the business model financially interesting? In the case of digital business models, they should be built from the following components: functional representation based on five core elements: people – users; business – the scope of services using "digitally connected companies/ groups of companies" forming the business ecosystem; things – digitally connected things (cars, bicycles, music players, etc.); data; and cloud computing (Blaschke et al., 2017, pp. 123, 126). Digital business models are revolutionising the approach to management processes. Innovative technologies mean that existing business formulas based on traditional value chain assumptions do not apply. The digital revolution makes business models dynamic. So-called bilateral markets develop, also known as the bilateral network, which is an economic platform with two separate groups of users that ensure mutual benefits. The benefits for each group demonstrate the economies of scale resulting from demand. Bilateral market platforms choose the right price to charge each group, where one group "drives" the other (Bataineh et al., 2016, p. 472). Social media plays a crucial role in this aspect. There are many reasons why people use social media. We see many mechanisms in the Internet through which their owners try to make money (Clemons, 2009, p. 51). Understanding the potential of the digital economy leads to opportunities for creating economic and social value. Such formulas of operation in the global market differ significantly from the "old" approach to business model design. Currently, attractive value should be created for stakeholders – usually of a social nature, generally speaking, and consequently for economic benefits. A symbiotic concept in this regard is possible (Jabłoński and Jabłoński, 2020). However, it should be clearly indicated that earning is an obvious requirement of every business model. The configuration of successful business models should include a set of interdependent activities that can be grouped around tasks related to customer identification, customer commitment, value chain relationships, and monetisation (Baden-Fuller and Mangematin, 2013, pp. 418–427). Monetisation is necessary to achieve the development goals of digital business models and should be built into the logic of the designed business model. The dynamisation of business models should be based on at least two pillars of business model utilisation:

1. The dynamics of interaction in the relational mode between the actors of the built-in value network in the business model.
2. Dynamics stimulated by the scheme of the adopted monetisation of created value.

These two areas of business model dynamics, mutually interpenetrating, should create a coherent structure of the business model as understood by the market. Otherwise, the sustainability of the business model will be shaken, and the business model will be characterised by an above-average level of volatility (Jabłoński, 2017, pp. 13–21). Monetisation is a factor that stimulates the dynamics of business models, and monetisation schemes strongly influence the attractiveness of digital business models. The types of monetisation are an element that supports the process of business model development, and are a condition for its survival. The sustainability and stability of the designed business model depends on the effectiveness of monetisation. The dynamics of business models depend on the consistency of the value created through the business model with monetisation schemes. Both of these issues must be symbiotic.

Dynamics in operating systems are of fundamental importance in the context of contemporary market conditions. The digital economy accelerates the ageing process of products and shortens their life cycle. Since products and services are currently interdependent on the business model life cycle, dynamics as a concept should be considered together with the concept of business models. The variability of exogenous and endogenous factors makes it necessary to condition the durability of products and services from the sustainability of the business model under which they are delivered to recipients. As part of the search for methods of ensuring the sustainability of business models, as well as making changes to them that extend their life cycle in the context of the variability of the external and internal environment, the assumptions of the System Dynamics method can be used. Digital business models develop their dynamics in the ecosystems of activity, and then regularly disrupt themselves, renewing themselves in constantly changing markets (Blaschke et al., 2017, p. 127). According to J.W. Forrester, System Dynamics are built in two directions in terms of communication between mental and simulation models. Mental models underlie everyday decisions and contain huge amounts of stored information. However, the human mind is not certain when it comes to understanding what the available information means in terms of behaviour. Computer simulation ensures the connection of data with mental models, and subsequently ensures the dynamic visualisation of consequences (Forrester, 2009, p. 9). The System Dynamics method enables the construction of continuous simulation models. It allows for the modelling of the structure and dynamics of complex systems and the processes occurring therein. It also takes into account the numerous instances of feedback occurring in these systems, which describe the cause-and-effect relationships between the elements of the examined system. The fundamental assumption of the method is to consider the examined system as a coherent whole in terms of its dynamics (Hoffmann and Protasowicki, 2013, p. 19). System Dynamics are based on the statement that the system structure which determines behaviour is responsible for changes and problems arising in the system. The cause of the problem is the entire system, and all areas therein. Therefore, the source of the problem should be sought in only one or more of its elements. The System Dynamics method abandons the linear theorem: cause – problem – effect. Thinking systemically, the system should be analysed as a whole, because it is its structure that generates the behaviour of the system leading to the problem (Żukowski, 2012, p. 334). The business model and its dynamics are relevant to the theoretical aspect of defining systems indicated. The conceptualisation of business models has gained much attention in the relevant literature, and the current focus of research shifts from a static perspective to a more dynamic one. Schaffer, Pfaff, and Krcmar define the dynamic business model as a complex system of interrelated components of the mechanisms of value creation, delivery, and capture that interacts with heterogeneous internal and external influences, leading to the evolution of its components and the system itself (Schaffer, Pfaff, and Krcmar, 2019). The concept is particularly important for the design and use of digital business models. The dynamics of complex systems such as digital business models are a distinctive feature which results from the nature of this type of ontological entity. Business models which are in synergy with business ecosystems determine the demand-side behaviour through scalability effects. Thus, they are able to increase the level of their impact in the social and economic space. The dynamics of changes in digital business models are determined by the concepts of the new economy. Cognitive computing, which describes technology platforms that are based on the scientific disciplines of artificial intelligence and signal processing, is of particular importance in terms of making the operation of new business entities dynamic. These platforms include machine learning, reasoning, natural language processing, speech and vision recognition (object recognition), human-computer interactions, dialogue, and narrative generation (Kelly, 2016). "Dynamics", in the context of this value creation formula, shape and operationalise the complex objects that digital business models are. Market changes force the need to adapt business models to market expectations, both through their digital transformation and fulfilling the assumptions of innovative concepts for the new economy. The concept of cognitive computing fits into the prospects of business model development in terms of the new, digital economy (Jabłoński and Jabłoński, 2019, pp. 174–175). As part of searching for new formulas for delivering value, complex technical creations emerge, characterised by expected functionalities, and capable of interacting dynamically with users.

Designing digital business models and monetisation mechanisms

Designing business models in the digital economy requires a different approach than in traditionally understood business. The starting point is the configuration of business model components designed to provide the expected functionality rather than the value chain as defined by Michael Porter. The condition is the choice of technology and the related environment, which constitutes the business ecosystem. Technology must ensure the ability to create and deliver value. There must be value providers and recipients at both ends of the digital platform. The design of the digital business model is created by technologically transforming the intentions of value business providers to ensure specific functionalities for potential users (see Figure 4.1).

The iterative nature of the design process is part of agile project management methodologies. The design process should be concurrent. In the first stage, users should assess their understanding of the business intention and then verify the attractiveness of the functionality of the proposed solution. The required resources and opinions of potential users should be used for this purpose. The iterations of designed solutions are based on the technological transformation of business intentions into functionalities with the active participation of potential users. Monetisation is not the subject of the design at this stage of the design process. Thinking about how to earn money at this stage can prevent the search for new functionalities that are attractive to potential users.

To understand digital business, the right thought context should be used in the process of digital business model design. According to Skilton, a broad

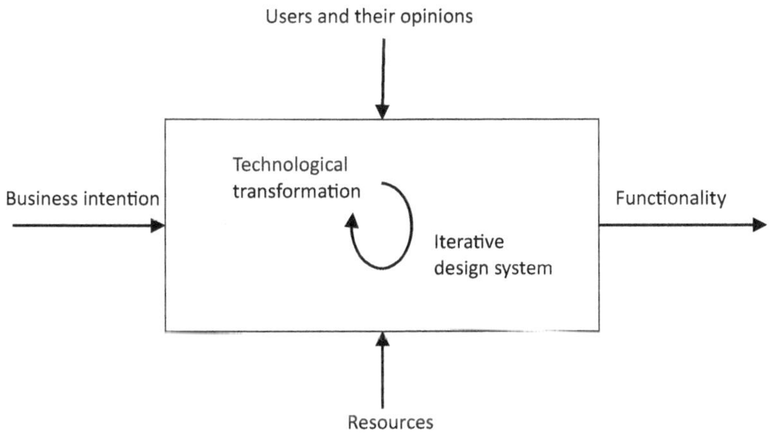

Figure 4.1 Diagram of the iterative digital business model design system.
Source: Own study.

look at digital business requires the identification of three approaches, namely a vertical integrated value network, horizontally integrated value network and value network ecosystem. The vertical approach covers the process from sub-suppliers through the provider to sellers, buyers, consumer, and consumers' consumers. The horizontal approach is based on order processing in the context of scaling sales volumes. In turn, the value network ecosystem includes a cycle of activities in a closed circulation using a multi-sided platform and a two-sided platform using a vertical value chain and a horizontal value chain (Skilton, 2015, p. 17). A critical analysis of this approach shows differences between the vertical value chain, horizontal value chain, and value network ecosystem. Each of these approaches occurs in digital business with varying degrees of saturation and use, and results from different theoretical assumptions, mainly in the context of theories such as complex network theory and actor-network theory. The use of network analysis will also be important (Scott, 2012, p. 21). The above approaches to business ecosystem design are based on the above theories, which should not be forgotten, because good knowledge of theoretical assumptions promotes better operationalisation of project activities. The interdependent implementation of business ecosystem configuration, supported by theoretical assumptions, allows for the conceptualisation of both the horizontal and vertical value networks, as well as for the construction of the entire network of connections. Most often, however, what should be paid attention to is that digital business ecosystems are based on relationship networks using multidirectional communication channels that contribute to the increased volume of network members.

Contemporary business models are characterised by an innovative approach to creating and delivering value to their recipients. In many cases, they require the use of sophisticated logic of human interaction with the use of innovative technological solutions. They often undermine the current economic rules. The market share of digital business models that change the current order is increasing dynamically, and not only on global markets (Ng, 2014, p. 92).

The classical economy of Adam Smith (2015) represented by the theories of free market economies and economic policy, the theory of economic growth, the theory of exchange value (market prices) and the theory of foreign trade is opposed to the assumptions of the digital economy, in particular the Sharing Economy, which is defined as a socio-economic system built around the distribution of human and material resources. It covers the joint creation, production, distribution, trade, and consumption of goods and services by various people as well as organisations. Factors such as the ubiquity of the Internet and mobile devices, the abundance of idle goods, the growing consumer awareness of environmental sustainability, as well as the economic recession leading to an increased unemployment rate, attracted consumers to transactions that allow them to access and profit from unused assets more conveniently (Parente, Geleilate, and Rong, 2018, p. 52). As regards the Sharing Economy, many issues require scientific research to better understand this trend and to explain this phenomenon of the modern economy. The effect of the Sharing Economy trend is the dynamic emergence of new business models based on these assumptions. Two key goals that can be achieved concurrently by using business models based on the Sharing Economy can be distinguished, namely a social goal which enables the possibility of sharing unused resources with other people and organisations and an economic goal used to generate wealth for the creators of these business models.

A scientific problem, but at the same time a practical one, is the analysis of profitability by means of the monetisation of digital economy business models. In many cases, the achievement of the expected ability to monetise a business model is the primary goal of modern business solution designers. This is evidenced by the words of Nicolas Brusson, the CEO and co-founder of BlaBlaCar. When asked how they earn, he answered:

> We do not earn in many countries yet. In some we haven't even started the monetisation phase. In countries where we already have a business model such as France, Spain, Great Britain and Benelux, we collect transaction commission. If this is large enough, we take 10 percent. So if the driver estimates the seat in the car at 20 euros, a passenger pays 22 euros, BlaBlaCar receives 2 euros from this. But the price includes not only the transaction and platform, but we also provide a guarantee in case of cancellation: if the passenger does not show up, the driver receives the money anyway.

Importantly, he also represents an interesting approach to shareholders. He says that: "We put employees first, then community members, and finally shareholders" (Wąsowski, 2017). This is crucial in the context of the social aspect of value creation by means of a business model, but difficult to accept in terms of business monetisation and creating value for shareholders. The profitability of business models is currently the subject of numerous studies, including by Kumar, Lahiri, and Bahadir Dogan (2018); Benitez et al. (2018); Müller and Welpe (2018); Kumar, Ananda, and Songaa (2017), and others. The authors highlight a significant problem in terms of new business formulas achieving profitability.

Legal and tax issues are a separate issue regarding the financial aspects of business models offering digital services. This state of affairs means that both operators of Internet platforms/mobile applications and their users (service providers and clients) have difficulties in assessing their tax obligations and consequences. For example, the business model which Sharing Economy platforms are based on seems quite simple: the platform usually connects people offering services or products with people who need these products or services. Thus, economic exchange takes place (e.g. service for service, goods for goods, money for accommodation, money for travel). From the legal point of view, it should first be determined who the entities are who are participating in the economic exchange based on the Sharing Economy. Subsequently, it would be necessary to determine legal relationships between economic agents operating within the framework of the Sharing Economy. Next, the result of such an analysis will affect the determination of the scope of their rights and obligations, and, in the event that the exchange proves to be defective, of possible liability for damages. In addition, regulations on consumer protection, personal data protection and rules for the provision of electronic services may affect these relationships (Raport PwC, 2016, pp. 2, 7). Legal, tax, and market aspects have a crucial impact on the development and future effects of these types of business ventures. The aspects of profitability, value estimation, and the monetisation of business models of companies operating in the digital economy are issues which increasingly require analysis.

The theoretical and practical framework for the monetisation of business models

The issue of the monetisation of business models is important from the point of view of seeking innovative methods of earning money and creating market value for companies. Monetisation is the transformation of something (assets, e.g. business model, data sets, etc.) into money. It is important to show the difference between the revenue model and the monetisation model. The revenue model is just one aspect of the business model – and it is simply the method or process in which the company intends to extract (not attract) money from the "market" for the value created. The revenue model is the way money flows from a paying customer to a company. For example, the basic revenue model is a single price (simple sale of a product at a fixed price). The general monetisation model is a continuous method based on the logic of a unique business model consisting of processing the delivered product or owned users for permanent sale. The fundamental condition for achieving the monetisation effect of a business model is to attract a large volume of recipients of the proposed business solution. The business model should attract them by using a unique service formula compared to other market proposals and specific value propositions. In business practice there are often so-called opposing monetisation models, for example offering software for free or cheaply, and making money (monetisation) by selling customised programming services, consulting, or updating. Monetisation is, therefore, the way in which a company makes money using a business model, and is not direct proof of a sales transaction. Monetisation methods include solutions such as *freemium*, *premium*, *trial*, subscriptions, and so on. Monetisation is included in the intention of business model designers and it is not always possible for it to be effective from the very beginning of the company's existence. It is often necessary, even for a few years, especially in the case of start-ups, to make efforts to create the possibility of monetising the business model, and this does not always turn out to be successful. Thus, monetisation becomes the core objective of innovative business model designers, and the financial aspect is of fundamental importance in this context. Based on the review of the relevant literature and the observation of market behaviour and

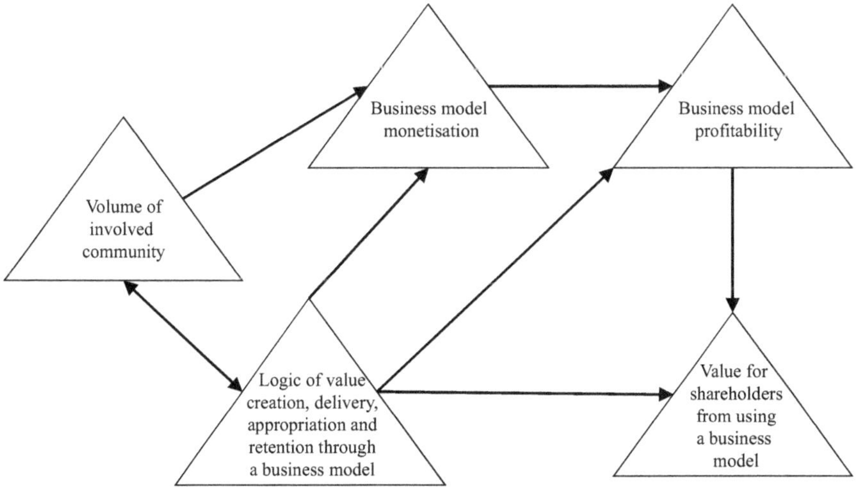

Figure 4.2 Financial triad of the Sharing Economy business models.
Source: Own study.

aspirations of modern companies, the concept of the author's financial proposal of the business model triad has been developed (see Figure 4.2).

The triad consists of three financial aspects: namely, monetisation, building profitability, and business model values, the results of which depend on two core variables such as the volume of the involved community and the logic of value creation, delivery, appropriation, and retention. This concept, therefore, is based on the assumption that the starting point for facilitating the ability of the business model to monetise is the logic of value creation, delivery, appropriation, and retention through the business model's functionality built into the structure. The condition for maintaining this logic is to build a business ecosystem around the business model. The volume of this community, and thus its scale of impact on revenues, monetises the business model. This, in turn, creates conditions for achieving profitability, which contributes to increasing the value for shareholders using the business model. This value-oriented logic of a business model in the case of the digital economy, and in particular the Sharing Economy, should – in addition to the financial aspect – create social values that should be positively received by actors of the sharing process using this business model. Thus, the volume of the community can grow dynamically.

Monetisation as a concept has many different definitions. Some treat it broadly as a revenue-raising scheme, while some treat it narrowly and say it applies only to so-called micropayments. Generally, the transformation of non-monetary resources into monetary resources appears in each approach. Monetisation is not only understanding how to make money but an idea that a business model should generate economic income, and a system by which it is made possible.

Table 4.1 Definitions of the monetisation of digital business models

Dollarisation	Dollarisation is translating the benefits that a product or service delivers to a customer into the actual dollars-and-cents impact.
Monetisation	Monetisation is the conversion of an asset into money or the establishment of something as a medium of exchange. It can refer to methods used to generate profit, and it also can mean the literal conversion of an asset into money.
Data monetisation	Data monetisation is the conversion of an asset into a revenue stream or into profit by creating greater quantified financial value for customers than the competition.

Source: Own study based on Liozu and Ulaga, 2018, p. 24.

The strength of the idea of monetisation lies in the fact that revenues must be created through a specific, essentially unique system. They cannot be forced into increasing the number of commercial transactions on the market, but they should be built into the system of relationships with users. Users, in turn, should accept this type of settlement for the value delivered. They will accept it only if the scale of the financial burden is acceptable to them and the price-quality ratio is optimal. The complexity of the concept of monetisation is presented in Table 4.1. The concept of monetisation is not tantamount to the concept of data monetisation although these concepts must overlap in the digital economy.

Therefore, attention should be paid to the important category of monetisation considered in terms of data monetisation. In the digital economy, data are often used for direct and indirect sales. Micropayments can also result from access to attractive data. The place and role of data monetisation in the digital economy is shown in Figure 4.3.

Data monetisation is based on the sale of stored and/or used data. The data are used within the business ecosystem. The need for access to data results from its useful value. Data usability shapes the business ecosystem based on data usage.

When undertaking a critical analysis of this model, it should be noted that data monetisation should result directly from the dynamics of the functioning business model. Thus, these data are not only attractive in the context of passive–historical data, but should, in particular, be dynamic, that is, result from the analysis of customer/user behaviour. The dynamics of the data subjected to verification and monetisation makes the added value of the data greater.

Data monetisation can be internal or external. Internal monetisation includes activities that lead to the use of the potential of your data, by better tailoring the offer to customers or predicting their behaviour more accurately. External monetisation refers to cooperation between companies aimed at obtaining a synergy effect from their data. For example, it may include the provision of services to third parties based on the data obtained.

Data monetisation is therefore the possibility of direct and indirect monetisation of knowledge of digital behaviour and interest profiles of the company's

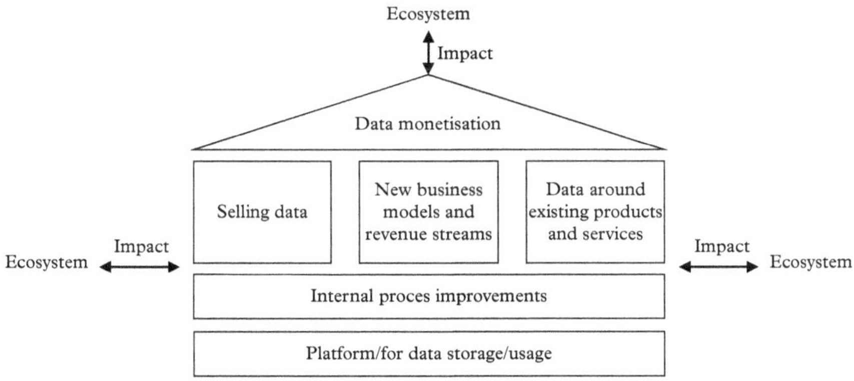

Figure 4.3 Models for data monetisation.
Source: Own study based on Liozu and Ulaga, 2018, p. 31.

customers or Internet users. Monetisation is the transformation of assets into an additional source of income (Portal Email Partners, 2017). Monetisation as an idea can be conceptualised and operationalised in relation to various industries and scopes of activity conducted through digital solutions. It may apply to content management processes in the case of publishing houses, website-assisted services, computer games or other activities. In any case, this monetisation will be based on different assumptions. Monetisation is stimulated by the processes of the digital transformation of the global economy. According to Kreft, the famous "free" access results from a business model based primarily on media content creation by users, sales to advertisers and data processing for business purposes. This relationship is the most market-oriented, and the price depends on many factors, such as the value of users from advertisers' perspective (Kreft, 2019) The potential of the monetisation logic of the sale of digital business models lies in understanding and estimating the value of consumer behaviour on the part of the value recipient. A crucial question that business model designers ask themselves is how to create an effective monetisation model? There are generally two ways to achieve monetisation, namely:

1. Additional revenue,
2. Reduced cost.

In addition, the key is to indicate behavioural factors that determine the behaviour of digital solution users. These are direct behaviours (e.g. reporting a need via a digital form), and indirect behaviours (a solution related to the idea of a business model that uses customer attraction to the application, thus creating value for those interested) (Conversion blog, 2010). The simplest example of the monetisation of direct behaviour is an online store. The most important measure in this respect is the conversion rate of a purchase. If it is, for example, 4% (the number of all visitors to the website), revenue is increased by increasing the rate thanks to conversion optimisation (without having to invest more money in advertising activities). Knowing the average value of the order, you can easily calculate how much revenue will increase thanks to conversion optimisation. Indirect behaviour is most common when selling offline. People often use websites to see what products and services are offered, and the final purchase (conversion) is made outside the website (Conversion blog, 2010).

To illustrate the concept of monetisation and its relationship to the entire business ecosystem, it is worth looking at the solutions tested in the digital publishing market (see Figure 4.4).

Digital content platforms are a good example of the monetisation of digital business models. The key to publishers being able to monetise their content is to experiment with them by using different models that are constantly evolving. The core technological architecture must be flexible as well as expandable so that publishers do not have to invest in new technologies whenever they need to experiment in the context of new content offer formulas. Only those publishers with the right architecture and technology solutions will succeed as

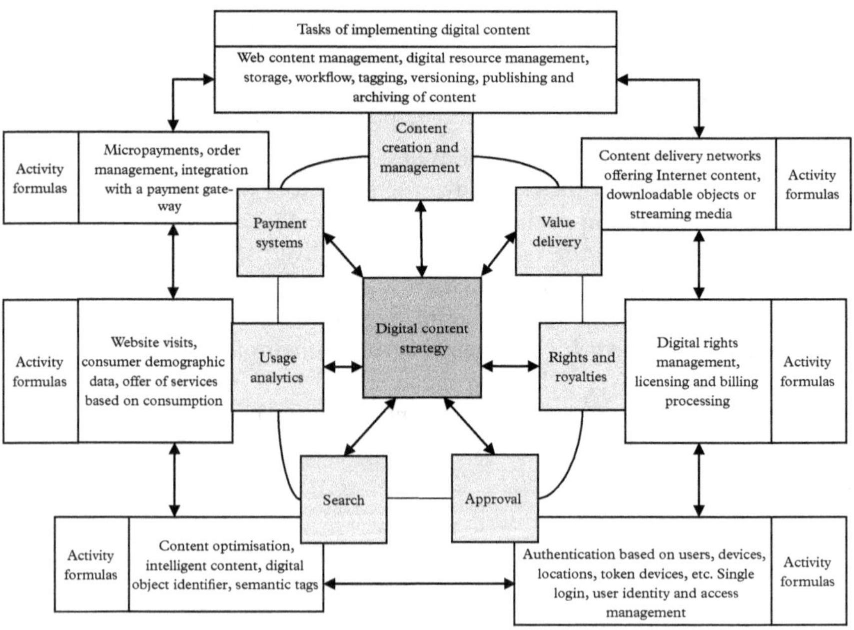

Figure 4.4 Technological components of the business model in the implementation of digital content.

Source: Own study based on Padmanabhan and Sriharsha, 2012.

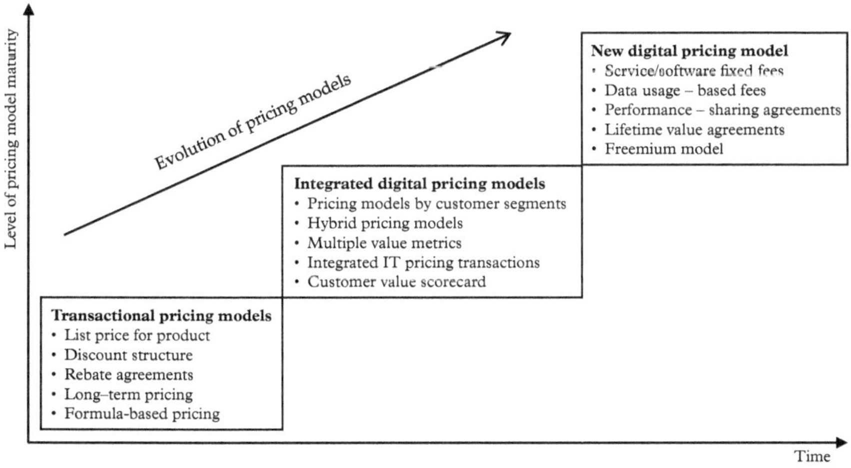

Figure 4.5 Different approaches to business monetisation in the context of company status in regard to development orientation towards the digital economy.

Source: Own study based on Liozu and Ulaga, 2018, p. 212.

recipients, and their business models will change over time (Padmanabhan and Sriharsha, 2012).

Generally, payment methods are traditional, digital, and hybrid and are used in traditional sectors of the economy, digital business ecosystems, and when companies implement digital transformation strategies, at which point they are hybrid (see Figure 4.5).

The evolution of pricing models is presented in Figure 4.5. The evolution presents the transition from the transactional pricing model through the integrated hybrid model to the new digital pricing model. The evolution takes place in real time showing the level of maturity of the adopted pricing model.

In this situation, one can talk about the life cycle of the company in the context of adapting the business model based on the assumptions of the digital economy. This naturally determines the approach to using the appropriate business monetisation formulas. The more saturated the business model with the components responsible for the digital economy, the greater the chance to apply innovative monetisation principles, including micropayments, in the product structure of digital business models.

Classification of monetisation formulas for digital business models

There are numerous solutions in the field of monetisation formulas for digital business models. Generally, they are based on the concept of so-called micropayments, or are more broadly defined as any means of generating revenue from resources owned and/or value created. One of the conditions for effective monetisation is the fulfilment of the system solution requirement, which in a way, thanks to built-in logic, makes users willing to pay. The examples of monetisation formulas commonly used in the digital economy are presented in Table 4.2.

Table 4.2 App Monetisation Models

No.	*Type of monetisation*	*Description*
1.	In-app Advertising	The digital advertising monetisation model has been adapted for mobile applications. This includes interstitial, banners, video, native, and text ads. Application developers can also advertise other applications by means of a wide range of so-called ad networks, where they can place ads on other applications and websites to target specific audiences and attract traffic to their applications.
2.	Interstitial Ads	This ad format applies to interstitial ads that are to occupy the entire smartphone screen to attract the attention of mobile users. The charging formula applies to earnings for every 1,000 views.
3.	Banner Ads	This mobile ad format is the equivalent of a computer banner that has its limitations. It takes up little space on the smartphone screen, so mobile users can pay less attention to it.
4.	Video Ads	Video ads are one of the most effective mobile ad formats. Currently, the leaders in this area are Google, Facebook, and Vungle. Mobile video advertising is a short movie lasting up to 15 seconds that presents the application and contains a direct link to download it.
5.	Native Ads	Native ads are considered the most effective. Native ads can be designed in many sizes and implemented differently on different media, so their average price varies significantly. Prices for native ads are set per 1,000 views.
6.	Text Ads	The simplest form of mobile advertising is text advertising. The cost includes one click.
7.	Paid Apps	When mobile application stores were launched, most mobile applications were paid and it was the only monetisation model. Later, advertising and shopping began to appear. Currently, there are still several categories of applications for which the paid application model is more profitable than others. These include Tools, Performance, Photo and video, and Navigation. This model is the foundation of the concept of the App Store application package for iOS, which allows iOS application users to buy and download multiple related applications from the same application developer simultaneously. In this model, the application publisher receives remuneration each time the application is downloaded separately or as part of the above-mentioned application package.

No.	*Type of monetisation*	*Description*
8.	Freemium (try before you buy)	In this monetisation model, application publishers offer mobile users free application downloads for use with a limited feature set. Additional content can be provided through their in-app purchases for premium features. This model is the direct equivalent of a free trial computer software model. The iOS App Store policies provide developers with many levels of in-app purchases, ensuring the flexibility to offer additional features at various levels to users.
9.	In-App Purchases	There are four types of in-app purchases available in the iOS App Store – Consumable, Non-Consumable, Auto-Renewable Subscriptions and Non-Renewing Subscriptions. Consumable purchase includes the purchase of various in-game consumables in the application that users must complete during the game. The non-mandatory type of in-app purchases refers to purchases that application users must make once to extend the set of features offered by the application. Thanks to the type of in-app purchases with the automatic renewal function, users can pay for specific services or periodically updated content of the application, and the latter means that users pay only once for the subscription, and then access the specific content of the application for a specified time. One of the application monetisation strategies that is particularly important for mobile games is the in-app currency. A typical example is offering mobile game users the in-app purchase of a set of coins for use in a selected game, for example, 50 coins for a specific amount.
10.	Subscriptions	Subscriptions with the option of automatic renewal provide users with access to content, services or premium features in a given application on an ongoing basis. At the end of each subscription period, the subscription will automatically renew until a user chooses to cancel it. In this model, application developers can offer many plans with options for upgrading, lowering, and moving to a higher level (when mobile application users switch from one subscription to a comparable one). With this subscription model, developers can offer discounts for a long subscription period.
11.	Affiliate Marketing and Lead Generation	Affiliate marketing is an effective way for application developers to make money on mobile resources. Affiliate marketing of mobile applications consists of paying commission for each instance when the mobile application has been downloaded or a specific action has been performed using a link in the application. There is one particular type of affiliate marketing, which is Lead Generation – in this case it is a process of not selling products or services, but capturing the contact details of

(continued)

Table 4.2 Continued

No.	*Type of monetisation*	*Description*
		people who are really and clearly interested in buying specific services or products. In this type of affiliate marketing programme, you earn money by capturing and providing this information to a company that is looking for such potential customers.
12.	SMS Marketing	SMS marketing is the delivery of marketing content via SMS. To monetise the application using this channel, application publishers use smartphone user contact databases that have been collected only with their express consent.
13.	Email Marketing	Email marketing is one of the oldest types of internet marketing and involves sending marketing content via email.
14.	Sponsorships	Sponsorship consists of acquiring one or several advertisers in a given application. The sponsor in a given application can be represented by an icon covering the greater part of the application interface with his/her logo, by means of a welcome screen that is visible to application users immediately after its launch or via push notifications.
15.	Licensing	If an application functionality requires the collection of user-generated data or there are technical means of collecting data, such as geographical locations, data licensing to other companies can be considered. This makes applications available to end users free of charge, though monetisation takes place through data licensing. This business model is based on the licensing of a community-collected data set for companies that need to place location-based advertising.
16.	Crowdfunding	Crowdfunding can be a good channel for making money on a mobile application. Such a channel can be a way to generate income by generating cash flow focused on achieving a specific business or social goal that a crowd of users wants to finance.

Source: Own study based on Dogtiev, 2019.

The above monetisation formulas do not exhaust their complexity. Interesting solutions in the field of the monetisation of digital business models are used by the computer games industry. Table 4.3 shows crucial monetisation formulas used by developers in this industry.

Monetisation formulas used by computer game producers, as well as combinations thereof which are built into computer game scenarios, are criticised by users in many respects, and in some cases their compliance with the law is even questioned. Some players become addicted to computer games, which exposes them to unreasonable expenses if the micropayment system associated

Table 4.3 Monetisation Models for games

No.	*Type of monetisation*	*Description*
1.	Offline shops	The traditional way to earn from the game is to sell the game in traditional game stores or department stores.
2.	Online shops	Selling a computer game in one of these online stores.
3.	Display advertising	Display advertising is a commonly used business model in free-to-play games. There are various forms of advertising banners used in computer games. A large audience is required for display advertising to be a successful business model. Revenue is calculated per click or per 1,000 impressions.
4.	Video pre-roll	Pre-roll video is a form of advertising banner. It displays a video ad while the game is loading. This monetisation strategy has the same rules as for general display ads: a large community is needed to deliver the expected revenue.
5.	In-game purchases	Social games or mobile games are often monetised by offering in-game purchases. When a user gets stuck at a certain level, they can buy tips or skip this level with the loans offered. Also virtual goods can be used to make purchases in a given game, such as decorating a virtual home or similar.
6.	Add-ons	Sale of add-ons for a given game. After purchasing a standard game, players receive many expansion packs to enjoy the game even more. This model is often used in mobile games as well. Add-ons can make the game more attractive, which gives additional value to its users.
7.	Branded content	Product placement in a given computer game. If there are any brands that are willing to pay for product placement or sponsored content in a given game, this could be an additional or main source of income.
8.	Recommendation engine	Fee for the recommendation. The designed recommendation engine can provide an income stream.
9.	Subscriptions	A monthly fee must be paid to use (additional) services. This can also be used for computer games.
10.	Pay walls	A strategy to encourage players to try a computer game by offering it for free for some time, after which they must pay to continue playing. The next challenge will be to interest players enough to convince them to pay.
11.	Merchandising	Sale of products not related to a computer game through the use of an information channel for such purchases. Establishing an online store or selling products in a traditional store when a computer game has loyal fans who are willing to spend their money on merchandising. This will not be a major source of revenue, but it can further increase the overall monetisation strategy.

Source: Website spilgames (accessed: 5 January 2020).

with an attractive computer game scenario is designed in such a way that it "pulls" the player into the spiral of expenses. For example, in FIFA the Ultimate Team mode has been built-in for several years, in which the main goal is to get the best players. This can be done either by buying them on the transfer market for the currency received for playing the match and other activities, or packs with players can be purchased with the currency earned by spending real cash. In some cases, players spend large amounts of money on this form of micropayment. Some national governments, for example Belgium, impose directives ordering the removal of micropayments from computer game scenarios sold in this country on the producers of certain computer games. Also, computer game users pay attention to this, which may have adverse consequences in the outflow of the volume of existing users as well as deterrence of new ones. Therefore, computer game manufacturers should reasonably design monetisation systems with an optimal price-versus-quality relationship.

As regards Internet blogs, there are four blog monetisation methods, namely:

- Advertisements (Google Adsense),
- Promotion of products in partner (affiliate) programmes,
- Publication of sponsored articles,
- Sale of one's own product or service.

The operationalisation of monetisation formulas may be based on specific solutions resulting from the possibilities inherent in technological solutions. The most popular solutions regarding the monetisation of computer applications include eCPM (effective Cost Per Mile), CPC (Cost Per Click), and CPA (Cost Per Action).

Effective Cost Per Mile (eCPM) is a model that is based on rewarding the publisher of the application, regardless of whether mobile users have actually taken any action in terms of advertising the mobile application or not. It can be calculated according to the following formula:

$$eCPM = \frac{Total\ Earnings}{Total\ Impressions} \cdot 1{,}000$$

The total earnings representing the value of the revenue that the publisher of the application generated from a particular advertisement is divided by the total number of impressions received by this advertisement during the advertising campaign.

Cost Per Click (CPC) model: compared to eCPM, the Cost Per Click (CPC) model is based on the action of a mobile user – a click on a mobile ad. The following formula is used to calculate this indicator:

$$CPC\left(Cost\ Per\ Click\right) = \frac{Total\ Ad\ Spend}{Total\ Measured\ Clicks}$$

The total expenditure on advertising is the amount spent on advertising divided by the number of clicks made. Publishers have the chance to attract a diverse group of advertisers through the CPC model, which allows you to monitor the behaviour of mobile users. It may turn out that mobile advertising will not provide a high click-through rate, making this solution unprofitable. Using this model, application developers find it more difficult to predict its revenues and build a scalable financial system.

The Cost Per Action (CPA) model includes a scheme where the publisher only earns when mobile users take certain actions, for example when they see a mobile ad, click on it, and then either download the application and run it at least once, make a purchase, or subscribe to the service. This model can generate high revenues for the advertiser, while the publisher of the application can expect a higher payout.

Thus, when determining the value of revenues in the digital business model, the following parameters can be taken into account:

- % inventory – proportion of ad space sold on sites,
- number of ad units,
- CPM – Cost per thousand impressions for ad volume deals,
- CPC – Cost Per Click for Pay Per Click Deals.

Eight digital ad revenue model options can be also distinguished:

1. Revenue from subscription access to content.
2. Revenue from Pay Per View access to document.
3. Revenue from CPM display advertising on site.
4. Revenue from CPC advertising on site (pay per click text ads).
5. Revenue from sponsorship of site sections or content types (typically fixed fee for a period).
6. Affiliate revenue (CPA, but could be CPC).
7. Subscriber data access for e-mail marketing.
8. Access to customers for online research (Chaffey, 2019).

Generally, the monetisation methods include the solutions described in Table 4.4.

This proposal highlights monetisation through the attributes of a business model, monetisation through the use of various sources of financing for development, monetisation through services, and monetisation through the benefits of having applications and access to Big Data sets.

The concept of monetisation can also be explained by the example of the process of monetising video content on the Internet. It involves the participation of four actors: a viewer, a platform, an advertiser, and a creator. Depending on the relationship between individual actors, different types of monetisation models can be distinguished. Monetisation of video content can be direct or indirect. Indirect monetisation involves the sales of generated traffic, while

Table 4.4 Division of monetisation formulas by various criteria

No.	*Monetisation method*	*Description*
Monetisation through the attributes of the business model		
1.	Advertising	The most common form of making money on websites is advertising, which works well on media websites, blogs, and other information and media services. The goal is to display ads on these websites. Several forms of advertising can be listed, including: • Contextual advertising • Display advertising • Targeted advertising • Text link advertising
2.	Sponsorship	Sponsorship is different in nature than advertising. Often, sponsors are introduced to websites or the media. Their operationalisation can be based on solutions such as information, live transmission, or a viral marketing campaign.
3.	Paid Content and Advertorials	Advertising sections can often be seen in magazines and newspapers, which at first glance seem to be publication editing. In these paid areas of content, useful or valuable knowledge that also leads the user towards marketing is shared. Media sites can offer advertising sections on their pages, allowing marketers to publish content.
4.	Syndication of Content	Changing the purpose of content from other channels or displaying content on other websites can result in revenues from micropayments or a fixed price. Viewing content from other sources may result in content providers paying providers.
5.	Affiliations	For many websites, providing recommended partner links can be a steady stream of links and commission revenue. An example is the Amazon book recommendation programme. It is important that the website is fully transparent about the link relationship and recommendations. Companies that aggregate content and distribute it to other companies may receive micropayments for such activities, for example Mozilla Firefox generates regular amounts of micropayments from users who use the search bar in the upper right-hand corner of the browser.
6.	Donations	Placing donation proposals usually takes place under the Marketing segment, since the same types of activities are required to obtain donations from groups or individuals. This common method requires the transfer of money for a good cause in exchange for goodwill for recognising (or placing an identifier on the website) tax relief or knowing that someone has supported something they believe in.

No.	Monetisation method	Description
7.	Conversion	Not all websites generate direct revenue, although marketers can bring potential customers closer to the point of sale. In some companies that provide qualified potential customers, they earn on those potential customers. Websites can generate interest from marketing activities, qualifying activities that ultimately lead to sales.
Monetisation through financing sources		
8.	Acquisition	The most frequently discussed transaction process in contemporary start-up conditions is the option of buying them through a large internet unit.
9.	Initial Public Offerings	An initial public offering is how a company sells its property to the public and buyers become shareholders so that eventually the value of shares (and companies) increases. This form of monetisation decreased significantly in 2007 and is now very rare.
10.	Investment and Partnership	Many start-ups receive funding waves from venture capital companies or large partners. Although this activity is not often considered a "monetisation" method, it actually gives those who run the site the opportunity to grow.
Monetisation through services		
11.	E-commerce	Selling goods online and giving recommendations provides the seller, wholesalers and brokers with the opportunity to profit from selling their own goods.
12.	Premium, Memberships, and Licensing	Full membership or exclusive membership, common to websites offering free services, provide users with additional benefits. Some examples include email services offering additional storage space, Flickr offering more photo upload capacity, or access to other websites. This may also include software licensing options.
13.	Virtual goods	This form of monetisation is constantly growing in social networks and virtual sites. Real and virtual objects combine value, have meaning from donor to recipient, and can be assigned a monetary value. Monetisation through the benefits of having applications and access to Big Data sets.
Monetisation through the benefits of having applications and access to Big Data sets		
14.	Selling Data	Many websites collect information that can be resold to third parties. Data types include internet traffic, term search, registration information, and e-mail information. When gathering information, it is necessary to be open and transparent to one's own users.
15.	Secondary Opportunities	Opportunities for brand extension to other media can generate revenue, in particular new job offers, opportunities for speaking, writing, and content syndication.

Source: Own study based on Owyang, 2007.

direct monetisation involves selling goods and services. Indirect monetisation formulas include:

- pay per click (PPC);
- cost per mille (CPM);
- cost per action (CPA), which includes:
  - cost per sale (CPS);
  - cost per lead (CPL).

The methods of video monetisation online, that is, advertising, crowdfunding, sponsorship, subscription, product placement, and e-commerce, are in a different order than the types of monetisation (direct and indirect). Therefore, they should not be treated as equivalent, as there is no obstacle to some sort of monetisation which combines the types of direct and indirect monetisation (Raport podsumowujący badanie, National Broadcasting Council Report, 2016, p. 96).

The types of monetisation regarding monetising video content online include the formulas described in Table 4.5.

As mentioned earlier, monetisation is a scheme of the flow of content, money, interactions, and connections between actors involved in this process. Monetisation, therefore, stimulates the relationships between actors in the network of connections determined by the logic of the adopted business model. Therefore, it is a core element of the adopted business solution, strongly connected with the proposed value offer. Monetisation makes the business model dynamic. From an economic point of view, the condition for the survival of a given business model is the necessity of fulfilling three conditions:

1. Actors gathered around the business model must recognise the benefits of the value proposition delivered within the business model.
2. Actors must accept the proposed monetisation method.
3. Cash flow does not have to be compatible with the number of customers/users of digital platform. Each user/customer can have unique conditions of using created value from a digital platform, for example a solution in the range of the freemium and premium monetisation formula. Usually the number of users who do not pay is greater than the number of users who pay.

Figure 4.6 presents the author's method of presenting how monetisation works in the context of digital business models. A customer/user transfers funds to the digital platform, which delivers the expected value through the operators supporting it. The flow of the proposed value can be symmetrical or asymmetrical, which results from the type of direct or indirect monetisation. In the case of direct monetisation, the delivered value is followed by the flow of money, and then the symmetry between these two variables is maintained.

When the revenue from value delivery through a business model is not related to this delivery, indirect monetisation occurs. In the case of indirect

Table 4.5 Types of monetisation regarding monetising video content on the Internet

No.	*Monetisation formula*	*Description*
1.	Market model	A creator produces video material which is published on a self-publishing platform. Then the video content is made available by the platform, which results in delivering it to viewers who have the ability to directly view the content on the site and distribute it to friends and on other platforms or social networks. The viewer becomes a consumer, potential customer – he/she moves from the video service to an external website, where he/she can buy a physical or digital product (ecommerce), the author and seller of which was the video creator. Money from the purchase goes to the creator (type of direct monetisation). In this particular model, the platform does not generate revenue because the creator published and shared the material for free.
2.	Return model	In the return model, an advertiser is responsible for the inflow of money, while a creator provides video material to the website. Importantly, the activities of advertisers and creators are independent of each other. Subsequently, the content is made available by the platform, which results in delivering it to viewers who have the ability to directly view content on the site and distribute it to friends and on other platforms or social networks. In addition to the target video content, viewers are shown promotional material for advertisers. The selection of ads for video content is not accidental.
3.	Popularisation model	The popularisation model is a model in which the effect of monetisation is funds that cannot be used (during transactions) on other markets. This model is basically similar to the market model, although it is clearly distinguished by the final good. The created video material is shared by the platform, which results in its delivery to viewers who have the ability to directly view content on the site and distribute it to friends and on other platforms or social networks. Then the viewer becomes a consumer – he/she browses the author's earlier work, goes to his/her website, comments on the material and shares it with his friends. All interactions performed by the consumer come back to the creator in the form of a wider audience. This, in turn, translates into the advertising potential of the creator (type of indirect monetisation), that is, it determines his/her future revenues.
4.	Popularisation and market model	A model which somewhat combines the two previously discussed schemes is the popularisation and market model. A popular creator is paid by the advertiser (through sponsorship or product placement), which is an example of direct monetisation. A company invests measurable funds to become more recognisable in a specific age group, to

(*continued*)

Table 4.5 Continued

No.	*Monetisation formula*	*Description*
		distribute or sell its product. The creator prepares video material which is published on the self-publishing platform. Then the video content is made available by the platform, which results in its delivery to viewers who have the ability to directly view the content on the site and distribute it to friends and on other platforms or social networks.
5.	Indirect market model	The model refers to the symbiotic relationship between creators. Both creator no. 1 and creator no. 2 receive a measurable material benefit. As in the previous model, creator no. 2 is the investor who provides funds to the more popular creator no. 1. Creator no. 1 produces video material that is published on a self-publishing platform. Subsequently, the video content is made available by the platform, which results in it being made available to viewers who have the ability to directly view the content on the site and distribute it to friends and on other platforms or social networks. The video content or description contains a link to an external website, where the viewer has the opportunity to buy creator no. 2's products (e-commerce). Finally, the viewers generate profit for creator no. 2, which is an example of direct monetisation.
6.	Indirect popularisation model	There are two creators in the indirect popularisation model. Creator no. 1 receives a measurable financial benefit for promotional activities for creator no. 2. The implementation of this model is as follows: creator no. 2 invests in advertising his/her work or video series – he/she transfers the money, however, to the better-known creator no. 1, who has suitable advertising potential. Creator no. 1 produces a video that promotes creator no. 2, which he/she publishes on a self-publishing platform. Subsequently, the video content is made available by the platform, which results in it being made available to viewers who have the ability to directly view the content on the site and distribute it to friends and on other platforms or social networks. Viewers interact with the advertised creator no. 2, which increases his/her popularity and advertising potential (indirect monetisation type). There is protocooperation between the creators – they work together, and this results in mutual benefits.
7.	Crowdfunding	Viewers provide the creator with funds that finance the production process of video content (type of direct monetisation). The creator creates the video material and then publishes it on the self-publishing platform. The platform provides the ability to play and share the video, which results in reaching viewers (distribution). Viewers who helped to fund the project receive a returnable benefit – a specific value, for example the expected (ordered) film.

Source: Own study based on National Broadcasting Council Report, 2016, pp. 97–104.

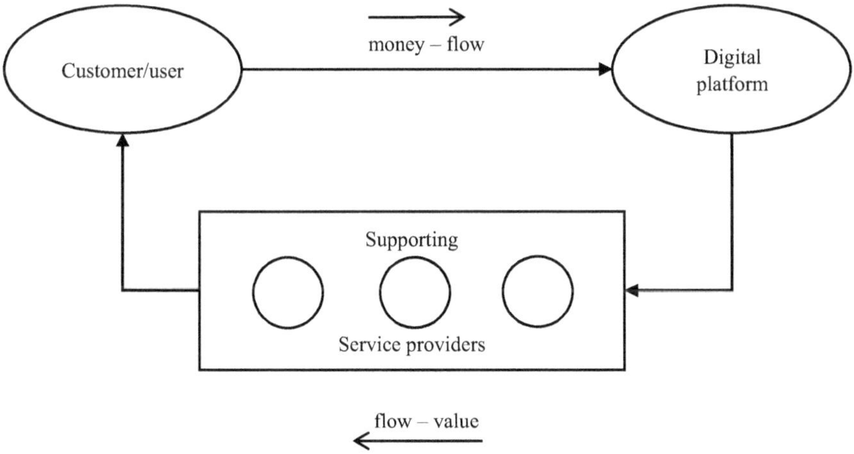

Figure 4.6 General formula of the monetisation of the digital business model.
Source: Own study.

monetisation, the phenomenon of lack of symmetry between the value delivery through the business model and the flow of money can be observed. Both of these solutions underlie the functioning of digital business models.

The presented general formula of the monetisation of the digital business model illustrates the relational nature of the functioning of the modern world economy. The transactional model is followed by a transition to the relational model (broadly on this topic: Hausner, 2019, pp. 205–208), which creates opportunities for the development of indirect monetisation formulas, for example, in the case of the monetisation of business models operating under the concept of the Sharing Economy. The Sharing Economy business model consists of a company or service enabler that acts as an intermediary between suppliers of goods or services (service provider) and customers who require it for unused goods and services. Mutually resolved systemic connections between actors build a monetisation formula of such defined business models (Kumar, Lahiri, and Bahadir Dogan, 2018, p. 148).

The models of generating revenue based on the monetisation of business services are the domain of online platforms in particular, and they are based on B2B or B2C relationships. It is necessary to use the Internet Platform Value Proposition supported by marketing strategies for business models in terms of the B2B and B2C relationship criterion. This relationship system uses optimal solutions in terms of monetising business services, deals, and the flow of required information accompanying transactional processes based on relational relationships (Muzellec, Ronteau, and Lambkin, 2015, pp. 139–150).

This model exposes the relationships between Internet users and the central role of the platform generating value proposition. The details of monetisation result from the type of services provided and the technologies used. They also depend on the type of business orientation in the context of B2B and B2C models.

When making a multidimensional analysis of the types and classification of digital business models, it should be noted that they are often ephemeral business models in terms of cash flows. Ephemeral business models in the digital economy are very short term and transient with a very short life cycle. However, this does not mean that it is impossible to achieve high rates of return and sometimes large, positive cash flows. An example of such ephemeral business models is the crowdfunding-based business model. Crowdfunding as a new mechanism of raising funds, however, it has certain distinctive features that allow it to be distinguished from public collections, donations, and other traditional forms. The first feature of crowdfunding is the transfer of cash, almost always in a dematerialised form. It is impossible to provide support in any other form, such as material or other means. The entire capital-raising process is conducted by means of ICT solutions. The goal of the crowdfunding-financed project is clearly defined, as are the allocation of funds and the effects of their spending. Crowdfunding does not require the consent of any state authority and may be conducted for personal, business, or public purposes (Kozioł-Nadolna, 2015, pp. 671–683). Hence, crowdfunding is an ephemeral business model, because after reaching the assumed goal the model ceases to exist. For social media-based digital business models, business models are business model platforms that are based, inter alia, on embedding ephemeral, short-term content that appears only once and then disappears from the platform. Snapchat is such an example of an ephemeral business model.

Unlike archived social media, ephemeral social media applications such as Snapchat, Instagram, and Facebook Stories or Xpire allow user content to be shared for a set amount of time before auto-deletion (see Table 4.6 for examples of ephemeral social media and the time limit given to messages before they auto-delete) (Wakefield and Bennett, 2018, pp. 147–159).

Table 4.6 Examples of ephemeral social media applications

Social Media Platform	*Time Limit Options*
Snapchat	1–10 s; 24 h
Instagram Stories	24 h
Facebook Stories	24 h
Xpire	Minutes to Years
Wickr	Seconds to Days
Jott	5 s; 10 s; 20 s
CyberDust	30 s
Clipchat	5 s
Bum Note	2–120 s
Bleep	10 s

Source: Wakefield and Bennett, 2018, pp. 147–159.

Scant research has delved into the power of ephemeral content in terms of identifying its antecedents and consequences in users' decision-making processes. The overarching questions remain in regard to the ways in which users are motivated to embrace ephemeral content and what outcome behaviours are engendered as a result of such motivations (Chen and Cheung, 2019, pp. 67–74).

The solutions described here indicate how much potential is built in the digital economy when it comes to the methods of the monetisation of business models. Therefore, the following questions should be asked constantly: What is a revenue model? What should a revenue model include? What are the different franchise models, and how do they operate? What are the different value propositions and revenue-sharing models? What is an example of a revenue model? What is a revenue model and business model? Are revenue streams and revenue models the same thing? What is a good revenue model? How do I determine the right revenue model for my company? What are the differences between a business model and a revenue model? How do I write it? What is the difference between a product-sharing model and a revenue-sharing model? These questions indicate how difficult and risky modern online business is. They also point to areas that require theoretical and practical studies and analyses.

Data monetisation provides space for the development of monetisation formulas in digital business models. The digital "me" is not only information such as one's date of birth, address, phone number, or email address, but also information about work, interests, health, and finances. In the future, innovative services may become solutions that will allow consumers to monetise information on which companies earn today by using them for advertising services.

Reversing the relationship in such a way that a customer can receive remuneration for sharing information about himself/herself can bring interesting results, and the relationship of strength in the individual customer-corporation arrangement would increase immeasurably on the side of the former. An example of such a view of the role of data sellers and buyers is the activity of Datacoup. Its mission is – as it describes on its website – to change the asymmetrical model in which companies use user data en masse, and the latter derive no benefits from it. In this case, a customer creates his/her own profile on Datacoup, and its components determine its market value. The information collected in the profile is then made available by Datacoup to interested buyers, mainly banks and insurance companies, which pay for it.

Digital wallets are another example. They take different forms – from digital cards to specialised applications installed on smartphones. They store data on users, their transactions, cards, accounts, and often their shopping habits and preferences as well. Currently, these data are made available to the portfolio producers, who subsequently sell the data in aggregated, anonymous form.

As previously noted, the monetisation model is the flow of content, money, interactions, and relationships between actors involved in this process (Raport podsumowujący badanie, National Broadcasting Council Report, 2016, p. 96). The monetisation of business models based on cognitive algorithms falls into such a category of monetisation that uses Big Data sets. Interactive systems based on these functionalities create new possibilities of generating cash flows. This approach to the monetisation process is different from its other forms because it consists of the direct application of functionalities based on the application of the idea of cognitive techniques which identify specific features/attributes attractive to dedicated recipients. The condition for the delivery of the proposed functionalities is the use of a number of data analysis techniques. These analyses are not only related to data, but also to trends, intuition, and behaviour, and so on. In sectors where the most data are found, the greatest difficulties also occur in their use and monetisation. This is a crucial problem because the goal of every business model should be effective monetisation. Monetisation should focus on supporting the company's vision by implementing a monetisation strategy, and not just on packing resale data. Marketing is the area of the wide application of cognitive business models in terms of their monetisation ability. Therefore, monetisation will also depend on the adopted concept of the new economy, such as the concept of the Sharing Economy, the Circular Economy, Big Data set systems, or other concepts. In each different approach to value creation, monetisation will be based on different assumptions which will refer to the concept of business model dynamics.

The process of designing the monetisation formula of the digital business model – the design of stages

The process of designing the monetisation formula of digital business models is complex. Its operationalisation should take into account experience in the areas of project and process management.

To indicate the assumptions of the design of the monetisation formula of a digital business model, a process approach was used, presenting its individual stages in the form of a process course chart (see Figure 4.7).

Based on the review of the relevant literature and observation of market practices, the stages of designing the digital monetisation formula of the business model have been identified. The first stage should focus on identifying the attributes of value created for users by the digital business model. If there is a chance to monetise the value proposition, monetisation formulas already functioning on the market should be identified. If it is possible to configure value proposition with monetisation formulas on the market into a coherent whole, best practices in the application of commonly known monetisation formulas should be used. After developing a monetisation formula consistent with value proposition for users, it should be subjected to market testing. For this purpose, a technique of improving product quality can be applied. This technique involves the repeated reviews, verifications, and validations of the designed or adopted monetisation formula of the digital business model. The review allows for the assessment of whether the input data are consistent with the output data. The verification provides evidence that the monetisation formula has fulfilled the expected requirements. Validation ensures that the monetisation formula

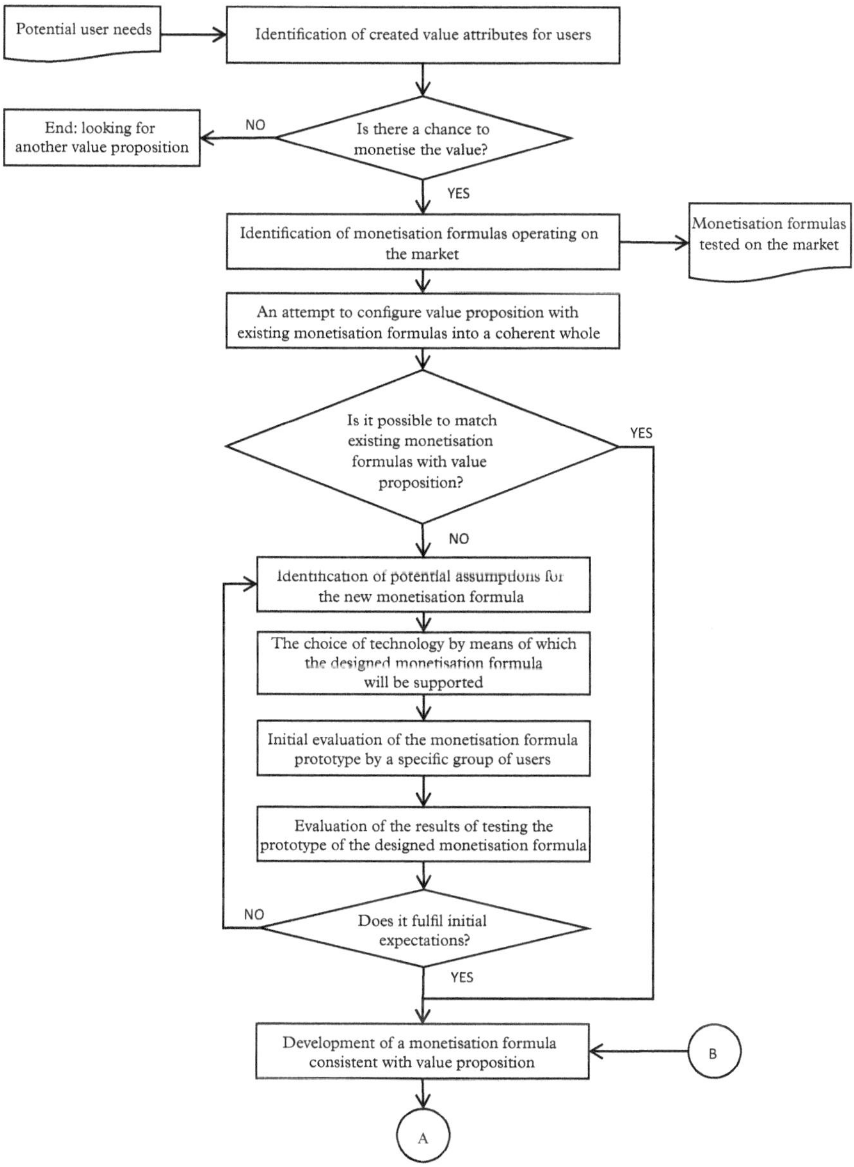

Figure 4.7 Stages of the design process of the monetisation formula of the digital business model.

Source: Own study.

(Continued)

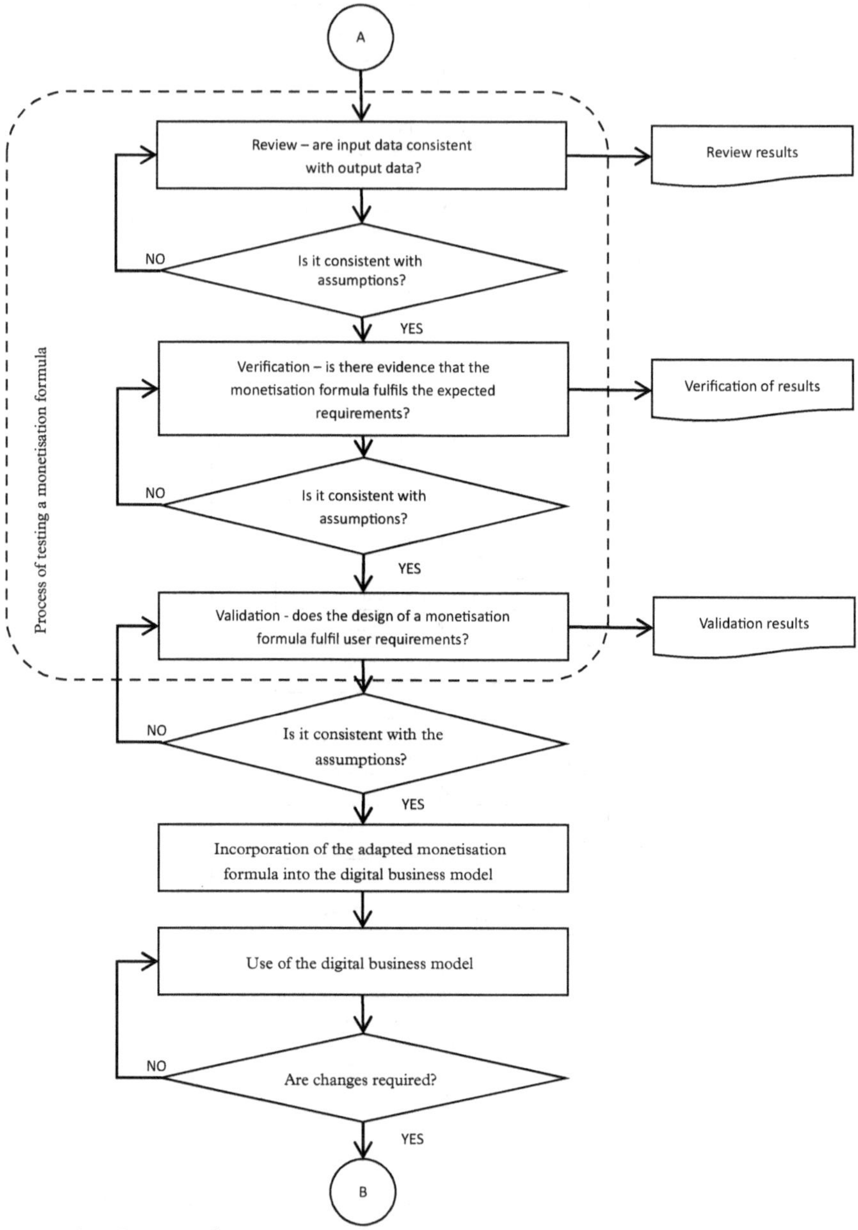

Figure 4.7 Continued

fulfils the expectations of specific user groups. If it is impossible to match the monetisation formulas on the market with the value proposition generated by the digital business model, a new, innovative monetisation formula of the digital business model should be designed. At the first design stage, potential assumptions for the new monetisation formula should be identified. The next step should be choosing the technology through which the planned monetisation formula will work. In the subsequent stage, the prototype of the designed monetisation formula should be evaluated by a specific group of users. A preliminary evaluation of the results of testing the monetisation formula should answer the question whether the further conduct of the project is justified. If the initial assessment shows that the expectations have been fulfilled, monetisation formulas already on the market should be adapted to the value proposition delivered by the digital business model. After conducting the testing process described above and achieving positive results, the designed monetisation formula should be included in the digital business model as a core component. When the use of the digital business model starts, the need to improve it should be monitored together with the adopted monetisation formula. If changes are required, the monetisation formula should be adapted to value propositions.

Controlling the monetisation of digital business models

Classical corporate financial controlling involves monitoring operating costs. In the case of functional controlling, it may also include aspects such as controlling R&D activities, projects, logistics, personnel, marketing and sales, investments, and so on. In the case of digital business models, the issue of controlling takes on a different character. Instead of the traditional revenue and cost accounting system, the concepts of Big Data analytics and Marketing Analytics should be used. It is necessary to use statistics, analyses, models, and Big Data. Controlling in the digital economy will be dealt with by business analysts, digital marketing specialists, price analysts, and monetisation formula designers, among others. Monetisation controlling will be strongly associated with the analysis of the behaviour of digital platform users. User behaviour is the foundation of a marketing strategy and verification of the effectiveness of monetisation formulas. The first step in implementing monetisation controlling will be to recognise user behaviour, their preferences, and financial constraints, as well as the choices they have made. Flexibility will be a core measure used in monetisation controlling. Flexibility is a scale-free measure, calculated as the percentage change in the value of the output variable in response to the percentage change in the value of the input variable (Grigsby, 2018). Volatility in transactions or individual financial operations describing the level of flexibility will express interest in the value proposition delivered by means of a digital business model. It will become the foundation of monetisation controlling. Growth charts will also be important in terms of expressing the level of effectiveness of the monetisation formulas used. The analytics of the effectiveness of monetisation formulas should consist of the creation of models that arrange databases. According to Grigsby, an effective marketing analytics tool based on the analysis of Big Data sets will be the RFM (recency, frequency, and monetary) triad, that is, the time since the last purchase, the frequency of purchases, and money paid (Grigsby, 2018). Designing experiments for the testing (review, verification, and validation) of designed monetisation formulas will also be justified. The use of multiple data sources as part of the Big Data concept will be crucial to designing an effective monetisation controlling system. They can include measures such as the number of clicks, the type of website displayed, time spent on the website, the type of browser used, and so on. Big Data analytics may include sophisticated tools such as neural networks, Deep Learning, executive and analytical algorithms, and others. All these methods focus on such variables that result from the behaviour of users and their habits. Collecting Big Data sets and drawing generalised conclusions from them aims to better understand trends in their calculations and to design executive and analytical algorithms that support monetisation processes. Monetisation controlling is an important link which supports the design and monitoring of the effectiveness of monetisation formulas of digital business models. The model for controlling the monetisation of digital business models is presented in Table 4.7.

A model of controlling monetisation of digital business models designed in this way can be universal and widely used. The range of solutions used can also be a starting point for improving business intelligence processes which are relevant to the specificity of the digital economy.

Table 4.7 Model of controlling the monetisation of digital business models

Big Data Analytics and Marketing Analytics assumptions		
Statistics	Analyses	Predictive and econometric models
Behavioural analytics of digital platform users		
Identification of user behaviour	Analysis of user preferences	Analysis of financial constraints of users
Use of analytical and statistical variables		
Assessment of flexibility	Growth charts	Application of statistical database models
Analysis of Big Data sets		
Recency	Frequency	Monetary
Defining performance measures		
Number of clicks	Type of website displayed	Time spent by the user on the website/system
Application of advanced data analytics methods		
Neural networks	Deep Learning	Executive and analytical algorithms
Conclusions, recommendations and improvement plans		

Source: Own study.

Digital performance management concept and monetisation strategies in digital business models

The concept of performance management, which takes into account the conditions of the digital economy, is also the subject of application for companies using digital business models. Performance monitoring can include at least economic aspects, that is, the results of the implementation of the monetisation strategy, but also the size of the community gathered around the digital business model and its value proposition. For example, as regards computer games, the monetisation strategy is very important because it is a very risky business. Game development is associated with high costs and only 5% of the best games on the market are profitable. As regards social games, players can create their own virtual characters and communities, and interact with friends. Companies involved in gaming activities have developed paid content models such as subscription, advertising, and micro-transactions for virtual goods. Basically, users are not interested in paying for virtual goods, but the few who pay for them really make this business model work. Ultimately, micro-transactions, especially in the life cycle of social games, have become the driving force behind incremental revenues. Key assumptions made in the implementation of the monetisation strategy of computer game producers focused on achieving the results of the digital business model are as follows:

- An organisation is able to successfully achieve its financial goals.
- An organisation is able to successfully apply saving strategies.
- An organisation is able to attract more players with smaller investments.
- An organisation uses in-depth mechanics to maximise conversion rate and life value in games.
- An organisation can successfully build multi-platform offers to reach players/consumers (Aleem, Capretz, and Ahmed, 2016, p. 28).

Since the concept of performance management is focused on monitoring effects, it is necessary to identify such performance measures that are appropriate for the digital business model. The effectiveness of the digital business model will depend on the performance of the digital business model covering at least three key areas (see Figure 4.8).

A condition of achieving a company's digitalisation capability is the availability and application of appropriate base technology and an attractive configuration of the digital business model. Only in this approach is it possible to fully use data, contractual and relational abilities, and full digital business analytics.

The core areas of digital capability include data, permission, and analytics. As regards data, the following must be monitored: data generation, data transmission, data storage, and data access. As regards permission, issues related to legislation, related to contracts and related to society should be taken into account. The area of analytics includes analysis, visualisation, and reporting (Ritter and Pedersen, 2019, p. 3). Digital capability will therefore be determined by access

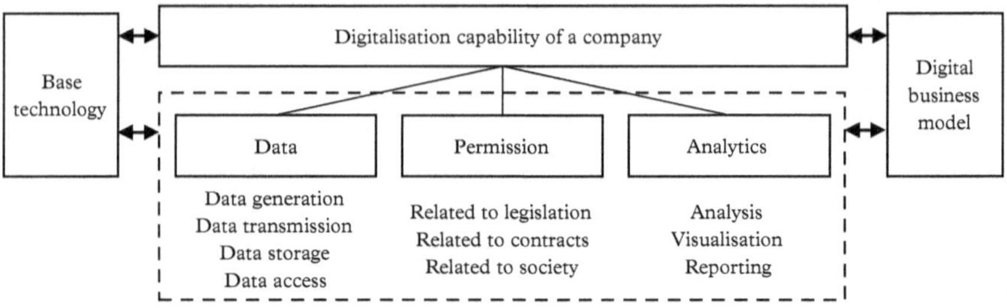

Figure 4.8 Dimensions of the digitalisation capability of a company in the context of digital business models.

Source: Own study based on Ritter and Pedersen, 2019, p. 3.

to their analytics data and legislation that will be different in different countries around the world. The combination of an effective and efficient monetisation formula with technological conditions will shape the company's ability to create economic value. Financial results for digital business models will depend on the quality and effectiveness of implementing a digital strategy dependent on the managerial capability and operational capability (Ukko et al., 2019, p. 4). In this context, it is reasonable to develop a structure for monitoring performance of the digital business model using the author's performance spiral (see Figure 4.9).

In the context of the designed concept of performance monitoring, a spiral of digital business model performance was designed. The monetisation strategy results directly from the adopted monetisation formula, and is implemented using defined core performance monitoring areas. Seven performance monitoring areas have been defined. The financial results of a company which uses the digital business model are the result of the implemented solutions which shape the configuration of the business model. First of all, performance indicators related to the value proposition area should be determined. Further areas include the area of data sets, the technology area, the area of organisation and management, the area of value visualisation, and the area of customer (user) relationships. The last area subject to monitoring is the area of business analytics. As part of the designed concept of the monitoring of digital business model performance, a spiral has been adopted, as the monetisation formula is implemented by means of a monetisation strategy, which is reflected in defined areas that are improved by an iterative method so that the financial effect and user volume are in the central space of the spiral. The improvement of individual areas should contribute to ensuring the consistency of the digital business model and the achievement of the expected financial results and the expected level of user volume. The more users of the digital business model there are, the greater the chance of achieving the expected financial results using the adopted monetisation formula. The areas are described in Table 4.8.

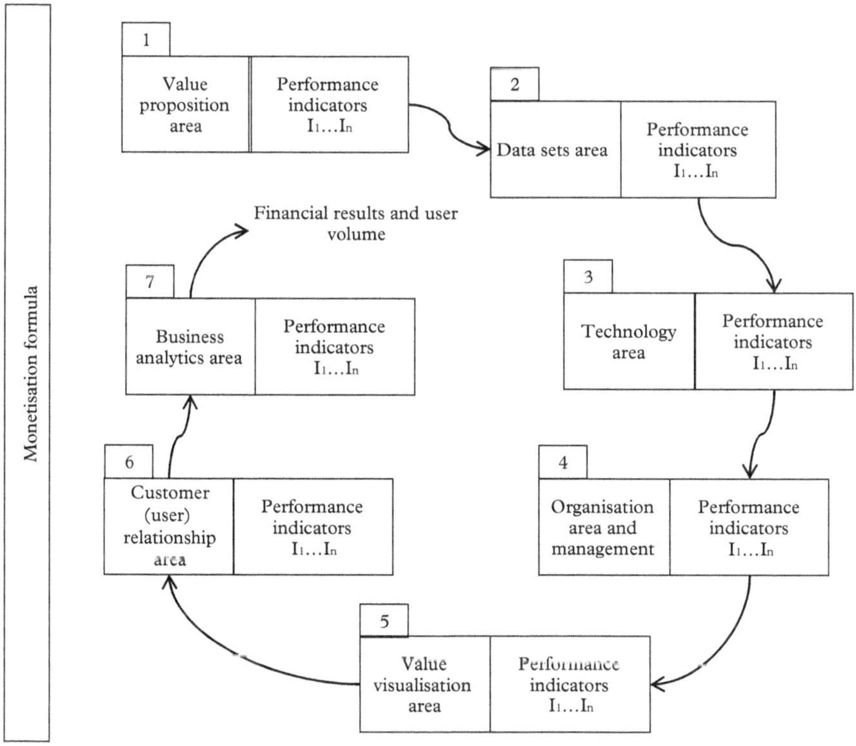

Figure 4.9 Spiral of digital business model performance.
Source: Own study.

The proposed concept of performance monitoring is based on the joint implementation of the assumptions of the monetisation formula, its implementation strategy, and areas constituting the configuration of the digital business model. It has an original character and strongly exposes the financial and quantitative aspects in relation to the volume of digital business model users. The spiral of digital business model performance is based on the process of iterative performance improvement through experience.

The mechanism of scaling the monetisation formula of digital business models

Scalability means the ability of a system (usually IT) to maintain its efficiency while increasing the load by increasing the number of components. The scalability of a business model is its ability to maintain similar or higher efficiency, while constantly increasing or reducing the number of its components and simultaneously adjusting its impact boundaries (e.g. in a network environment) (Jabłoński, 2016, p. 194). Scaling in a business model refers to the addition or

Table 4.8 Areas of monitoring the spiral of digital business model performance

No.	*Area of monitoring digital business model performance*	*Description*
1.	Value proposition area	It covers the scope of monitoring the quality of the created functionality delivered to the customer (user).
2.	Area of data sets	It covers the quality of all databases used in the digital business model.
3.	Technology area	It includes monitoring the efficiency, effectiveness, and efficacy of the underlying technology used.
4.	The area of organisation and management	It includes monitoring the efficiency of managing the digital business model by means of a set of appropriate management methods and techniques.
5.	Value visualisation area	It includes monitoring the perception of delivered value through accepted functional and aesthetic solutions embedded in digital applications.
6.	Customer (user) relationship area	It includes monitoring customer (user) communication processes, including a complaint system.
7.	Business analytics area	It includes monitoring the effectiveness and efficiency of adopted analytical models including statistical methods, Big Data analysis, and other related to customer behaviour, customer segmentation and other endogenous and exogenous issues.

Source: Own study.

subtraction of a component and/or components of a business model to improve its effectiveness. Scalability is a core parameter determining the company's ability to grow; it is based, among others, on the statement that not every unit of revenue is generated by an equal unit of cost. When assessing the ability of business models to increase company value, investors appreciate above all such models that allow companies to achieve increasingly higher profitability by obtaining ever higher revenues. However, a common feature of e-business models in particular is that they have high market value with little or even no long-term profits. The market value is high because of the attributes that these business models have, such as an innovative solution in the field of social networks, a unique technical solution that creates interesting added value and so on. Therefore, their scalability is important. The business model scaling mechanism results from the essence of digital business models and poses a significant challenge for them. In this approach, monetisation refers to the processes of creating financial wealth from human and systemic solutions (Skilton, 2015, p. 177).

In the relevant literature, Amit and Zott (2001, pp. 493–520), Rappa (2004, pp. 32–42), and Bouwman and MacInnes (2006) defined scalability as a core factor in innovative business models contributing to the results achieved by a company. Scalability, therefore, is an important feature of the business model, as it is embedded in its configuration, while the strategy puts the business model in motion and sets its resources in the right direction, as expected by business model decision-makers, and scalable business processes are used to achieve operational goals and will be more effective when the business model is also characterised by high scalability. According to Green, a scalable business model is a simple concept. In a scalable model, increased revenue costs less than current revenue. In other words, the operating margin increases as the company's revenues increase (Green, 2014). In the logical interpretation of the application of the scalability of business models, the mechanisms of analogy can be used, referring to Moore's law and Wright's law, which are widely used, not only in computer science. Moore's law is an empirical law that results from the observation that the economically optimal number of transistors in an integrated circuit increases in subsequent years according to the exponential trend (doubles in almost equal periods of time). The author of this law is Gordon Moore, one of the founders of Intel, which in 1965 observed a doubling of the number of transistors every 18 months. This number was then adjusted, and today it is assumed that the number of transistors in microprocessors has doubled about every 24 months for many years. By analogy, Moore's law also applies to many other computer hardware parameters, such as hard disk capacity and memory size. Moore's law, which originally referred to the number of transistors in one integrated circuit, is now used properly to determine virtually any technological progress (Moore, 1965). In this sense, core assumptions for the scalability of business models using the principles of Moore's law and Wright's law can be developed.

1. We treat a company embedded in the network as an organisation capable of achieving high performance through it.
2. We define the basic resources, processes, and stakeholders of the company embedded in the network as required to construct a scalable business model.
3. We set technological and organisational boundaries of the business model of the company embedded in the network.
4. We convert the business model of the company embedded in the network to a discrete model.
5. Using Moore's law and Wright's law, we analyse how it is best possible to expand the business model in terms of components and apply the principle of how much we can reduce the costs of its operation.
6. We simulate the development of the business model, assuming the boundary conditions for the developed measurement system, which is a tool for assessing the business model of the company embedded in the network.
7. We then change the parameters of the business model and the structure of its components for as long as we adapt the assumed discrete model to the actual situation in business.
8. We validate the designed scalable business model, implementing it.

By further analysing the concept of the scalability of the business model, it can be assumed that the business model subject to scalability consists of two groups of components:

1. Primary components,
2. Secondary components.

Primary components form the core of the business model, which is the basis of its construction at the design stage.

Secondary components are added to the business model to improve company performance. They are the development of primary components. Their addition or subtraction are important in order to ensure the scalability of the business model. The growing complexity of the business model in terms of a scalability criterion consists of the incremental change in the number of business model components in time.

To sum up, contemporary strategic management mechanisms focus on the relationship between the monetisation rate of the business model and its scalability. The monetisation of the business model related to the methods of providing cash through this business model is and should be closely correlated with the economic effect which generates a financial surplus based on an appropriate correlation of revenues and costs. The scalability of the business model is the result of the right proportion between many of its attributes, mainly in economic and financial terms. One should be aware that the monetisation ability and the rate thereof depends on the construction of the business model that ensures the logic of monetisation, which results in the inflow of cash into the company's account.

Monitoring of risk in digital business models

Digital business models generate very high business risk, which results directly from the specificity of this type of project. When attempting to define risk areas, several core areas can be assumed, which include: innovative value proposition, the choice of technologies underlying the functioning of the digital business model, and the monetisation formula used. These three areas generate the greatest risk of failure. As regards value proposition, there may be distortions resulting from a failed idea or its incorrect operationalisation. Customers (users) may not accept the proposed value because of the unattractive or poorly designed value visualisation–application aesthetics. A significant risk of failure of the digital business model project relates to the choice of technologies. Errors, defects, and failures in the application may result from badly chosen technology which is unsuitable for the expected functionalities of the digital business model. Another core area which generates the risk of project failure as well as the exploitation of the digital business model is making mistakes in the designed monetisation formula. Both the mismatch of existing monetisation formulas and the adoption of erroneous market assumptions can be a significant problem in the implementation and operation of the digital business model.

Critical analysis of the monetisation processes of digital business models

The issue of the monetisation of digital business models plays a fundamental role in the overall perception of the economisation of the digital economy. The following conclusions, recommendations, and suggestions, which are related to numerous issues and problems that occur in the process of designing effective monetisation formulas implemented by means of the monetisation strategy, can be presented:

1. An effective monetisation formula is a condition for the success of the digital business model.
2. The digital business model is configured, among others, through the use of components such as: a value proposition area, a data set area, a technology area, an area of organisation and management, a value visualisation area, a customer (user) relationship area, and a business analytics area.
3. The main achievements responsible for the success of the digital business model include the profitability of the digital business model through the use of an optimal effective monetisation formula and the achievement of the expected volume of digital business model users. The number of users is a condition for the success of the business model and its monetisation.
4. In terms of recognising the digital business model as a complex system, a strong relationship occurs between the choice of the monetisation formula, the implementation of the monetisation strategy, and the choice of the configuration of digital business model components.
5. The process of designing the monetisation formula for the economisation of the digital business model should have the character of a technical design using a system of tests, measurements, and validation of the proposed solutions.
6. The process of monetisation controlling plays a crucial role in the use of the digital business model, which is an important element supporting the design and monitoring of the effectiveness of the monetisation formulas of digital business models.

The configuration of monetisation activities for digital business models refers not only to choosing a monetisation formula. It requires a holistic and eclectic approach to building the digital business model which is consistent in all aspects, using the optimal monetisation strategy while ensuring that the requirements of customers (users) interested in the delivery of the expected value proposition for reasonable business financing principles are fulfilled.

Monetisation, understood as a scheme of the flow of content, money, interactions, and connections between actors involved in a business relationship within a specific technology platform, stimulates relationships between actors participating in a network of connections determined by the logic of the adopted business model.

The modern monetisation formulas of digital business models fit into the relational nature of the functioning of the modern global economy, departing from the transactional model. Monetisation as a scheme for generating economic results is different from the standard model of generating revenues from operating activities, because its assumptions are based on a systemic approach consisting of building a scheme of generating cash flows into the logic of the digital business model and using its attributes in the context of direct or indirect use of this business model functionality. Cash flow does not have to be linked to a value chain.

As regards indirect monetisation, a phenomenon of lack of symmetry between the value delivered through the business model and the flow of money occurs. It does not affect the effectiveness of the adopted solution.

As regards the improvement of the effectiveness of digital business models, a condition for their survival is the need to satisfy three fundamental conditions:

- Actors gathered around the business model must recognise the benefits of the value proposition delivered within the business model.
- Actors must accept the proposed monetisation method.
- The cash flow does not have to be sufficient in terms of value to the value delivery scheme.

The following methods of monetisation can be distinguished:

- Monetisation through the use of business model logic attributes;
- Monetisation through financing sources;
- Monetisation through services;
- Monetisation through the benefits of having applications and access to Big Data sets.

Particular attention should be paid to the fact that monetisation formulas are supported by extensive structures of relationships between actors participating in the system of the dynamic exchange of values in a network of connections. Here, monetisation results from the cooperation of entities constituting the configuration of relationships between them within the business model.

Conclusions

The comprehensive presentation in this chapter of various approaches to the concept of monetisation indicates the complexity and difficulties in designing effective solutions in this area. Matching the logic and attributes of digital business models to the adopted monetisation formula is a condition for the success or failure of a business venture in many cases. The monetisation of digital business models is a leading aspect in assessing the effectiveness of designed business solutions. Digital platforms and built-in algorithms for their operation enable companies to obtain the expected economic effects. The condition is to ensure that the solution is attractive to users and available for the maximum possible number of users. The volume of users which determines the scale of impact of a given digital business model is strongly correlated with the ability to obtain above-average economic results. The ability to acquire new recipients of the proposed value depends on the method of delivery and economic conditions on the basis of which it can be transferred to the customer. The success of the digital business model depends on the quality of the monetisation formula and the consistency of its integration with the configuration of the digital business model.

References

Aleem, S., Capretz, L.F., and Ahmed, F. (2016). "Empirical Investigation of Key Business Factors for Digital Game Performance", *Entertainment Computing*, 13, 25–36. DOI: 10.1016/j.entcom.2015.09.001.

Amit, R. and Zott, C. (2001). "Value Creation in E-Business", *Strategic Management Journal*, 22(6–7), 493–520. DOI: 10.1002/smj.187.

Baden-Fuller, C. and Mangematin, V. (2013). "Business Models: A Challenging Agenda", *Strategic Organization*, 11(4), 418–427. DOI: 10.1177/1476127013510112.

Bataineh, A.S., Mizouni, R., Barachi, M.E., and Bentahar, J. (2016). "Monetizing Personal Data: A Two-Sided Market Approach", *Procedia Computer Science*, 83, 472–479. DOI: 10.1016/j.procs.2016.04.211.

Benitez, J., Chen, Y., Teo, T.S.H., and Ajamieh, A. (2018). "Evolution of the Impact of e-Business Technology on Operational Competence and firm Profitability: A Panel Data Investigation", *Information and Management*, 55(1), 120–130. DOI: 10.1016/j.im.2017.08.002.

Blaschke, M., Cigaina, M., Riss, U.V., and Shoshan, I. (2017). "Designing Business Models for the Digital Economy", in G. Oswald and M. Kleinemeier (eds.), *Shaping the Digital Enterprise*, Switzerland: Springer International Publishing, pp. 121–136. DOI: 10.1007/978-3-319-40967-2_6.

Bouwman, H. and MacInnes, I. (2006). *Dynamic Business Model Framework for Value Webs*, 39th Annual Hawaii International Conference on System Sciences (HICSS2006), Hawaii. DOI: 10.1109/HICSS.2006.131

Chaffey, D. (2019). *8 Online Revenue Model Options for Internet Businesses*. Available at: www.smartinsights.com/digital-marketing-strategy/online-business-revenue-models/online-revenue-model-options-internet-business/

Chen, K.J. and Cheung, H.L. (2019). "Unlocking the Power of Ephemeral Content: The Roles of Motivations, Gratification, Need for Closure, and Engagement", *Computers in Human Behavior*, 97, 67–74. DOI: 10.1016/j.chb.2019.03.007.

Clemons, E.K. (2009). "The Complex Problem of Monetizing Virtual Electronic Social Networks", *Decision Support Systems*, 48(1), 46–56. DOI: 10.1016/j.dss.2009.05.003.

Conversion blog (2010). *Artykuł Pokaż mi pieniądze cz. 2, czyli jak stworzyć model monetyzacji*. Available at: www.conversion.pl/blog/pokaz-mi-pieniadze-cz-2-czyli-jak-stworzyc-model-monetyzacji/ (accessed 20 October 2019).

Dogtiev, A. (2019). *App Monetisation Models*, Website Business of Apps. Available at: www.businessofapps.com/marketplace/app-monetisation /research/app-monetisation - models/#2 (accessed 5 January 2020).

Forrester, J.W. (2009). "Some Basic Concepts in System Dynamics", *Sloan School of Management Massachusetts Institute of Technology*, Cambridge.

Green, R. (2014). *Scalable Business Model*. Available at: www.briefing.com/investor/learning-center/general-concepts/scalable-business-models/ (accessed 20 October 2019).

Grigsby, M. (2018). *Marketing Analytics: A Practical Guide to Improving Consumer Insights Using Data Techniques*, London: Kogan Page.

Hausner, J. (2019). *Społeczna czasoprzestrzeń gospodarowania, w kierunku ekonomii wartości*, Warszawa: Wydawnictwo Nieoczywiste.

Hoffmann, R. and Protasowicki, T. (2013). "Metoda dynamiki systemowej w modelowaniu złożonych systemów i procesów", *Biuletyn Instytutu Systemów Informatycznych*, 12, 19–28.

Jabłoński, A. (2016). "Scalability of Sustainable Business Models in Hybrid Organizations", *Sustainability*, 8(3), 194. DOI: 10.3390/su8030194.

Jabłoński, A. and Jabłoński, M. (2019). *Modele biznesu przedsiębiorstw, Perspektywy rozwoju – ujęcie koncepcyjne*, Warszawa: CeDeWu.

Jabłoński, A. and Jabłoński, M. (2020). "Social Business Models in the Digital Economy, New Concepts and Contemporary Challenges", *Palgrave Macmillan, Springer Nature*. DOI: 10.1007/978-3-030-29732-9.

Jabłoński, M. (2017). "Labilność modeli biznesu a zarządzanie interfejsami w koncepcji ekonomii współdzielenia", *Przegląd Organizacji*, 9, 13–21.

Kelly, J.E. III (2016). "Computing, Cognition and the Future of Knowing: How Humans and Machines Are Forging a New Age of Understanding", *IBM Research: Cognitive Computing. IBM Corporation*, New York.

Kozioł-Nadolna, K. (2015). "Crowdfunding jako źródło finansowania innowacyjnych projektów", *Zeszyty Naukowe Uniwersytetu Szczecińskiego, Finanse, Rynki Finansowe, Ubezpieczenia*, 854(73), 671–683.

Kreft, J. (2019). *Władza algorytmów, u źródeł potęgi Google i Facebooka*, Kraków: Wydawnictwo Uniwersytetu Jagiellońskiego.

Kumar, V., Ananda, A., and Songaa, H. (2017). "Future of Retailer Profitability: An Organizing Framework", *Journal of Retailing*, 93(1), 96–119. DOI: 10.1016/j.jretai.2016.11.003.

Kumar, V., Lahiri, A., and Bahadir Dogan, O. (2018). A Strategic Framework for a Profitable Business Model in the Sharing Economy", *Industrial Marketing Management*, 69, 147–160. DOI: 10.1016/j.indmarman.2017.08.021.

Liozu, S.M. and Ulaga, W. (2018). *Monetizing Data: A Practical Roadmap for Framing, Pricing and Seeling your B2B Digital Offers*, Arizona: Value Innoruption Advisors Publishing.

Moore, G.E. (1965). "Cramming More Components onto Integrated Circuits", *Electronics Magazine*, 38(8), 114–117.

Müller, S.C. and Welpe, I.M. (2018). "Sharing Electricity Storage at the Community Level: An Empirical Analysis of Potential Business Models and Barriers", *Energy Policy*, 118(C), 492–503. DOI: 10.1016/j.enpol.2018.03.064.

Muzellec, L., Ronteau, S., and Lambkin, M. (2015). "Two-sided Internet Platforms: A Business Model Lifecycle Perspective", *Industrial Marketing Management*, 45, 139–150. DOI: 10.1016/j.indmarman.2015.02.012.

Ng, I.C.L. (2014). *Creating New Markets in the Digital Economy, Value and Worth*, Cambridge: Cambridge University Press.

Owyang, J. (2007). *Explaining What the Social Graph Is to Your Executive (Web Strategy)*. Available at: www.web-strategist.com./blog/2007/11/10/ (accessed 15 December 2019).

Padmanabhan, V. and Sriharsha, B.V. (2012). "Content Monetisation Strategies for the Digital Publisher: A Step by Step Approach for Successful Digital Transformation", India: Wipro Technologies.

Parente, R.C., Geleilate, J.M.G., and Rong, K. (2018). "The Sharing Economy Globalization Phenomenon: A Research Agenda", *Journal of International Management*, 24(1), 52–64. DOI: 10.1016/j.intman.2017.10.001.

Portal BiznesTuba (2016). *Article 4 kroki do monetyzacji danych w firmie*, http://biznestuba.pl/biznes-na-zywo/4-kroki-do-monetyzacji-danych-w-firmie/ (accessed 15 December 2019).

Portal Email Partners (2017). *Artykul Monetyzacja – czym jest i jak na niej zarabiać?* (accessed: 20 October 2019).

Raport podsumowujący badanie (2016). *Wideo w sieci – Modele dystrybucji i monetyzacji plików wideo w języku polskim w sieci Internet*, National Broadcasting Council.

Raport PwC (2016). (Współ)dziel i rządź! Prawno-podatkowe aspekty ekonomii współdzielenia w Polsce.

Rappa, M.A. (2004). "The Utility Business Model and the Future of Computing Services", *IBM Systems Journal*, 43(1), 32–42. DOI: 10.1147/sj.431.0032.

Ritter, T. and Pedersen, C.L. (2019). "Digitization Capability and the Digitalization of Business Models in Business-to-business Firms: Past, Present, and Future", *Industrial Marketing Management*. DOI: 10.1016/j.indmarman.2019.11.019.

Schaffer, N., Pfaff, M., and Krcmar, H. (2019). "Dynamic Business Models: A Comprehensive Classification of Literature", *MCIS Proceedings*, 13, https://aisel.aisnet.org/mcis2019/13 (accessed 20 December 2019).

Scott, J. (2012). *What is Social Network Analysis?* New York: Bloomsbury Academic.

Skilton, M. (2015). *Building the Digital Enterprise: A Guide to Constructing Monetisation Models Using Digital Technologies*, New York: Palgrave Macmillan.

Smith, A. (2015). *The Wealth of Nations: A Translation into Modern English*, Manchester: Industrial Systems Research.

Teece, D.J. (2018). "Business Models and Dynamic Capabilities", *Long Range Planning*, 51(1), 40–49. DOI: 10.1016/j.lrp.2017.06.007.

Timmers, P. (1998). "Business Models for Electronic Markets", *Electronic Markets*, 8(2), 3–8. DOI: 10.1080/10196789800000016.

Ukko, J., Nasiri, M., Saunila, M., and Rantala, T. (2019). "Sustainability Strategy as a Moderator in the Relationship between Digital Business Strategy and Financial Performance", *Journal of Cleaner Production*, 236. DOI: 10.1016/j.jclepro.2019.117626.

Wakefield, L.T. and Bennett, G. (2018). "Sports Fan Experience: Electronic Word-of-mouth in Ephemeral Social Media", *Sport Management Review*, 21, 147–159. DOI: 10.1016/j.smr.2017.06.003

Wąsowski, M. (2017). *Jak zarabiać na dzieleniu się? CEO BlaBlaCar: Model biznesowy nie jest naszą obsesją [wywiad]*, Portal Business Insider Polska, artykuł z 18.04.2017 (accessed December 2019).

Website spilgames, *11 monetisation strategies for game developers*, https://spilgames.com/11-monetisation-strategies-for-game-developers/ (accessed 5 January 2020).

Żukowski, P. (2012). "Podstawy budowy modelu dynamiki systemu zarządzania oraz jego symulacja w organizacji gospodarczej (na podstawie metodologii dynamiki systemów J.W. Forrestera)", *Przedsiębiorczość – Edukacja, Rola przedsiębiorczości w edukacji*, 8, 331–347. DOI: 10.24917/131.

5 Analysis of the digital business models of the new economy

Introduction

The functioning of digital business models in practice goes to prove that the digital economy creates great business opportunities for modern entrepreneurs. The possibilities offered by new technologies are vast. These contemporary conditions create prospects for building global companies which use digital business models. There are many examples of great successes by companies operating on global markets. The concepts of the Sharing Economy, Big Data, and the Circular Economy, broadly discussed in the monograph, create opportunities to design such global companies. The joint implementation of the assumptions of the concept of the new economy and unique digital business models affects the development and growth of innovative companies characterised by above-average market capitalisation and user volume. The number of customers clearly influences the level of the monetisation of these companies. From the point of view of theory and practice, these issues are of fundamental importance to understanding the contemporary conditions and principles of doing business.

The aim of the chapter is to present case studies on the effective solutions of business models that use the monetisation of business models.

There are many good practices in the field of business models in the world; however, they do not always meet all the criteria for classification in the Digital Economy. In various geographical areas of the world, the understanding of digital aspects is different. Therefore, the features of business models will also be different. The aim of the chapter is to indicate good practices in the field of designing business models and their assessment from the point of view of a broad spectrum of selected criteria.

The operationalisation of digital business models

A canvas for describing digital business models was designed to operationalise and present digital business models in terms of the criterion of monetisation. The canvas includes quantitative and qualitative aspects. Such a dual description of digital business models allowed for the identification of factors related to the scalability of business models as well as determinants which characterise their configuration. Quantitative attributes include the volume of recipients

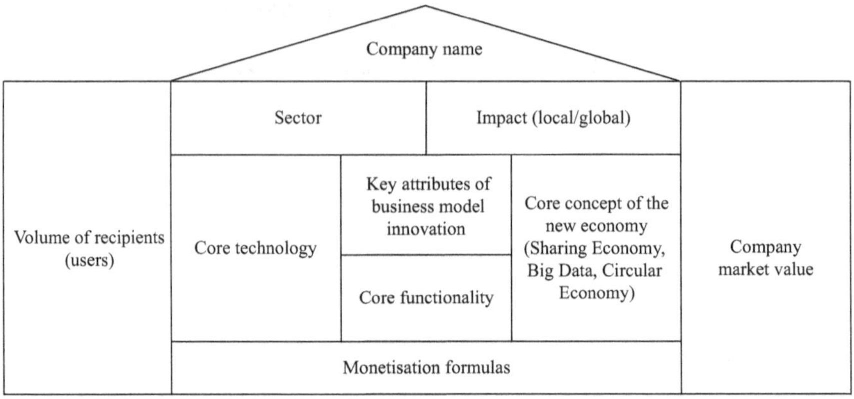

Figure 5.1 Canvas for the description of digital business models.
Source: Own study.

(users), the market value of the company, and the scope of market impact (local/global). The qualitative parameters of the description of digital business models include the sector where a company operates, the core technology of the digital business model, the key attributes of business model innovation, the core functionality, the core concept of the new economy within which the digital business model operates, and, in particular, the monetisation formulas used. To illustrate the specificity of digital business models, such models which represent three key concepts of the new economy, namely the Sharing Economy, Big Data, and the Circular Economy, were described by means of the above-mentioned approach. Twelve examples of digital business models in the Sharing Economy have been identified and described, namely Uber, Lime, JustPark, Zipcar, Fon, Spotahome, Stashbee, Fiverr, Snap, Couchsurfing, BlaBlaCar, and Silvernest. Five Big Data companies, namely Amazon, Google, IBM, Teradata, and Oracle, and ten companies in the Circular Economy, namely Winnow, DyeCoo, Close the Loop, Enerkem, Schneider Electric, Cambrian Innovation, Lehigh Technologies, HYLA Mobile, TriCiclos, and MINIWIZ have been described as well. Figure 5.1 illustrates the adopted formula of the canvas which describes digital business models.

Examples of the monetisation of Sharing Economy companies

Uber technologies, Inc.

Uber technologies, Inc. is an American company based in San Francisco (California), the creator of the Uber mobile application used to order car transport services by associating passengers with drivers using the application. Uber services are available in 528 cities around the world.

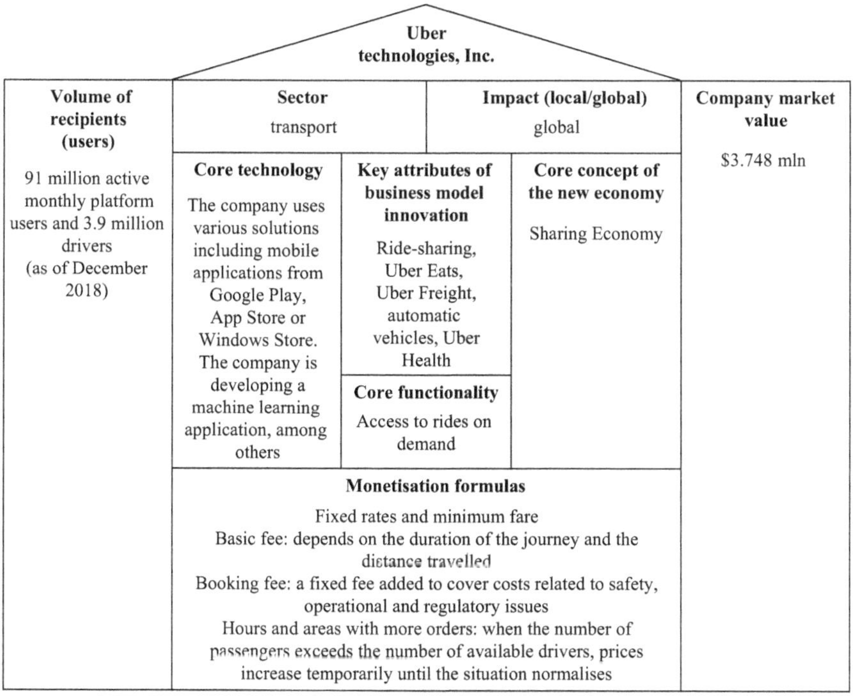

Figure 5.2 Model of the description of Uber business model components in terms of monetisation.

Source: Own study based on www.uber.com/pl/ (accessed: 3 January 2020).

Lime

Lime cooperates with neighbourhood organisations to cultivate community development and improve living conditions in the city. They possess scooters, bicycles and transit vehicles and strive to reduce dependence on passenger cars in short-distance transport and leave a cleaner, healthier planet to future generations. The system offers vehicles that users can find and unlock using a mobile application that knows the location of available vehicles via GPS (www.li.me/pl/ [accessed 9 January 2020]).

JustPark

JustPark is the UK's favourite parking service. You can rent someone your parking space and earn easy, tax-free money. Over 300 hotels use JustPark for smarter and more efficient parking management.

The application uses data from many sources (payments, camera transmissions, sensors, online search traffic), and historical occupancy rate to forecast the expected occupancy on a given day (www.justpark.com/car-park-management/ [accessed 9 January 2020]).

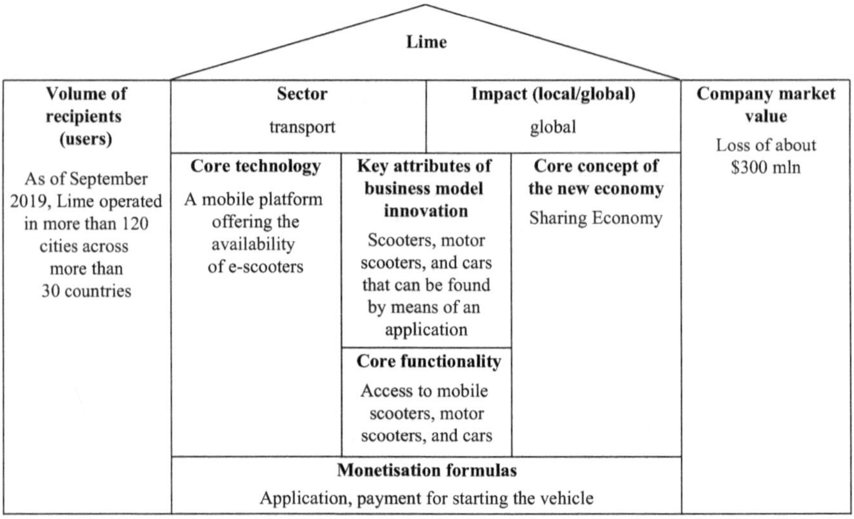

Figure 5.3 Model of the description of Lime business model components in terms of monetisation.

Source: Own study based on Mhatre, 2019 (accessed: 9 January 2020).

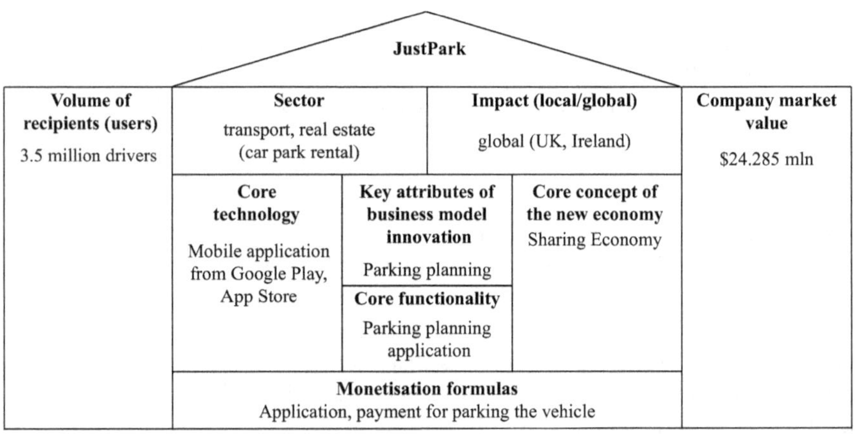

Figure 5.4 Model of the description of JustPark business model components in terms of monetisation.

Source: Own study.

Zipcar

Zipcar is an American car-sharing company founded in 2000, a subsidiary of the Avis Budget Group. Zipcar provides its members with car reservations, billed by the minute, hour, or day; members can pay a monthly or annual membership fee

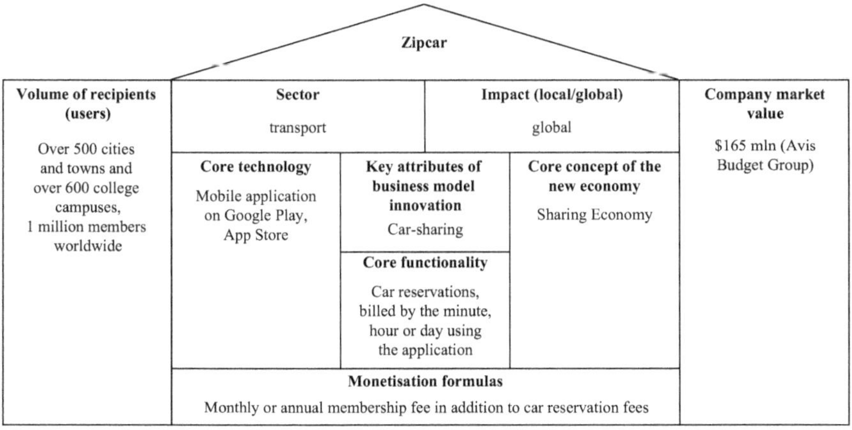

Figure 5.5 Model of the description of Zipcar business model components in terms of monetisation.

Source: Own study.

in addition to car reservation fees. Members can book vehicles using the Zipcar mobile app, online, or in certain places by phone at any time, immediately or one year in advance. Zipcar members have automated access to cars via an access card that unlocks the door; the keys are already inside (Mack, 2009).

Fon

Fon was founded in 2006 in Spain with the mission of covering the world with Wi-Fi. Driven by the Wi-Fi social approach and through strategic partnerships with leading telecommunications companies and Wi-Fi providers, including British Telecom, Deutsche Telekom Group, SFR, SoftBank, Telstra, KPN, Proximus, Vodafone, Virgin Media, and The Cloud, they created a globally connected Wi-Fi network.

Currently, it covers over 23 million hotspots around the world and grows every day. This increase has been achieved, including both residential and major public Wi-Fi traces, as well as facilitating connections between Wi-Fi services. The Fon Wi-Fi app is used to seamlessly connect to millions of Wi-Fi hotspots around the world (https://network.fon.com/ [accessed 10 January 2020]).

Spotahome

Spotahome is a platform on which you can rent real estate in the medium or long term in 29 cities in Europe and Asia. Spotahome draws inspiration from a similar business model that works very well in the tourism industry, but focuses on finding a home for 30 days or more. It is a 100% Internet-based platform offering flats, rooms, studios, and student flats for rent. Spotahome offers real

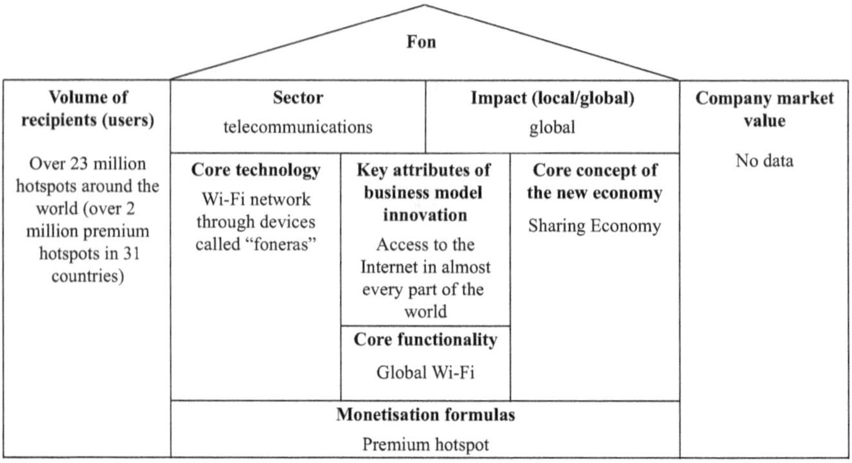

Figure 5.6 Model of the description of Fon business model components in terms of monetisation.

Source: Own study.

estate in the following countries and cities: Spain (Madrid, Barcelona, Bilbao, Valencia, Granada, Seville), Belgium (Brussels), United Kingdom (London), Italy (Rome, Milan, Florence, Bologna, Turin), France (Paris, Lyon), Ireland (Dublin), United Arab Emirates (Dubai), Germany (Berlin), Austria (Vienna), Poland (Warsaw, Kraków, Gdańsk, Łódź, Wrocław), and Turkey (Istanbul). It has over 200 employees and over 45,000 properties registered for rent. The site is available in six languages: English, Spanish, Italian, French, German, Turkish, and Polish.

Stashbee

The company's operations are based on building a platform that connects people who have unused space with people who need it for storage and parking to make it easier for their hosts to put their empty space to good use (and helping them earn a bit of extra cash too!) (https://stashbee.com/ [accessed 10 January 2020]). It has 18,500 registered users and hosts.

Fiverr

Fiverr is a global marketplace connecting freelancers and businesses for their digital service needs. Their mission is to change how the world works together. Fiverr was founded in 2010.

Snap

Snap Inc. is a camera company. They contribute to human progress by empowering people to express themselves, live in the moment, learn about

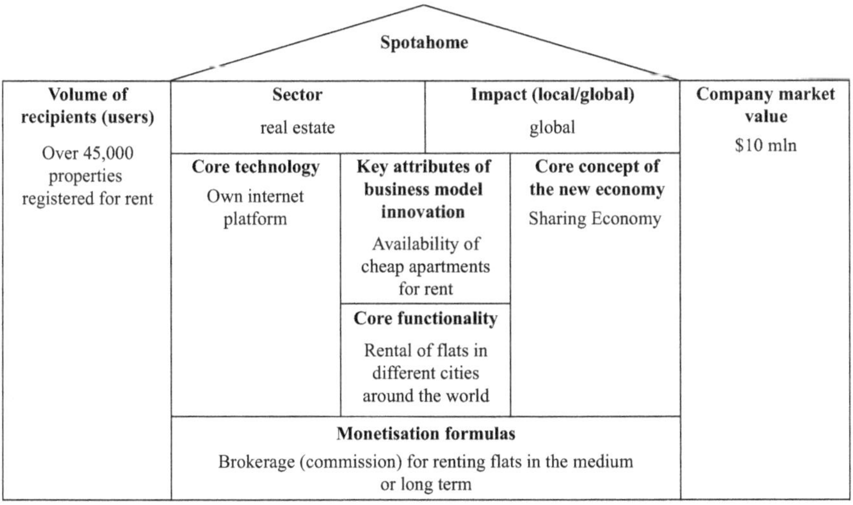

Figure 5.7 Model of the description of Spotahome business model components in terms of monetisation.

Source: Own study.

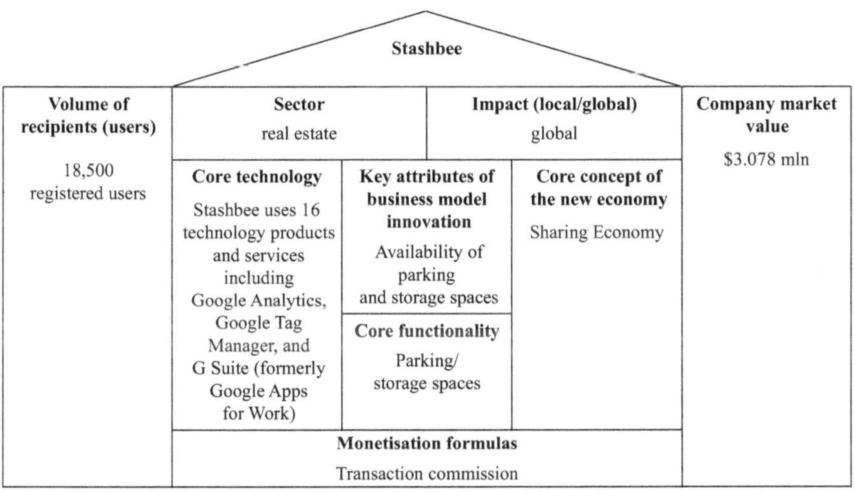

Figure 5.8 Model of the description of Stashbee business model components in terms of monetisation.

Source: Own study based on Loritz, 2019 (accessed: 10 January 2020).

the world, and have fun together (https://investor.snap.com/company-profile [accessed: 15 January 2020]).

Their flagship product, Snapchat, is a camera application that helps people communicate visually with friends and family through short videos and images

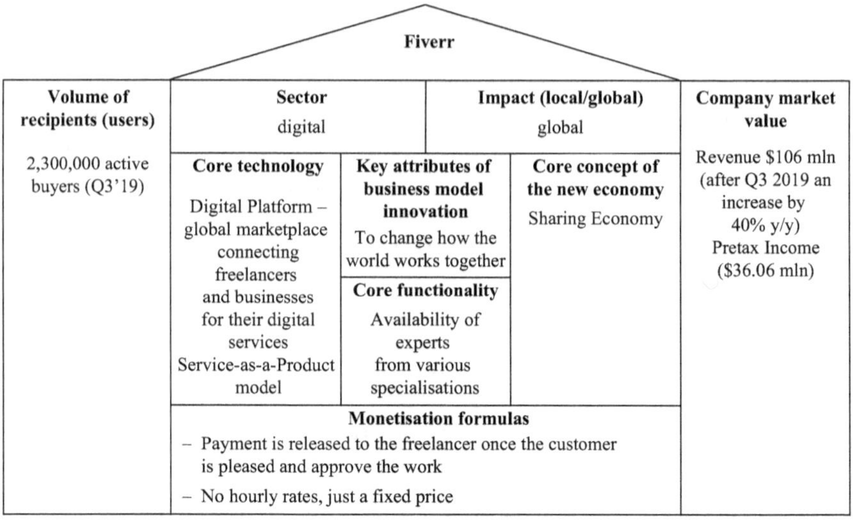

Figure 5.9 Model of the description of Fiverr business model components in terms of monetisation.

Source: Own study based on www.marketwatch.com/investing/stock/fvrr/financials (accessed 10 January 2020).

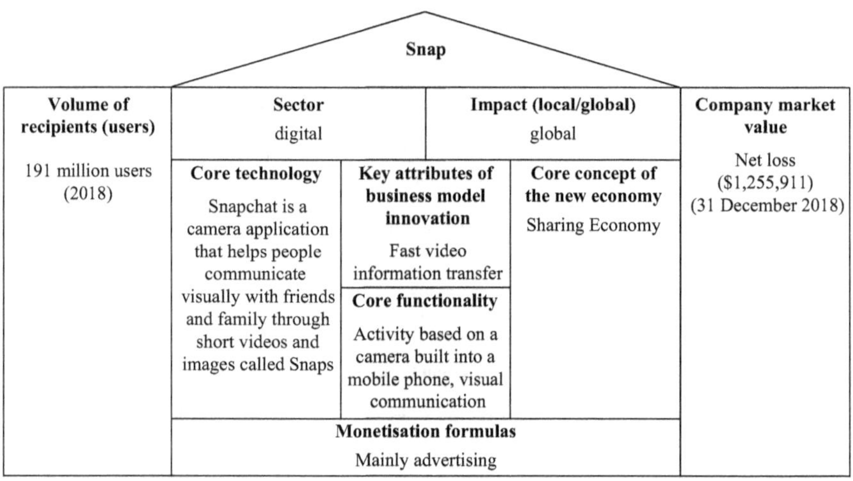

Figure 5.10 Model of the description of Snap business model components in terms of monetisation.

Source: Own study based on Hayes, 2018 (accessed: 15 January 2020).

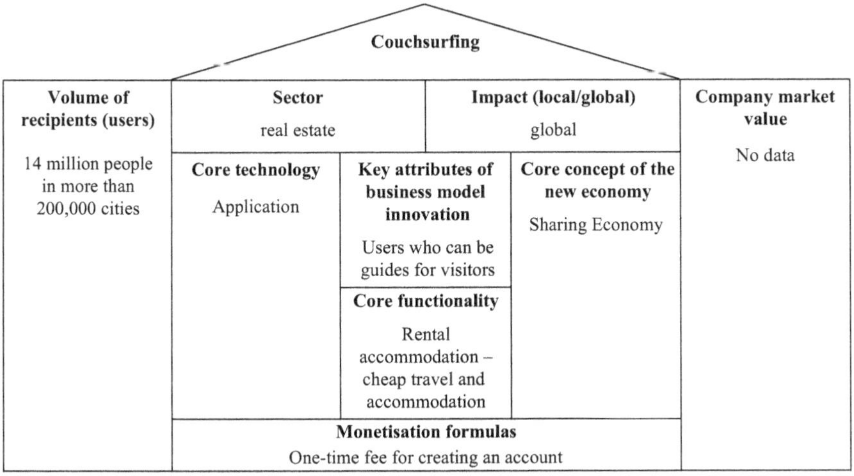

Figure 5.11 Model of the description of Couchsurfing business model components in terms of monetisation.

Source: Own study.

called Snaps. By opening directly to the camera, they empower users to express themselves instantly. Snaps are deleted by default, so there is a lot less pressure to look pretty or perfect when creating and sending images on Snapchat. By reducing the friction typically associated with creating and sharing content, Snapchat has become one of the most-used cameras in the world.

Couchsurfing

Couchsurfing is a global community of 14 million people in more than 200,000 cities who share their life, their world, their journey (www.couchsurfing.com/ [accessed 15 January 2020]).

By creating a profile on Couchsurfing.org, users can use the beds offered by other users, popularly called hosts, or make space in their own flat available to guests of their choice, or both, in accordance with the idea of couchsurfing.

BlaBlaCar

BlaBlaCar is a trust-based social network that connects drivers who have free spaces in their cars with passengers travelling in the same direction. Many people use BlaBlaCar every month, thus creating a whole new way of travelling. BlaBlaCar has 70 million users in 22 countries: Benelux, Brazil, Croatia, the Czech Republic, France, Spain, India, Mexico, Germany, Poland, Portugal, Russia, Romania, Serbia, Slovakia, Turkey, Ukraine, Hungary, Italy, and the UK. The service is used by approximately 25 million travellers per quarter, and the average travel distance is 310 km.

Silvernest

Silvernest lets you choose how you want to homeshare, including the option to reduce your rent in exchange for help around the house. Silvernest help to draw up a homesharing agreement, make rent payments, and even speak with a certified relationship counsellor or licensed attorney. The service is dedicated to the elderly (www.silvernest.com/ [accessed: 15 January 2020]).

Examples of the monetisation of Big Data companies

Amazon

Google LLC - an American company from the IT industry. Its flagship program is Google search engine. Their mission is to organize global information resources so that they become available and useful to everyone (*Alphabet Announces Fourth Quarter and Fiscal Year 2018 Results*, 2019). Amazon had attracted over 130 million customers to its US website per month by the start of 2016. Amazon had over 162 million unique mobile browser visitors in December 2018 to the app's 122 million. Its mobile web base is still growing faster, adding more than 14 million users in the five months ending January 2019 while the app brought in a little more than 9 million (Keyes, 2019 [accessed 15 January 2020]).

Google

Amazon.com is an American trading company, a joint-stock company founded in 1994 in Seattle. It deals with B2C e-commerce and runs the world's largest online store.

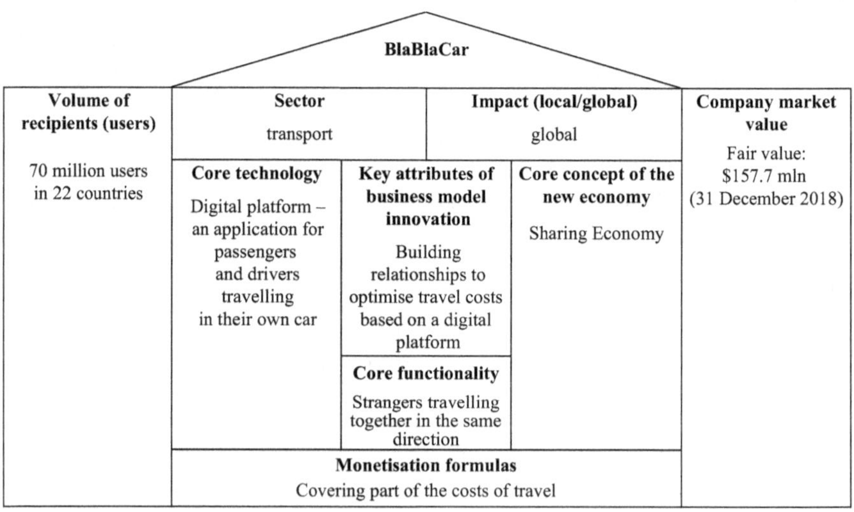

Figure 5.12 Model of the description of BlaBlaCar business model components in terms of monetisation.

Source: Own study based on *Annual Report 2018 BlaBlaCar.*

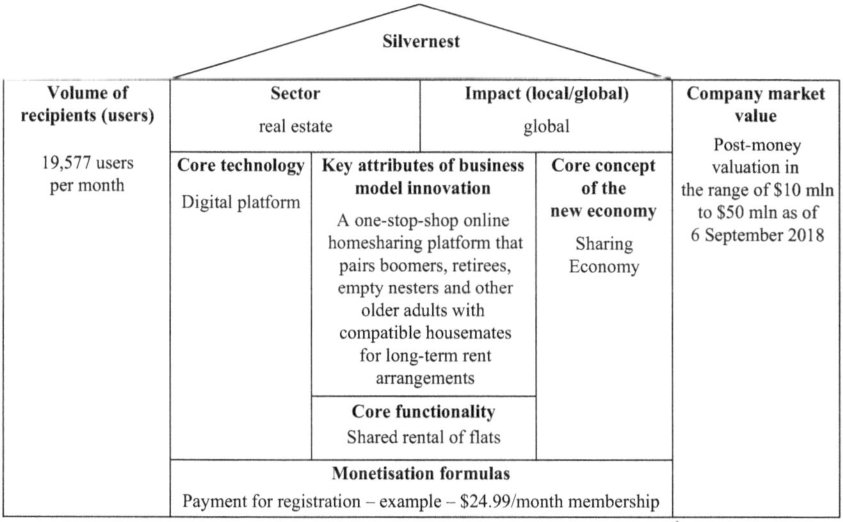

Figure 5.13 Model of the description of Silvernest business model components in terms of monetisation.

Source: Own study based on www.crunchbase.com/organization/silvernest (accessed: 15 January 2020).

According to Internet Live Stats as of October 2019, the search engine handles around 77,500 queries per second. This translates to about 2.4 trillion searches a year. Across all its properties – including Google Search, YouTube, Gmail, and Hangouts – Google Sites topped the ranking of the most popular multi-platform web properties in the US in July 2019 with more than 250.5 million unique visitors.

With close to seven billion searches handled on average by Google in a day, the number of people using Google on a daily basis comes to roughly 1.7 billion.

Google's global revenue in 2018 was $136.2 billion. This was an increase of about 23% from the company's 2017 revenue and a far cry from the $19.1 million made by Google in 2000 (Dündar, 2019 [accessed: 15 January 2020]).

IBM

International Business Machines Corporation is an American company that is one of the oldest IT companies in the world. IBM deals with virtually every segment of the IT market, ranging from mainframe computers (a class of computers used mainly by large organisations for critical applications) to nanotechnology. IBM is the world's enterprise AI leader. Solutions enabled by IBM Watson help to produce better decision-making and business outcomes through more than 20,000 client engagements across 20 industries to date. IDC ranked IBM number one in terms of AI market share. They continue to pioneer innovations in natural language processing, speech processing, computer vision, and machine learning. Their investments have reshaped IBM to

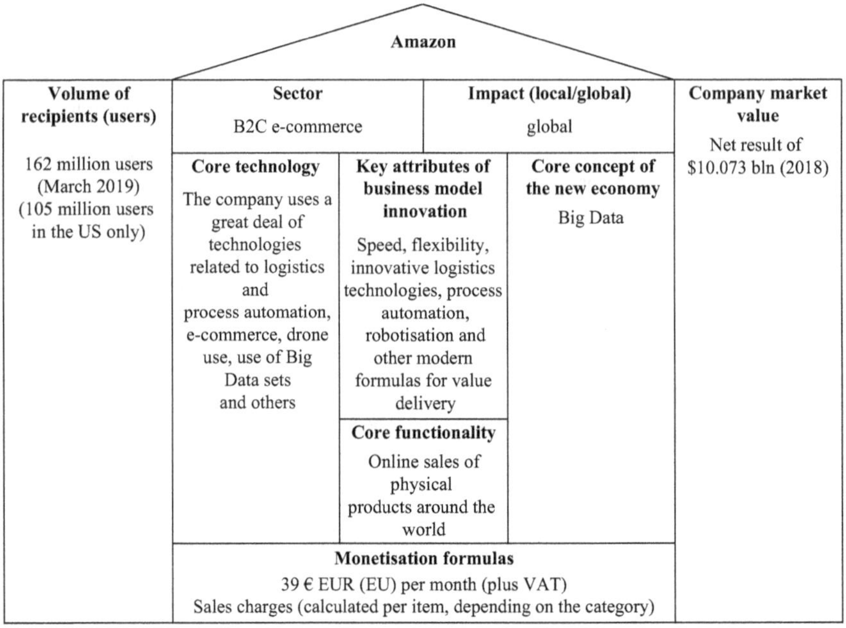

Figure 5.14 Model of the description of Amazon business model components in terms of monetisation.

Source: Own study.

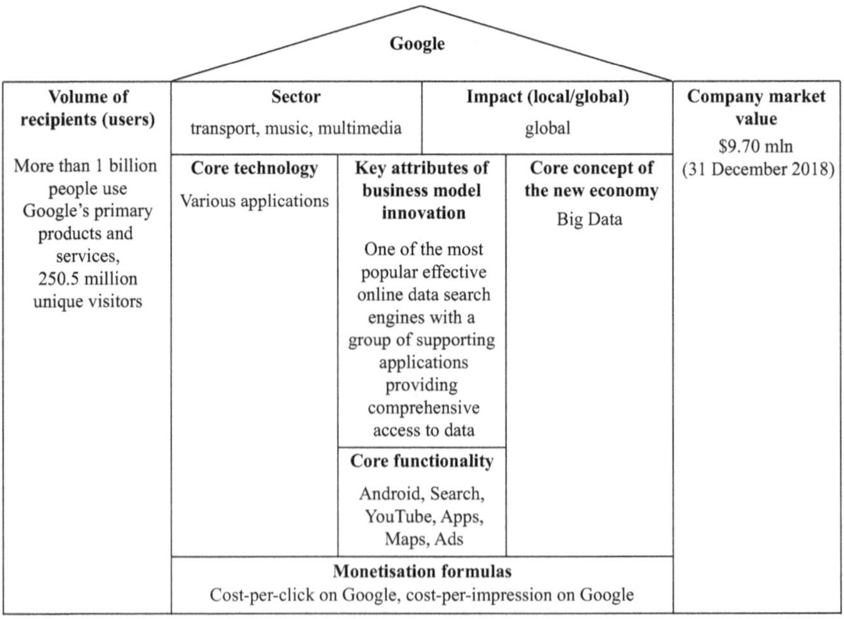

Figure 5.15 Model of the description of Google business model components in terms of monetisation.

Source: Own study.

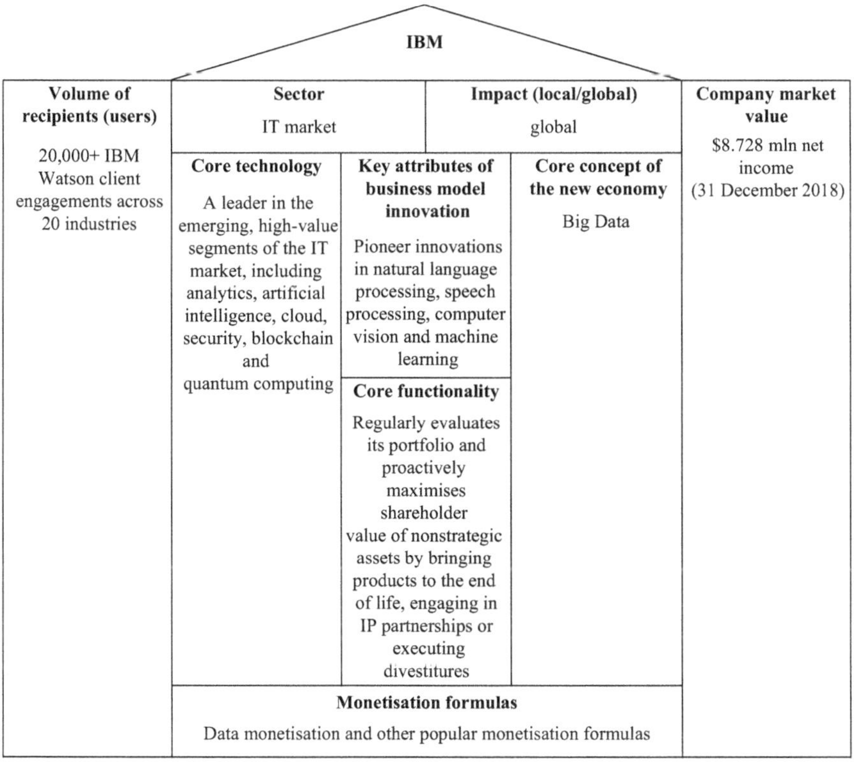

Figure 5.16 Model of the description of IBM business model components in terms of monetisation.

Source: Own study.

lead in the emerging, high-value segments of the IT market, including analytics, artificial intelligence, cloud, security, blockchain, and quantum computing. IBM Security, the world's largest cybersecurity enterprise, has 8,000 subject matter experts serving more than 17,000 clients in more than 130 countries. IBM Security manages 70 billion cybersecurity events per day for clients in more than 130 countries (*2018 Annual Report IBM*).

TeraData

Teradata Corporation is a leading hybrid cloud analytics software provider which focuses on delivering pervasive data intelligence to their customers, which they define as the ability to leverage 100% of a company's data to uncover real-time intelligence, at scale (*Teradata 2018 Annual Report*; www.teradata.pl).

In 2003 more than 120 industry-leading companies migrated from Oracle to Teradata after the launch of the Oracle-to-Teradata migration programme. Teradata University Network was created to advance awareness of data warehousing in the academic community. Nearly 170 universities from 27 countries

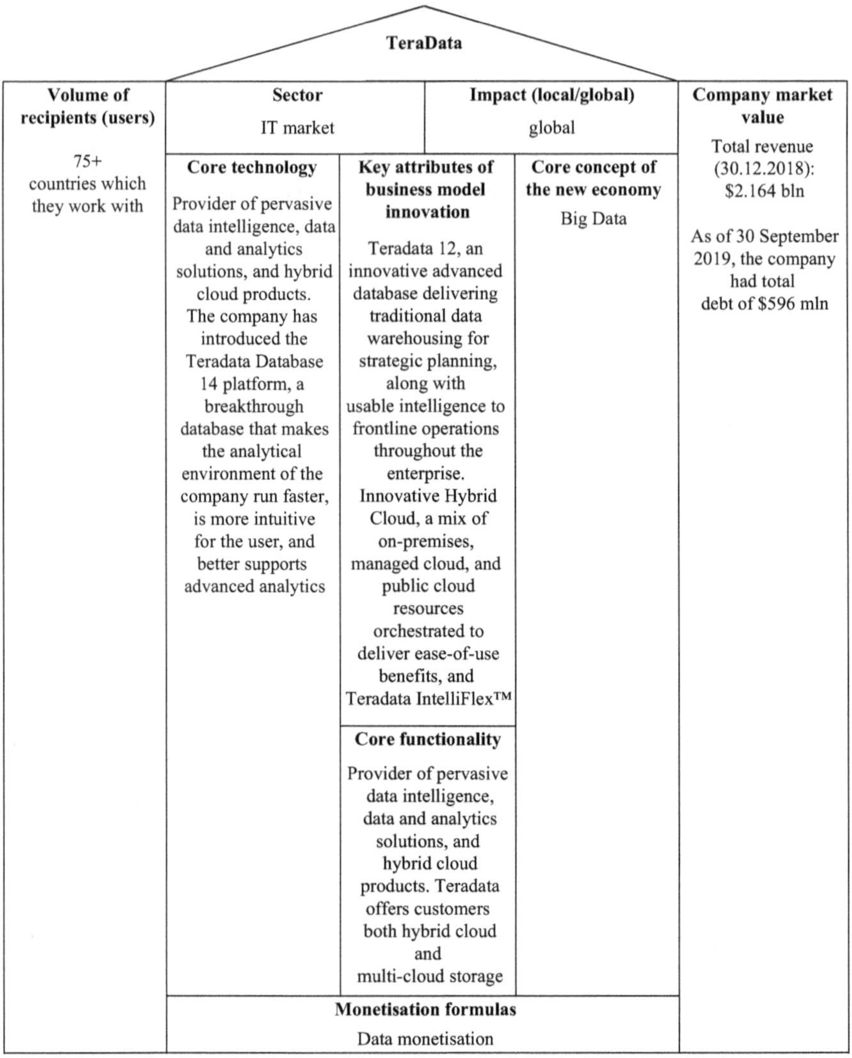

Figure 5.17 Model of the description ofTeraData business model components in terms of monetisation.

Source: Own study based on *Teradata Reports Third Quarter 2019 Financial Results* (2019).

were represented in the network. Teradata ended the third quarter of 2019 with $528 million in cash. As of 30 September 2019, the Company had a total debt of $596 million, including $108 million of outstanding finance lease obligations.

Oracle

Oracle is an American company that develops software for broadly defined company services, in particular database management systems. It is the second

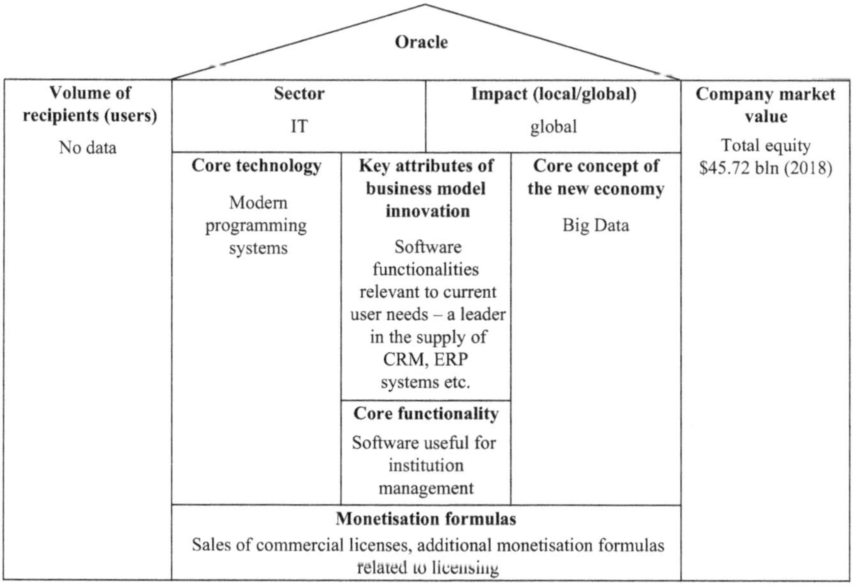

Figure 5.18 Model of the description of Oracle business model components in terms of monetisation.

Source: Own study.

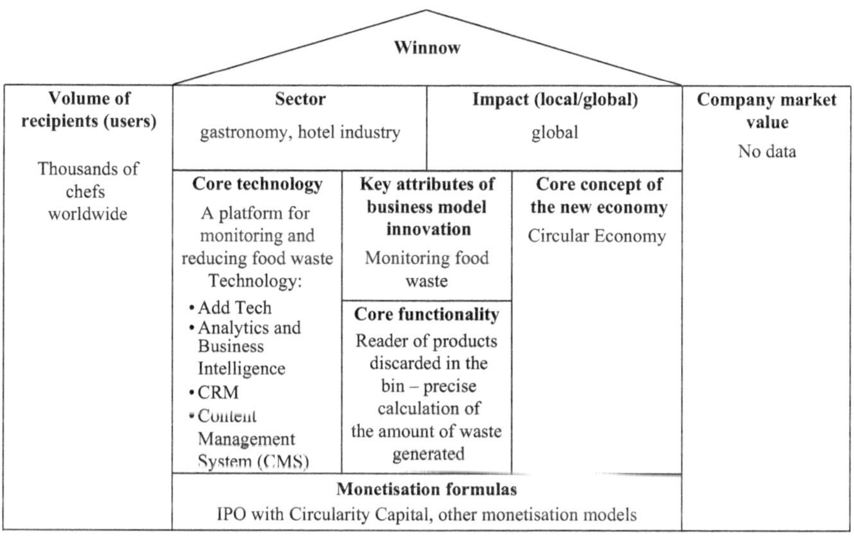

Figure 5.19 Model of the description of Winnow business model components in terms of monetisation.

Source: Own study.

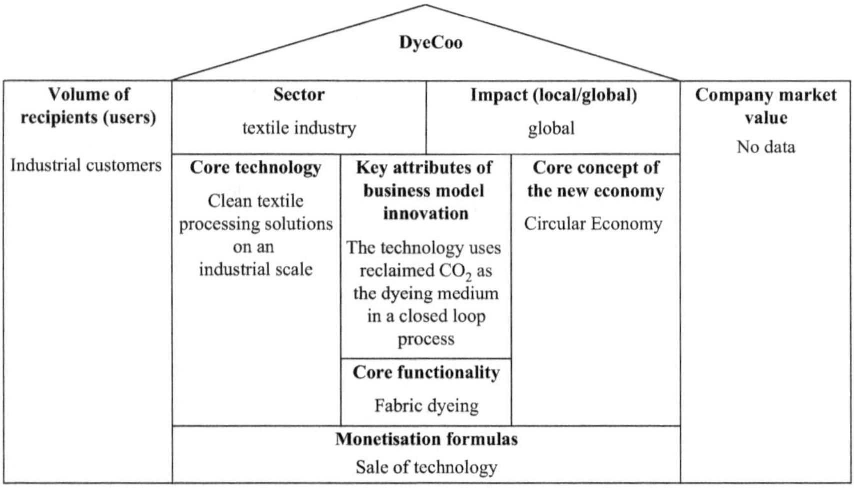

Figure 5.20 Model of the description of DyeCoo business model components in terms of monetisation.

Source: Own study based on www.dyecoo.com/co2-dyeing/ (accessed: 17 January 2020).

largest software vendor in the world (after Microsoft) in terms of revenue. The company has achieved this by focusing on software development for Linux; it also has its own distribution (Oracle Linux) (www.oracle.com/linux/).

Examples of the monetisation of Circular Economy companies

Winnow

Their mission is to connect the commercial kitchen, create a movement of chefs and inspire others to see that food is too valuable to waste and that technology can transform the way they use food. At Winnow, they help the food service and hospitality industry cut down on food waste by making the kitchen smarter. Winnow Vision uses computer vision to help chefs easily pinpoint waste, cut costs, and save time. Winnow is designed to scale quickly and easily and their international reach across 30 countries, with four global offices, makes them perfectly placed to assist global businesses.

DyeCoo

DyeCoo, based in Weesp, the Netherlands, has more than 15 years of experience in CO_2 technology. With extensive knowledge in design and engineering of CO_2 equipment, DyeCoo provides clean textile processing solutions on an industrial scale. DyeCoo's CO_2 technology is the world's first 100% water-free

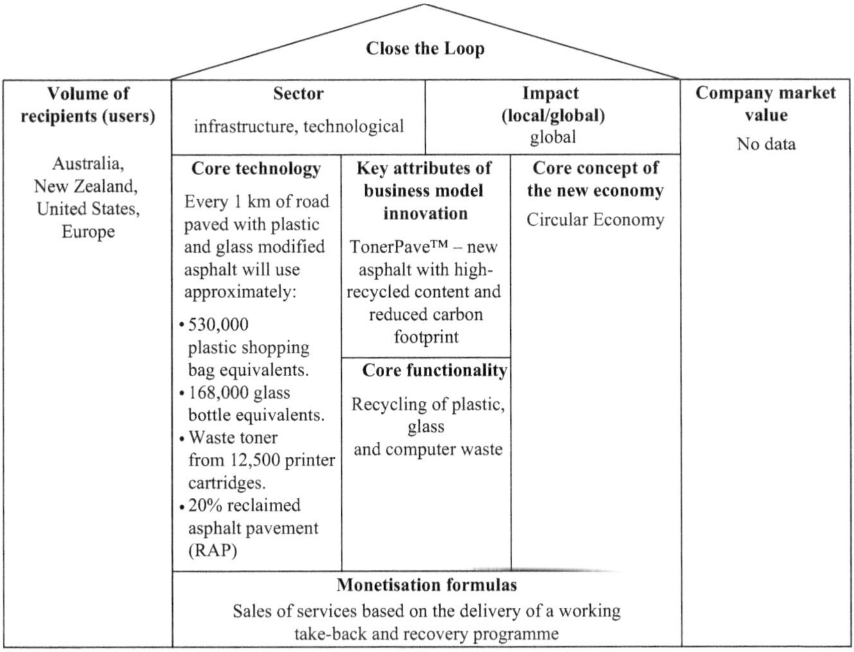

Figure 5.21 Model of the description of Close the Loop business model components in terms of monetisation.

Source: Own study based on www.closetheloop.com.au/ (accessed: 17 January 2020).

and process chemical-free textile processing solution. The technology uses reclaimed CO_2 as the dyeing medium in a closed loop process.

Close the Loop

Close the Loop helps companies gain control over their sustainability processes. They make it easy to take back, recover, and reuse your high-value products – so they don't end up in rivers, landfills, or on someone else's assembly line. These partnerships are with Fortune 500 companies such as Xerox, Staples, HP, and Konica Minolta. Close the Loop understands the best form of recycling is firstly reusing

Enerkem

Enerkem offers an innovative, sustainable solution in the field of waste management, energy diversification, and implementation of the Circular Economy. Their Business Model is structured along two pathways to allow the flexible deployment of Enerkem Technology:

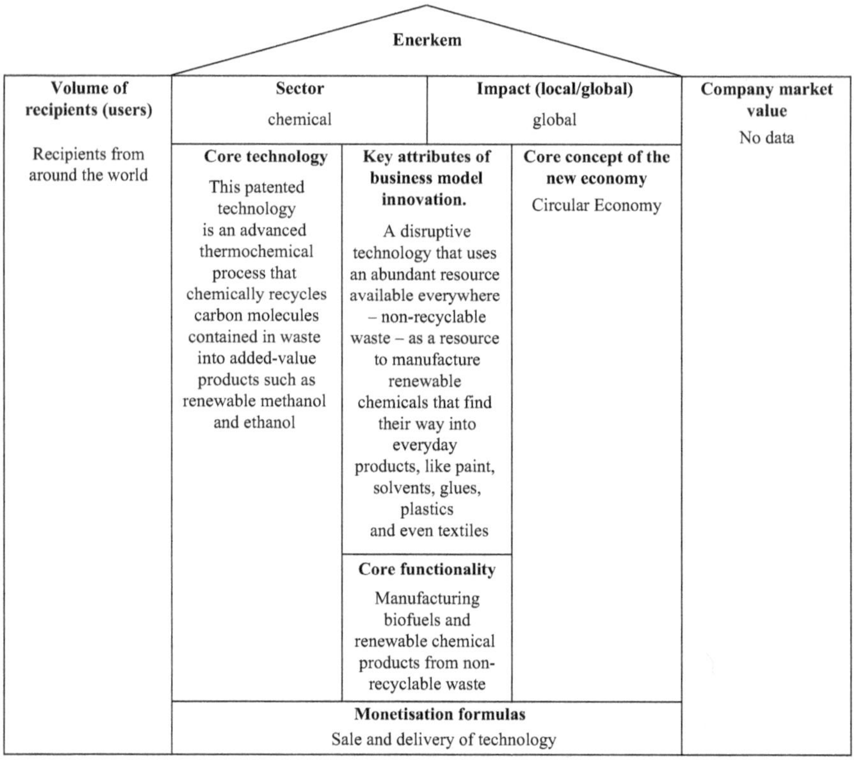

Figure 5.22 Model of the description of Enerkem business model components in terms of monetisation.

Source: Own study based on https://enerkem.com/process-technology/ (accessed: 17 January 2020).

Enerkem Technologies	*Enerkem Biofuels*
Licensing the technology and supplying equipment/modules	Participation in plant equity in addition to the technology and equipment provision of the Enerkem Technologies business

Source: https://enerkem.com/process-technology/technology-comparison/ [accessed: 17 January 2020].

Schneider Electric

Schneider Electric provides digital solutions in the field of energy management and automation, combining the world's best energy technologies, real-time automation, software and services as part of integrated solutions for homes, buildings, data centres, infrastructures, and industry. Their presence is balanced across four geographical regions and four diversified end-markets: North

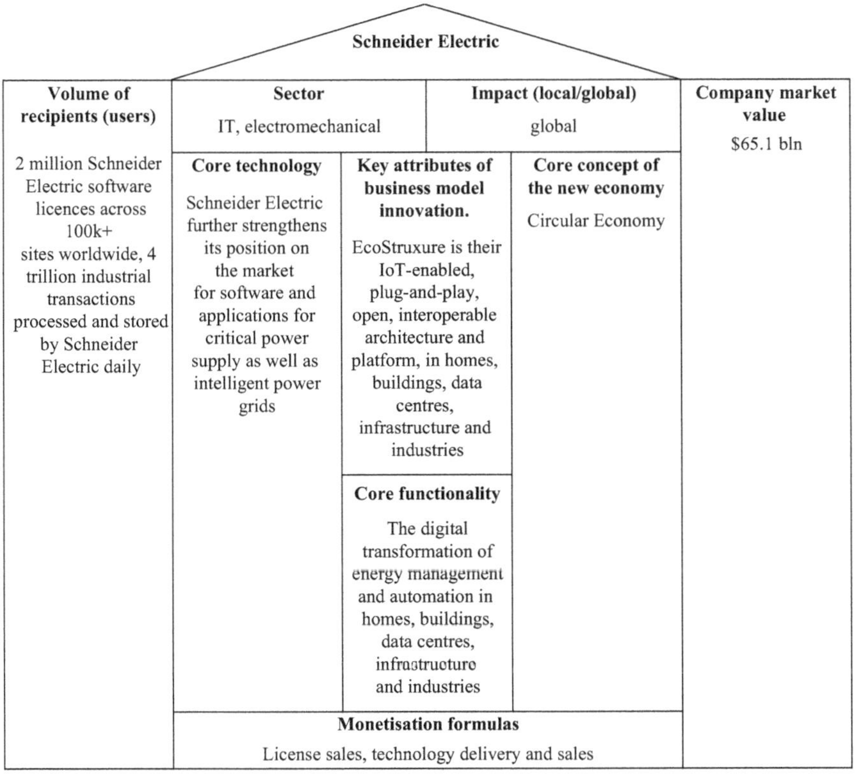

Figure 5.23 Model of the description of Schneider Electric business model components in terms of monetisation.

Source: Own study based on *Schneider Electric Innovation Summit Paris 2018 Research Report*, https://markets.businessinsider.com/stocks/schneider_electric-stock (accessed: 5 February 2020] and www.se.com [accessed: 5 February 2020).

America (28%), Western Europe (27%), Asia Pacific (29%), and Rest of World (16%) (www.se.com. [accessed 5 February 2020]).

At Schneider Electric, they develop innovative solutions that enhance both your home's appearance and your lifestyle, reduce your energy bills, and safeguard your family and memories (www.se.com [accessed 5 February 2020]).

The share price was $103.34 on average, while the volume of shares was 1,139,758 (www.se.com/ww/en/about-us/investor-relations/share-information/share-price.jsp [accessed 4 February 2020]).

Cambrian Innovation

Cambrian Innovation helps businesses across a number of sectors transform their wastewater streams into value, generating clean energy and clean water with their EcoVolt solutions (https://cambrianinnovation.com/ [accessed: 5 February 2020]).

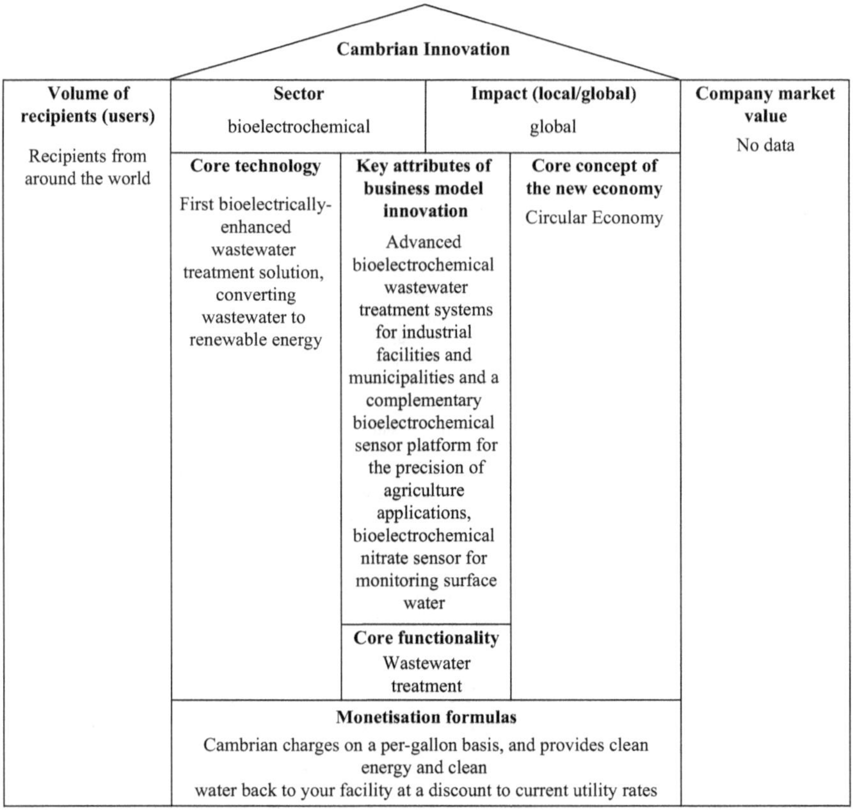

Figure 5.24 Model of the description of Cambrian Innovation business model components in terms of monetisation.

Source: Own study.

Cambrian Innovation is a commercial provider of distributed wastewater treatment and resource recovery solutions. Dedicated to solving critical water, wastewater, and energy management challenges for industrial producers, it is the standard for some of the top names in food and beverage processing including: Domaine Chandon, Tree House Brewing Company, and AB InBev.

Cambrian Innovation is developing and marketing a portfolio of environmental products with support from government and industry partners. New products include advanced bioelectrochemical wastewater treatment systems for industrial facilities and municipalities and a complementary bioelectrochemical sensor platform for precision agriculture applications.

Lehigh Technologies

Lehigh Technologies is a specialty chemicals company that produces highly engineered, versatile raw materials called micronised rubber powders (MRP) that can replace oil- and rubber-based feedstocks in a wide range of applications.

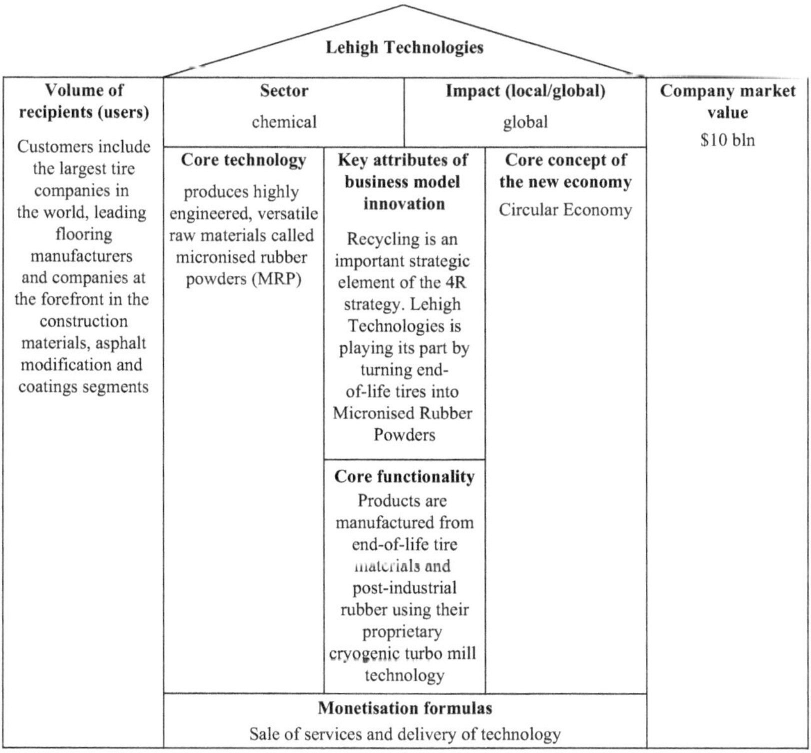

Figure 5.25 Model of the description of Lehigh Technologies business model components in terms of monetisation.

Source: Own study based on http://lehightechnologies.com/ (accessed: 5 February 2020).

By transforming waste materials into high-value products, Lehigh provides a sustainable solution to the important environmental problem of end-of-life tyres and other post-industrial rubber material.

They have two main product lines: PolyDyne™ and MicroDyne™, which are manufactured from end-of-life tyre materials and post-industrial rubber using their proprietary cryogenic turbo mill technology. Their customers include the largest tyre companies in the world, leading flooring manufacturers, and companies at the forefront in the construction materials, asphalt modification, and coatings segments. Today, Lehigh serves a wide range of global markets totalling more than $10 billion in revenue, including asphalt, construction materials, industrial rubber, plastics and polyurethanes, and tyres.

HYLA Mobile

HYLA Mobile exists to provide industry-leading technology, analytics, and logistics solutions to help the mobile ecosystem maximise their sustainability efforts in a manner that builds exceptional value for customers and shareholders, while benefiting the environment. HYLA Mobile is a privately held, US-based

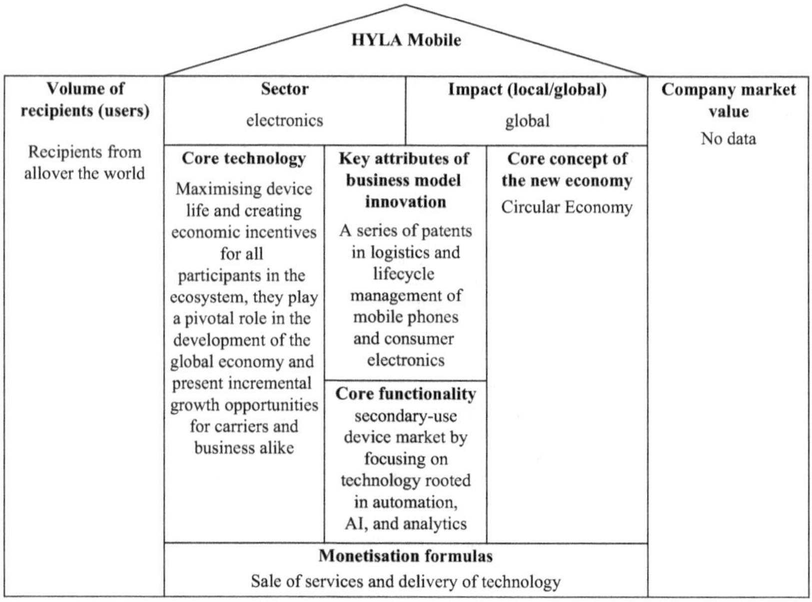

Figure 5.26 Model of the description of HYLA Mobile business model components in terms of monetisation.

Source: Own study.

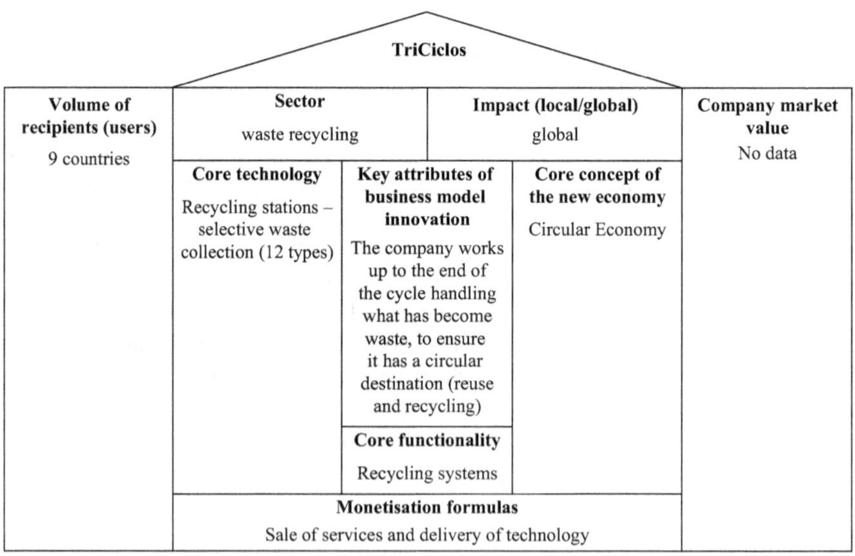

Figure 5.27 Model of the description ofTriCiclos business model components in terms of monetisation.

Source: Own study based on https://triciclos.net/en/ (accessed: 5 February 2020).

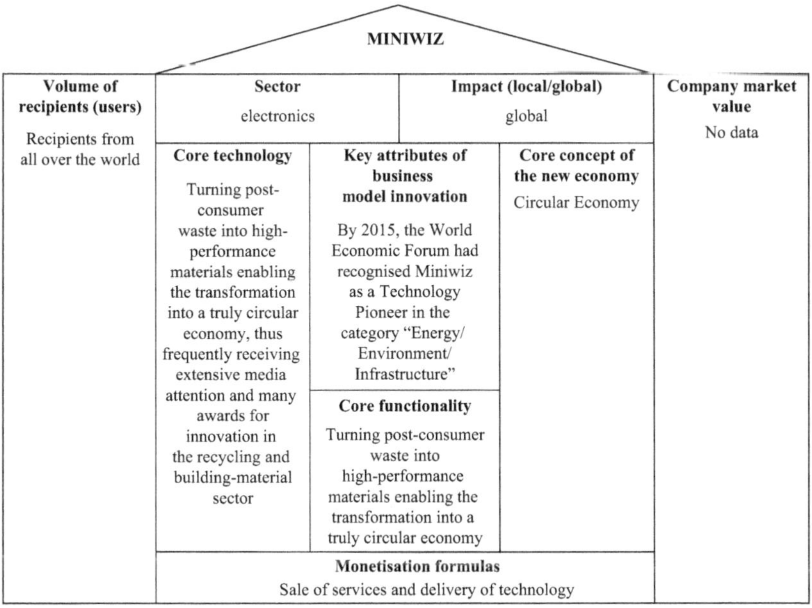

Figure 5.28 Model of the description of MINIWIZ business model components in terms of monetisation.

Source: Own study.

technology company backed by several well-known and widely respected private equity and venture capital firms. They service the $17 billion secondary-use device market by focusing on technology rooted in automation, AI, and analytics. HYLA Mobile is a pioneering leader in the wireless industry, with a history of delivering industry firsts. They own or have filed for a series of patents in logistics and life cycle management of mobile phones and consumer electronics.

HYLA specialises in processing, repairing, and liquidating mobile devices collected through trade-in, upgrade, warranty, and insurance programmes (www.hylamobile.com/ [accessed: 5 February 2020]).

TriCiclos

The company creates solutions to review waste generation before its design, that is, from the beginning of the material production chain. The company works up to the end of the cycle, handling what has become waste, to ensure it has a circular destination (reuse and recycling) (https://triciclos.net/en/ [accessed: 5 February 2020]).

MINIWIZ

MINIWIZ was founded in March 2005. In 2007, MINIWIZ developed its breakthrough project, the HYmini – a ground-breaking portable wind, solar, and hand-crank power generator made from recycled electronic waste plastic and post-consumer recycled paper. This device, a zero carbon footprint charging product, was the first of hundreds of MINIWIZ projects to follow, which truly encapsulated all MINIWIZ stands for – performance efficiency at zero carbon cost.

By 2015, the World Economic Forum had recognised MINIWIZ as a Technology Pioneer in the "Energy/Environment/Infrastructure" category, highlighting the positive impact that the company's activity has had upon the world's environment and economic development. Today, MINIWIZ focuses on turning post-consumer waste into high-performance materials, enabling the movement into a truly Circular Economy, thus frequently receiving extensive media attention and many awards for innovation in the recycling and building-material sector (www.miniwiz.com/ [accessed: 5 February 2020]).

MINIWIZ conceives, innovates, develops, and executes projects for brand, business, institutions, and governments at every step of their respective supply chains, to ensure total operational efficiency.

Conclusions

The descriptions of digital economy companies that fulfil the assumptions of the concepts of the Sharing Economy, Big Data, and the Circular Economy clearly confirm that their digital business models – which may include hybrid ones, that is, those which combine the functions of digital business models but still embedded in traditional forms of activity – in particular Circular Economy companies, are complex. Relationships between the defined components of these business models, that is, the operating sector, the scope of geographical impact, volume and type of users, core technology, the key attributes of business model innovation, the core functionality of the business model used, the core concept of the new economy, and finally the market value are strongly dependent on the adopted monetisation scheme. In each digital or hybrid model (which combine the features of a digital business model but are embedded in a traditional economy in part or in full), the principles of charging arise either from the idea used in this respect or are forced by practices occurring in the specific concepts of the new economy (the Sharing Economy, Big Data, or the Circular Economy). These concepts mainly determine the choice of monetisation formula. Most companies surveyed and analysed achieve success. They are often successful on a global scale and these companies have a very well-known brand recognised all over the world, which therefore means that it is appropriate to assess them in terms of the criteria developed. The conclusions for this area of research are as follows:

1. Digital business models of the companies surveyed are characterised by consistency, which is visible due to the analysis of the individual components of defined business models as well as their mutual synergistic relationships.
2. Belonging to the individual concepts of the new economy defines their specific identity.
3. The relationship between the volume of users and the monetisation scheme affects the market value of companies using the individual configurations of business models.

4. Other components, in particular the functionality of business models as well as core technologies and innovations, determine the level of investment attractiveness of these business models and their ability to raise capital.
5. The impact aspect is primarily global, which means that these business formulas are universal and not limited by political and legal conditions to the extent that they cannot overcome barriers in this respect.

To sum up, the examples of companies presented are a representative group of these digital business models that are worth examining in terms of their impact on changes in contemporary global business, proving the dynamically occurring processes of the digital transformation of companies and the strong use of new digital economy technologies for the market expansion of new formulas of value creation and delivery with the wide acceptance of recipients/users and other stakeholders.

References

2018 Annual Report IBM (accessed 17 January 2020).

Alphabet Announces Fourth Quarter and Fiscal Year 2018 Results (2019), MOUNTAIN VIEW, Calif. Alphabet Inc.

Annual Report 2018 BlaBlaCar

Annual report 2018 Snap Inc.

Bond, S. (2018). *Uber Gears Up for Shift to Bikes on Short Trips, CEO Expects Short-term Financial Hit*, CNBC LLC. Available at: www.cnbc.com/2018/08/26/uber-gears-up-for-shift-to-bikes-on-short-trips.html (accessed: 9 January 2020).

British Parking Awards l Landor LINKS Ltd. (2017). *Congratulations to the Winners of the British Parking Awards 2017!*. Available at: www.britishparkingawards.co.uk/2017/winners2017.php [accessed: 9 January 2020].

Brown, D. (2019). "LinkedIn Hails These Startups as the Best, Most Sought After in 2019", USA TODAY, https://eu.usatoday.com/story/money/2019/09/04/top-10-startups-2019-linkedin/2139023001/ [accessed: 9 January 2020].

Curtis, S. (2015). "JustPark Invites Users to Become Shareholders in £1m Crowdfunding Campaign", *The Telegraph*. Available at: www.telegraph.co.uk/technology/news/11408609/JustPark-invites-users-to-become-shareholders-in-1m-crowdfunding-campaign.html [accessed: 9 January 2020].

Diffey, Ch. (2019). "Stashbee Secures £2.5m for Equity Investment Round", *TechRound*, https://techround.co.uk/news/stashbee-secures-2-5m/ [accessed: 10 January 2020].

Dündar, T. (2019). *Google Search Statistics 2019*, https://99firms.com/blog/google-search-statistics/#gref [accessed: 15 January 2020].

Fiverr – Company Presentation November 2019

Hayes, D. (2018). *Snap Inc. Posts Slowest Quarterly User Growth in Its History; Shares Plunge*, Deadline Hollywood (Deadline.com), https://deadline.com/2018/05/snap-inc-snapchat-slowest-growth-earnings-stock-plunges-1202380663/ (accessed: 15 January 2020).

https://cambrianinnovation.com/ (accessed: 5 February 2020).

https://enerkem.com/process- technology/ (accessed: 17 January 2020).

https://investor.snap.com/company-profile (accessed: 15 January 2020).

http://lehightechnologies.com/ (accessed: 5 February 2020).

https://markets.businessinsider.com/stocks/schneider_electric-stock (accessed: 17 January 2020).

https://network.fon.com/ (accessed: 10 January 2020).

https://services.amazon.pl/ (accessed: 15 January 2020).
https://stashbee.com/ (accessed: 10 January 2020).
https://triciclos.net/en/ (accessed: February 2020).
www.aboutamazon.com/ (accessed: 15 January 2020).
www.closetheloop.com.au/ (accessed: 17 January 2020).
www.couchsurfing.com/ (accessed: 15 January 2020).
www.crunchbase.com/organization/silvernest (accessed: 15 January 2020).
www.dyecoo.com/co2- dyeing/ (accessed: 17 January 2020).
www.fasttrack.co.uk/company_ profile/justpark-2/ (accessed: 9 January 2020).
www.hylamobile.com/ (accessed: 5 February 2020).
www.justpark.com/car- park- management/ (accessed: 9 January 2020).
www.li.me/pl/ (accessed: 9 January 2020).
www.marketwatch.com/investing/stock/fvrr/financials (accessed: 10 January 2020).
www.miniwiz.com/ (accessed: 5 February 2020).
www.oracle.com/linux/ (accessed: 17 January 2020).
www.se.com (accessed: 5 February 2020).
www.silvernest.com/ (accessed: 15. January 2020).
www.spotahome.com/pl (accessed: 10 January 2020).
www.statista.com/statistics/546894/number-of-amazon-prime-paying-members/ (accessed: 15 January 2020).
www.teradata.pl (accessed: 17 January 2020).
www.uber.com/pl/ (accessed: 3 January 2020).
www.winnowsolutions.com/ (accessed: 17 January 2020).
www.zipcar.com/?redirect_ p=0 (accessed: 10 January 2020).

Keyes, D. (2019). *Mobile App Users Are Key to Amazon's Success*, Insider Inc. Available at: www.businessinsider.com/mobile-app-users-amazon-2019-3?IR=T (accessed: 15 January 2020).

LLB Reporter (2015). *JustPark Just Crowdfunded £1m in FOUR DAYS. We Ask Its Founder How He Did It*, LondonlovesBusiness.com, https://londonlovesbusiness.com/justpark-just-crowdfunded-1m-in-four-days-we-ask-its-founder/ (accessed: 9 January 2020).

Loritz, M. (2019). "London-based Online Storage Marketplace Stashbee Raises €2.8 Million on Seedrs", *EU-Startups.com*. Available at: www.eu-startups.com/2019/07/london-based-online-storage-marketplace-stashbee-raises-e2-8-million-on-seedrs/ (accessed: 10 January 2020).

Mack, B. (2009). "Zipcar iPhone App Makes Car-sharing a Breeze", *Wired*. Available at: www.wired.com/2009/06/zipcar-iphone/ (accessed: 10 January 2020).

McKay, T. (2019). "You Lost How Much on Scooters?", *GIZMODO*. Available at: https://gizmodo.com/you-lost-how-much-on-scooters-1839245178 (accessed: 9 January 2020).

Mhatre, A. (2019). *The Great Electric Scooter Backlash*, CBS Interactive Inc. Available at: www.cbsnews.com/news/the-great-electric-scooter-backlash/ (accessed: 9 January 2020).

Schneider Electric Innovation Summit Paris 2018 Research Report

Teradata 2018 Annual Report

Teradata (2019). *Teradata Reports Third Quarter 2019 Financial Results*, https://investor.teradata.com/news-and-events/investor-news/press-release-details/2019/Teradata-Reports-Third-Quarter-2019-Financial-Results/default.aspx (accessed: 17 January 2020).

Wayman, R. (2019). *Storage Startup Exceeds Investment Target with £2.5m Funding Round*, Bdaily Ltd, https://bdaily.co.uk/articles/2019/08/22/storage-startup-exceeds-investment-target-with-25m-funding-round (accessed: 10 January 2020).

6 Case study of a digital business model

Introduction

Some digital economy companies achieve above-average results. The chances of creating unique value on this market are not high, but sometimes success is simply unimaginable. In some cases, building a global brand based on the digital economy is much faster than it was in the era of the traditional economy. Good solutions can enter global circulation via social media, digital platforms, and the Internet at a very fast pace. Such spectacular successes are noted in the business world. Both management theoreticians and practitioners try to understand the phenomenon of the success of some companies, which quickly become global and whose market value is growing rapidly. Such situations occur especially in the area of the functioning of digital economy companies. Such spectacular success has been achieved by a joint-stock company listed on the Stock Exchange, namely CD Projekt S.A., which operates in the computer games industry. The significant market success of this company, which is characterised by a dynamic increase in market value and global impact in the area of computer game enthusiasts (in particular, caused by the market success of the computer game Witcher 3), prompted the authors of the monograph to analyse this company as a case study that is attractive for scientific and practical assessment.

The purpose of the chapter is to indicate key success factors as well as the conditions for creating the success of a company which operates on the electronic market and uses modern methods of sales monetisation. An optimal approach to value creation for users has created a unique product appreciated around the world.

Case study of a digital business model

The case study method is used when a researcher wants to indicate one isolated case that can be a source of comparative analysis in relation to other objects which implement similar strategic assumptions expressed in the business model and/or strategy. Yin proposes the use of the case study method to find answers to questions that are revealing in their nature, that is, how and why the phenomenon occurs. At the same time, it indicates that a case study may apply when the following occur:

- An early stage of knowledge development in a given research area.
- The current phenomenon is recognised in real conditions.
- Blurred boundaries between the phenomenon and the circumstances of its occurrence (Yin, 1984).

According to Lee, a single case reflects a single set of circumstances, and conclusions drawn on its basis can be generalised to other cases with similar circumstances. Conducting subsequent research using single cases may confirm these conclusions in other circumstances (Lee, 1989). As regards the research conducted based on the case study, the authors followed the definition of Czakon, where a case is understood as a single research object, recognised for a specific purpose, located at a specific time and place, taking into account its specific circumstances, studied by means of many data collection and analysis techniques. This definition emphasises that no universal regularities are expected from a case (Czakon, 2013, p. 93).

The adopted procedure for theory-forming case studies was applied according to Czakon's adopted model, which covers the following steps (Czakon, 2006, p. 10).

1. Formulation of the research question.
2. Case selection.
3. Development of data collection tools.
4. Conducting field studies.
5. Analysis of collected data.
6. Formulation of generalisations.
7. Comparison with the literature.
8. Closing the research – generalisation.

As part of the adopted case study research method, CD Projekt was selected, due to it being an excellent example of the success of the digital business model. This company has achieved spectacular success on the global market in recent years. As a producer of iconic computer games, it has increased its value and volume of users above average. It delivered the high-quality computer game Witcher (which has sold over 40 million copies) to the global market, which became even more popular and widely recognised after the broadcast of the Netflix series of the same name.

CD Projekt

Company history and key successes of CD Projekt

CD PROJEKT S.A., based in Warsaw, operates in the global, dynamically developing electronic entertainment industry.

The business adventure which marks the beginning of CD PROJEKT began in 1994, when Marcin Iwiński and Michał Kiciński founded CDP.pl – the first company in the CD PROJEKT capital group. Currently CDP.pl exists outside the group. At the beginning, the company mainly supplied software on CDs imported from the United States to the Polish market. In 1996, CDP.pl was the first company in Poland to start publishing games with Polish instructions and in Polish boxes.

The next milestone for the company was the creation of the first full Polish localisation of the game "Baldur's Gate", sales of which exceeded 100,000 copies. Actors lending their voice to the game included Wiktor Zborowski, Jan Kobuszewski, Marian Opania, Piotr Fronczewski, and Krzysztof Kowalewski.

In 2002, another company from today's CD PROJEKT Group – CD Projekt Red Studio Sp. z o.o. – was founded. In September 2003, the CD PROJEKT RED development studio began working on its first RPG set in the world created by Andrzej Sapkowski, "The Witcher". With a budget of nearly $5.2 million, the project was the most expensive domestic production of those times. It took five years to create the game and nearly 100 people were involved. Tomasz Bagiński (nominated for an Oscar for the film *The Cathedral*), Przemysław Truściński (a popular comic book author), and the band Vader – one of the most famous Polish heavy metal bands in the world – were among many who cooperated during the production.

The premiere of the first part of "The Witcher" in October 2007 turned out to be a commercial success. Within three days of the premiere, the game had been bought by 35,000 people in Poland alone. In 2012, "The Witcher" was also released for Apple computers and Linux. Since its release, the game has won over 100 international awards, including prestigious awards such as GameSpot, GameSpy, and IGN for the best role-playing game.

In 2008, the Good Old Games English-language website was launched, which initially sold iconic, classic PC games adapted to the requirements of modern operating systems. As of March 2012, the company began selling newer and premiere titles, and as of October 2012, games for Apple computers as well. Therefore, in 2012, Good Old Games changed its name to GOG.com. Currently, the platform offers a catalogue of over 2,000 titles, and most of its clients are users from the United States and Western Europe.

In 2008, the holding company CDP Investment, the parent company of the CD PROJEKT Group, was spun off. It included companies such as CD Projekt, CD Projekt RED and GOG Ltd. On 21 October 2009, CDP Investment and Optimus S.A., a company which has been continuously listed on the Warsaw Stock Exchange since 1994, concluded an investment agreement. As a consequence, on 1 May 2010, Optimus acquired 100% of the shares in CDP Investment. Since the turn of 2008/2009, Optimus has not conducted activities in the field of production and distribution of IT equipment, and the activity of the companies belonging to the CDP Investment Group has become its core business. The formal merger of CDP Investment and Optimus S.A. took place on 28 December 2010. On 25 July 2011 the District Court for the Capital City of Warsaw registered a change to the Company's Statute, and thus its name changed from Optimus S.A. to CD Projekt RED S.A. At the beginning of

October 2011, CD Projekt RED S.A. merged with its subsidiary CD Projekt Red Sp. z o.o.

At the turn of 2007 and 2008, work on the second part of "The Witcher" began. An original RED Engine was created especially for the game. CD-Action announced "The Witcher" as the most anticipated game of the year in 2011. The premiere of "The Witcher 2: Assassins of Kings" for PCs was held on 17 May 2011.

In 2012, CD Projekt RED released "The Witcher 2" for the Xbox 360 console and for Apple computers. In October 2012, the Company proudly announced that it had already sold a total of over 2 million copies of the second part of "The Witcher" trilogy. This was almost twice as many copies as the first part of "The Witcher" in the corresponding period.

In 2012, CD Projekt RED announced the start of work on its second major title. "Cyberpunk 2077" will be based on the iconic RPG system "Cyberpunk", which is widely known and popular all over the world. As part of their work on the game, the CD Projekt RED team actively cooperates with Mike Pondsmith, the creator of "Cyberpunk".

In 2012, CD Projekt changed its name to CDP.pl, and launched a digital distribution platform, while in November 2012, the General Meeting of CD Projekt RED decided to change the name of the company to CD PROJEKT S.A.

In November 2014, CD PROJEKT S.A. sold the controlling interest in its local distribution company. As a result of the transaction, the share of CD PROJEKT S.A. in cdp.pl decreased to 8.29% and the company was spun off outside the group. In 2014, a new CD PROJEKT logo was also presented: the Scarlet Cardinal (or REDbird). It embodies such qualities that identify the company in the video game industry and give their business the character of independence and indomitability. It shares the colour red with the fiery bird which appears in Slavic legends – the saker. This is to bring happiness and prosperity to people.

On 19 May 2015, the world premiere of "The Witcher 3: Wild Hunt" took place. The game debuted in 15 languages for PCs, PlayStation 4 and Xbox One consoles. During the first six weeks of release (i.e. until 30 June 2015), sales of the game worldwide amounted to 6,014,576. By the end of 2015, the game had won over 300 awards around the world, including five awards in the prestigious Golden Joysticks Awards 2015 and two awards in The Games Awards 2015. An award was also given to the CD PROJEKT RED studio, which was recognised as "Developer of the Year 2015".

In 2015, GOG.com introduced the new GOG Galaxy technology, which allows for online entertainment in multiplayer mode, among others. On 13 October 2015, CD PROJEKT released the first game expansion in its history – "Heart of Stone". Two weeks after its release, the average rating on Metacritic remained at 90 – this is one of the best-rated add-ons in history. On 31 May 2016, the premiere of the second and last add-on to "The Witcher 3: Wild Hunt" – "Blood and Wine" – took place. The add-on offers players more than 30 hours of gameplay in a completely new region – picturesque Toussaint, full of captivating vineyards and free of war turmoil, which, however, hides a dark secret. The add-on received critical acclaim and positive reviews from industry journalists. Foreign PC Gamer and XGN websites rated it 94/100 and 96/100 respectively.

On 14 June 2016 (on the eve of E3, the largest video game fair in the world) CD PROJEKT announced "GWENT: The Witcher Card Game". "GWENT" is a network game in the universe of Geralt of Rivia for PCs, Xbox One and PlayStation 4 consoles. "GWENT" is also a free, dynamic game (F2P) (offering optional micro-transactions), full of card intrigues, and duels of powerful armies known from the "Witcher world". In the game, victory is determined not only by luck, but above all by the player's skills: intuition, improvisation, and tactical construction of one's own deck. The game can be conducted in multi-player mode or as several-person single campaigns. The closed beta tests of "GWENT: The Witcher Card Game" for PCs and Xbox One consoles began on 25 October 2016. On 24 May 2017, the Public Beta of "GWENT: The Witcher Card Game" began, and all interested PC, Xbox One, and PlayStation 4 owners could participate.

In 2017, during gamescom in Cologne, CD PROJEKT announced "Blood War" – a multi-hour single-player story campaign combining elements of GWENT and RPGs. Blood War is a new, independent, single-player role-playing game, which is the result of the work of a consortium comprised of CD PROJEKT RED and GOG.com. GWENT Masters – a series of professional esports games that included two GWENT Open and 2 GWENT Challenger tournaments in 2017 – was also announced. The GWENT Masters series ended in January 2019 with the world championship of "GWENT: The Witcher Card Game". The total prize pool was USD 850,000.

On 3 September 2017, during PAX West in Seattle, a special discussion panel was held to mark the 10th anniversary of the premiere of the first game from "The Witcher" trilogy, during which representatives of the CD PROJEKT RED studio shared their memories of how their adventure with "The Witcher" trilogy began and the challenges they encountered while working on "The Witcher" games with the audience.

On 16 March 2018, CD PROJEKT S.A. debuted on the WIG20 index, which brings together the 20 largest blue-chip companies on the Warsaw Stock Exchange in Poland. In the second half of 2017, CD PROJEKT also debuted on two prestigious international indexes – FTSE Mid-Cap Index Emerging Europe and MSCI Emerging Markets. In June, during the largest computer games industry fair, the Electronic Entertainment Expo (E3), CD PROJEKT RED revealed the trailer of the game "Cyberpunk 2077". By the end of July 2018, the trailer had been shown more than 20 million times on all available channels. "Cyberpunk 2077" is a game set in the universe of the classic RPG "Cyberpunk 2020" system, offering dynamic gameplay based on a multi-thread plot. It is a story about the rising star of the mercenary world, taking his first steps in the most dangerous city of the future – Night City. As a result of shows at E3, this game has won over 100 industry awards, given to the best games presented during this event.

In August 2018, a new company named Spokko, a development studio specialising in projects for mobile devices, was established within the Capital Group.

On 23 October 2018, "GWENT: The Witcher Card Game" (PC version) premiered on the GOG platform. The premiere was the end of the Homecoming project, which is the largest update in the history of "GWENT", introducing a number of changes aiming to further emphasise the atmosphere known from "The Witcher 3: Wild Hunt".

On 23 October 2018, the PC version of the game "Thronebreaker: The Witcher Tales" premiered on GOG.com, and on 9 November 2018 on Steam.

On 14 January 2019, a new company was established within the CD PROJEKT Capital Group, which operates as CD PROJEKT RED STORE sp. z o.o. At the end of June 2019, the CD PROJEKT Capital Group consisted of the parent company CD PROJEKT S.A. and five subsidiaries – GOG sp. z o.o., CD PROJEKT Inc., CD PROJEKT Co., Ltd., Spokko sp. z o.o. and CD PROJEKT RED STORE sp. z o.o. (See Table 6.1.)

The phenomenon of "The Witcher" as a brand

The structures of CD PROJEKT S.A. (national holding company of the CD PROJEKT Capital Group), CD PROJEKT Inc. (USA) and CD PROJEKT Co., Ltd (China) include the CD PROJEKT RED studio, which produces computer games. This activity is based on the brands owned by the company: "The Witcher" and "Cyberpunk".

In 2002, work began on the company's debut in the RPG genre – "The Witcher". The first game, based on the story created by Andrzej Sapkowski, was released in October 2007. It received over 100 awards and was a global success. Currently, the portfolio of the studio's main products includes the following video games: "The Witcher", "The Witcher 2: Assassins of Kings", "The Witcher 3: Wild Hunt", and two add-ons – "Hearts of Stone" and "Blood and Wine". In 2018, the network game "GWENT: The Witcher Card Game" and "Thronebreaker: The Witcher Tales" premiered. The company released the game "The Witcher 3: Wild Hunt" on the Nintendo Switch console on 15 October 2019 (CD Projekt, 2019c [accessed: 9 January 2020]) and "GWENT: The Witcher Card Game" on iOS phones on 29 October 2019 (CD Projekt, 2019a [accessed: 9 January 2020]).

Market strategy

CD PROJEKT Group

Operating since 1994, CD PROJEKT is currently a group of electronic entertainment industry companies, which focus on two business areas, namely:

- Production and publishing of the highest class video games by the CD PROJEKT RED studio, known by fans around the world thanks to "The

Table 6.1 Summary of business activities of the parent company and other members of the CD PROJEKT Capital Group as of 30 June 2019

Company	*Activity*
CD PROJEKT S.A.	The core activities of the company, carried out by its CD PROJEKT RED studio, include the development of videogames, publishing its own videogames, selling the associated distribution rights as well as manufacturing, selling and/or licensing tie-in products which exploit the popularity of brands owned by the company. CD PROJEKT S.A. also acts as the holding company of the CD PROJEKT Capital Group and coordinates the activities of other companies belonging to the group
GOG sp. z o.o.	This company concerns itself with the online distribution of videogames, enabling customers from around the world to purchase games, remit payment, and download game binaries to their personal devices. To this end the company owns and maintains the global digital distribution platform at GOG.com. In addition, GOG sp. z o.o. has formed a consortium with CD PROJEKT S.A. to develop and operate "GWENT: The Witcher Card Game". Within the framework of this consortium, GOG sp. z o.o. is responsible for the game's online features and handling in-game transactions in the PC edition.
CD PROJEKT Inc.	This company coordinates publishing and promotional activities covering the group's own products and the GOG.com platform throughout North America. To facilitate this goal, the company operates an office in Los Angeles.
CD PROJEKT Co., Ltd.	This company coordinates publishing and promotional activities covering the group's products in the People's Republic of China, which includes managing a local team tasked with coordinating publishing and promotional activities related to "GWENT: The Witcher Card Game".
Spokko sp. z o.o.	Gamedev studio focusing on mobile releases.
CD PROJEKT RED STORE sp. z o.o.	A company which engages in online marketing of tie-in products associated with CD PROJEKT RED releases throughout the European Union.

Source: CD Projekt, 2019b.

Witcher", and currently working on the Cyberpunk 2077 megaproduction, among others;

- Digital sales of games to customers around the world as part of the GOG.com website and the GOG Galaxy platform.

CD PROJEKT RED Studio

Established in 2002, the CD PROJEKT RED studio creates and publishes video games for personal computers and the latest generation consoles "The Witcher" series, the studio's flagship brand, has sold over 40 million copies so far.

The studio's latest game, "The Witcher 3: Wild Hunt", was released in 2015 on PCs, PlayStation 4, and Xbox One consoles, winning a total of over 800 awards, including 250 as the best game of the year. The title was published in 15 languages in all major markets in Europe, the Americas, Asia, Australia and Africa. The box version of the game hit stores in 109 countries, and the digital version was available worldwide.

The largest CD PROJEKT RED productions are based on the original REDengine software. It is a continuously developed engine that uses the latest technologies to create complex role-playing games set in the open world.

CD PROJEKT RED is headquartered in Warsaw, with offices in Kraków and Wrocław, where teams responsible for subsequent studio productions work, as well as offices in Los Angeles, Berlin, Tokyo and Shanghai, whose task is to coordinate marketing and sales activities in the United States, Germany, Japan, and China respectively. The studio's international team consists of over 750 world-class specialists in programming, animation, graphics, design, production, and the publishing and marketing department which deals with global promotion.

THE MISSION OF THE CD PROJEKT RED STUDIO

The creation of revolutionary role-playing games that reach the hearts of people around the world.

THE GOAL OF THE CD PROJEKT RED STUDIO

To be among the three most recognised video game producers in the world, and for our brands to be at the forefront of global popular culture.

GOG.COM

GOG.com is a store that sells computer games in the digital distribution model worldwide. The store has been operating since 2008, and its offer includes new and classic titles from over 600 creators and publishers, including the largest ones, namely Activision, Bethesda, Disney, Electronic Arts, Ubisoft, Square-Enix, and Warner Bros.

The year 2015 marked the launch of the GOG Galaxy platform, which is an ecosystem for purchasing and managing your own collection of games, as well as for online games and using online services.

GOG.com is created by an international team of over 150 gaming enthusiasts who put players at the centre of their activities, following their opinions while developing their offer and platform.

THE MISSION OF GOG.COM

We combine passion for games and respect for players, providing the best titles supported by online services.

THE GOAL OF GOG.COM

To build a catalogue of new AAA titles fully supported by GOG Galaxy. To create a technology centre with GOG Galaxy which connects games produced by CD PROJEKT RED with a community of players, as well as players with each other.

THE PHILOSOPHY OF THE CD PROJEKT GROUP

A specific philosophy underlies our thinking and our business activity. Most of its elements are common to everything we do, although some naturally relate more to CD PROJEKT RED and others to GOG.com.

The CD PROJEKT group is based on the principle of fair play. The fair treatment of employees, players, and business partners lies at the heart of actions and decisions taken. They think the team is the greatest strength. They employ people with passion who care about working on games and products at the highest level. They are supporters of full world-view tolerance. They believe that tolerance is an important element which supports creativity and innovation. The CD PROJEKT Group builds a strong, direct relationship with the gaming community.

What is important in games

The CD PROJEKT Group believes that a game is a work of art rather than a product that is consumed without reflection. They create non-linear and intriguing games with an in-depth plot and designed for players who value real emotions. They want to develop role-playing games (RPGs). Productions of this type are some of the most difficult from a creative point of view, which accentuates their uniqueness. They develop original game creation technologies, which form the basis of their titles. They carefully select titles for the GOG.com catalogue, playing all the games they sell.

The CD PROJEKT Group believes that their creative and financial independence is key to success. This enables them to run the company and create games according to their own rules. They develop their own digital distribution platform and online games.

Development

The CD PROJEKT Group believes that the greatest successes will be achieved if the business plan follows the creative vision. Quality is the basis of their long-term value-building strategy. They are interested only in ambitious and unique projects with a global reach, and do not compromise in the implementation of these principles. They overcome standards and limitations and prove that they can do what many consider impossible. Wanting to create ground-breaking and truly innovative things, they are not afraid to enter unknown areas, take risks, and make mistakes. In their opinion, the most important capital is the creative energy and creativity of the team, the skilful use of these extremely rare resources and focus on key projects.

Focusing on a small number of brands, they intend to develop them further in other fields. Such an approach will allow them to simultaneously use creative and business synergies, as well as achieve critical mass effects in marketing activities which support their flagship projects, namely games.

They create synergies that will allow them to build an increasingly stronger competitive advantage for the CD PROJEKT Group, due to the fact that CD PROJEKT RED produces games, while GOG.com deals with digital distribution and develops technology to support online gaming.

Business model – a digital business model

The philosophy of the CD PROJEKT Capital Group activity is based on two pillars, namely:

- focusing on the highest quality of games and services produced,
- maintaining the independence necessary for this, including creative and financial independence.

According to the Management Board, these factors are crucial for the group to succeed in the competitive global electronic entertainment industry. The business model of the activity conducted by CD PROJEKT RED assumes control over every important stage of game development and sales – from a creative vision, to production processes and technological solutions, to the publishing process, promotion, distribution, and direct relationships with players. An integral element of the business model is the development of its own digital distribution platform and online gameplay, which is part of an ecosystem created with players in mind. The systematic popularisation of this type of entertainment, making it available and attractive to the mass user; the constant development of technology, which enables the creation of increasingly better and more realistic products; the increasing availability and affordability of gaming devices, as well as new methods of reaching potential players and the distribution of games are extremely important to the development of the group.

Monetisation formulas used by CD Projekt

CD PROJEKT S.A. cooperates with recipients from around the world (e.g. Microsoft, Sony, Warner Bros. Home Entertainment, BANDAI NAMCO Entertainment Europe, VALVE Corporation) and from Poland (cdp.pl, GOG) on the basis of long-term license and distribution agreements. The digital distribution agreements concluded by the company provide for reporting on a monthly basis, while physical distribution agreements provide for reporting on a quarterly basis.

Within the framework of the CD PROJEKT RED segment, the group actively sells its productions to individual hardware platforms through traditional distribution channels via leading distributors, as well as leading global digital video game distribution platforms (including Steam, Xbox Games Store, PlayStation Store, App Store, Origin, Amazon, Humble Bundle or its own GOG.com platform).

The core business models of CD PROJEKT RED:

- The sale of distribution rights in a given territory (in boxed or digital versions) settled *post factum* on the basis of monthly or quarterly sales reports/license reports prepared by the company's partners.
- The sale of physical box products (box games) to distribution partners.
- Sales through optional micropayments within "GWENT: The Witcher Card Game" (for example, barrels with cards, meteorite dust) via GOG and console platform owners.
- The sale of code packages that allow you to download and install the game.

The GOG.com platform was launched in September 2008. Its original mission was to revitalise the most iconic PC games and offer them to clients from all over the world, with particular emphasis on English-speaking countries, that is, the United States, Canada, Great Britain, and Australia. Currently, the service is available in English, French, German, Russian, Chinese, and Polish, offering clients not only a fully localised website or games, but also dedicated customer service, technical assistance, direct marketing in a given language, and popular local payment methods (in 13 currencies). Games on macOS and Linux operating systems are also available on the GOG.com platform.

The activity within the GOG.com segment consists of:

- The digital distribution of games via their own GOG.com platform and the GOG Galaxy application based on agreements concluded by GOG sp. z o.o. with producers, rights owners or game publishers. The platform allows you to purchase a game, pay for the game and download it to your own computer.
- The development of and support for the operation of the original GOG Galaxy application, designed to provide maximum comfort and functional experience related to the purchase, playing, and updating of games offered in the GOG.com catalogue and enabling online gaming between platforms, among others. GOG Galaxy technology is also responsible for the GWENT network functionalities, sales support, and payments in the PC version of the game.
- The participation of GOG sp. z o.o. in a consortium with CD PROJEKT S.A., which created and operates "GWENT: The Witcher Card Game" and the "Thronebreaker: The Witcher Tales" games. As part of the consortium, GOG sp. z o.o. is responsible for sales of GWENT on PCs and for the broadly defined technical infrastructure and network functionality of the game.

Due to paid access to games, GOG sp. z o.o. receives payment from users, part of which is transferred on the basis of concluded agreements to the company's suppliers. The company's digital distribution agreements provide for reporting sales obligations in monthly or quarterly billing cycles up to 30 days from the end of the reporting period. In addition, in the case of older products, the company may be entitled to adapt digitally distributed computer games to current operating systems or to provide the possibility of multiplayer games, if the game originally offered such a possibility. The level of revenues generated in the GOG.com segment in a given period is directly influenced by the attractiveness of the offered catalogue, the premieres of new games and promotional campaigns. GOG constantly strives to expand the group of game providers and add new, attractive titles to their offer. In addition, cyclical and occasional commercial campaigns are organised on GOG.com, such as summer, autumn, or holiday promotions, as well as other promotions introducing new features for engaging players.

The important revenue-generating products of the segment are also co-created by GOG as part of the "Thronebreaker: The Witcher Tales" and "GWENT: The Witcher Card Game" consortium. Revenues disclosed in this segment include:

- Part of the revenues earned by GOG from sales to final recipients on PCs (excluding the Chinese market), for GOG sp. z o.o. as stipulated in the consortium agreement.
- Part of the royalties earned by the group from sales made by external partners, as stipulated in the consortium agreement.

Market capitalisation, charts and financial data

CD PROJEKT has been listed on the Warsaw Stock Exchange since 2010. In March 2019, the Warsaw Stock Exchange began publishing the WIG.GAMES sector index. The share of the company's shares in the index portfolio is 41.78% (as of 29 July 2019).

The premieres of new titles have a significant impact on the segment's revenues and results. The production cycle of computer games developed by the CD PROJEKT RED segment is usually between two and four years. Usually, initial work on production of the next game starts before the end of production and the market launch of the previous game.

CD PROJEKT RED is also involved in smaller productions, for example add-ons to its own games or the adaptation of already released products to new platforms. Such projects can be conducted directly by the company and external partners, and their implementation time ranges from several to a dozen or so months.

As regards games already published, the distribution of their sales throughout the year is influenced by participation in periodically organised promotional

Table 6.2 Financial results of CD PROJEKT for the years 2015–2018

	2015	*2016*	*2017*	*2018*
Net sales revenues (thousand $)	181,474.98	123,756.21	85,311.24	58,539.83
Operating profit (loss) (thousand $)	105,919.95	76,996.23	57,862.25	29,500.19
Gross profit (loss) (thousand PLN)	107,484.34	80,301.75	59,608.58	32,305.39
Net profit (loss) (thousand $)	87,381.42	64,899.81	47,982.59	28,447.30
Number of shares	94,950,000	96,120,000	96,120,000	96,120,000
Earnings per share ($)	0.92	0.68	0.50	0.30

Source: www.bankier.pl/gielda/notowania/akcje/CDPROJEKT/wyniki-finansowe [accessed: 9 January 2020].

campaigns. Usually, the second and fourth quarters are the most intense periods, while lower sales are generated in the first and the third quarter (including holidays) of the year. The revenues of the CD PROJEKT Capital Group in 2018 reached $95.3 million, and net profit was $28.3 million. For the next year in succession, the group's results were built on very good sales of "The Witcher 3: Wild Hunt". In the GOG segment, the best revenue title was also a title from "The Witcher universe – GWENT". Thanks to the results achieved and the continuous development of operations over the past year, both the group's total assets and the level of equity exceeded the symbolic figure of $260 million for the first time in history. (See Table 6.2.)

Share price at the beginning of 2015 was about $4.16 per share. The value of the exchange rate fluctuated, but for these five years it increased significantly to finally reach $73.71 per share at the beginning of 2020. At the end of 2019, during the trading session on the Warsaw Stock Exchange, the quotation of CD Projekt shares was the highest in their history. The calculations of Bankier.pl show that the producer of "The Witcher" has just overtaken Bank Pekao to become the fifth largest Polish company on the Polish stock exchange in terms of capitalisation. On the stock exchange, CD Projekt is currently valued at $6.9 billion. The growth recorded since mid-December allowed the company to reach its highest value yet and overtake Bank Pekao ($6.8 billion), a giant of Polish commercial banking, in terms of capitalisation. In June 2018, CD Projekt was worth half the value of Pekao, while at the beginning of 2016 (i.e. after the premiere of "The Witcher 3") Pekao was worth as much as 14 times more than CD Projekt. However, the bank has been in a downward spiral for a long time, while the value of the game developer regularly reaches new heights. (See Figure 6.1.)

The recent growth in the value of CD Projekt can be linked to the premiere of the "The Witcher" series on Netflix. Although CD Projekt itself was

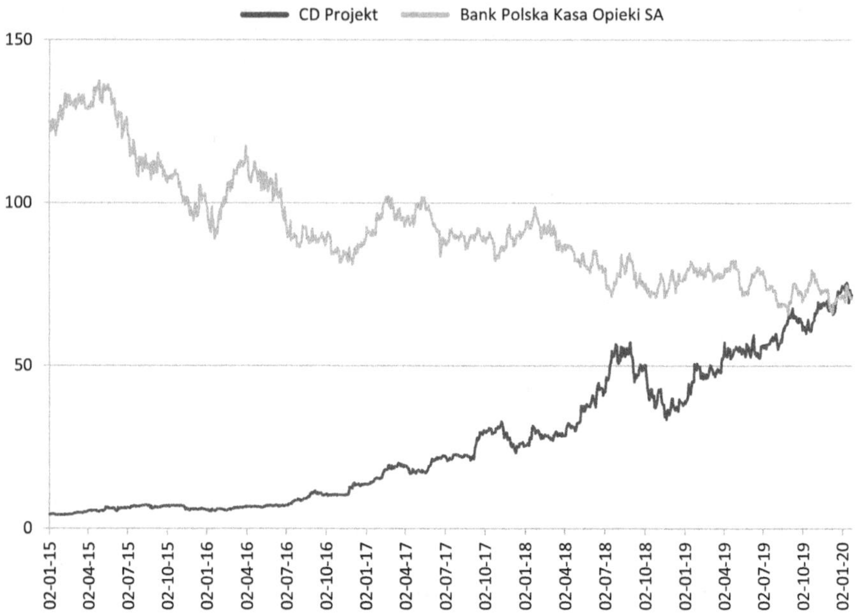

Figure 6.1 Comparison of Pekao and CD Projekt capitalisation (in billion $).
Source: Torchała, 2019 [accessed: 9 January 2020].

not involved in its production, Witcher games are currently the most important brand that CD Projekt owns, so interest in the series can translate into more games purchased. In October 2019, the company found itself on the elite list of "50 companies worth observing in 2020" by Bloomberg. The distinction and the fact that it is valued higher than Pekao show how great the scale of expectations associated with "Cyberpunk", to be released on 17 September 2020, is. Investors hope that if the game is successful, the company will make another leap forward. Not everyone, however, shares this enthusiasm, even among those predicting the success of "Cyberpunk". At the end of 2019, CD Projekt was the fifth largest Polish company on the Warsaw Stock Exchange. Only Orlen, PKO BP, Santander, and PZU were valued higher. On the other hand, the producer of "The Witcher" is followed by companies such as Pekao, ING, KGHM, Lotos, PGNiG, LPP, or mBank (Business Insider Polska, 2019 [accessed: 9 January 2020]).

The model of the description of CD Projekt business model components is shown in Figure 6.2.

In the first edition of the "Initiator of Innovation" competition organised by the weekly "Newsweek Polska" and the consulting company PwC, CD Projekt received an award in the "small and medium sized enterprises" category as the producer of one of the most famous games in the world, "The Witcher",

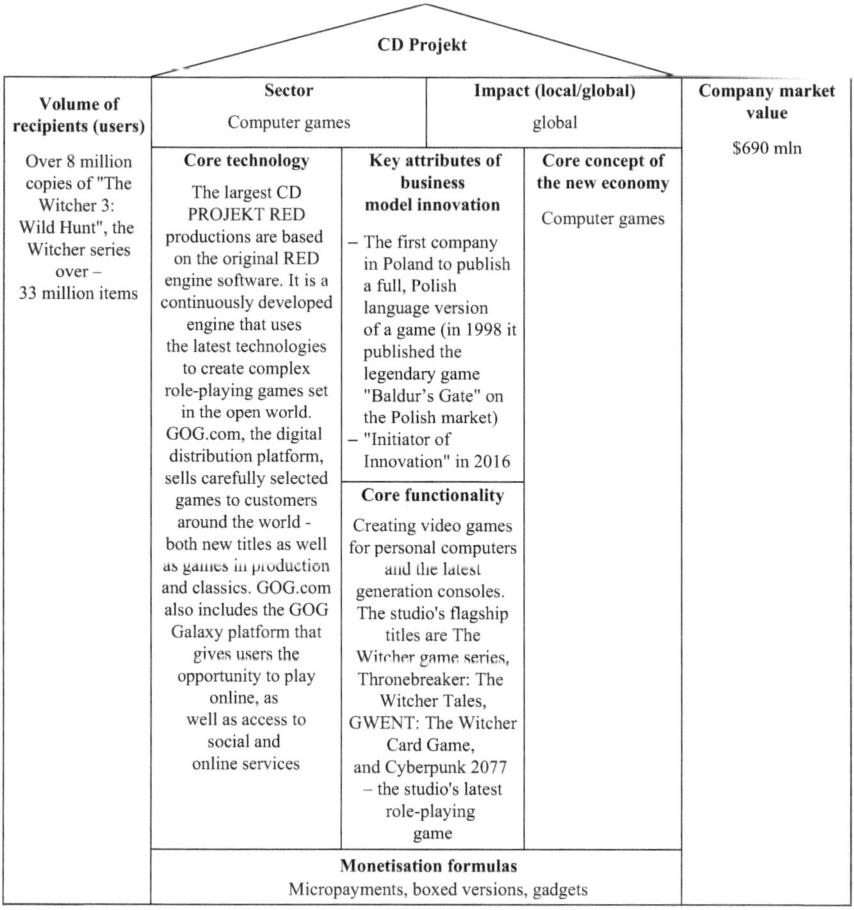

Figure 6.2 Model of the description of CD Projekt business model components in terms of monetisation.

Source: Own study based on Aquma, 2020 [accessed: 9 January 2020]; Wańtuchowicz, 2018 [accessed: 9 January 2020] and www.cdprojekt.com/pl/ [accessed: 9 January 2020].

which was awarded on the basis of an innovative ecosystem and the effective commercialisation of research and development (PwC, 2015 [accessed: 9 January 2020]). The computer games industry plays a special role in the development of technologically innovative branches of the economy. According to the Global Games Market Report, the Polish video game market is developing very dynamically compared to other countries in the region (LABportal.pl, 2015 [accessed: 9 January 2020]).

The closing share value (taking into account shares from January 2020) was $73.59, and the total number of shares was 9,377,679. Thus, the market value of

CD Projekt at the end of January 2020 was $690,122,672.52 (www.money.pl/gielda/spolki-gpw/PLOPTTC00011.html [accessed: 9 January 2020]).

Conclusions

The presented case study of CD Project proves that a company's success in the digital economy depends on many factors. In the case of CD Project, the development of a computer game based on the novel by Andrzej Sapkowski, "The Witcher", which is considered a classic of the fantasy genre, has been decisive. The high quality of the game together with the recognisable brand and solid game distribution system resulted in a product that generated over 8 million users from around the world, and the company achieved above-average market capitalisation. The technology used and the functionality of the business model helped both the company's business model and its value proposition to be accepted by computer game fans and investors. Therefore, a steady marked increase in share prices is observable. Monetisation formulas are optimally used to ensure the expected results of the company and to obtain customer acceptance.

References

Aquma (2020). *Ponad 8 mln kopii Wiedźmina 3 na Steam, sprzedaż rośnie dzięki serialowi.* Available at: www.gry-online.pl/newsroom/ponad-8-mln-kopii-wiedzmina-3-na-steam-sprzedaz-rosnie-dzieki-ser/z31d347 [accessed: 9 January 2020].

Business Insider Polska (2019). *CD Projekt jest już wart więcej niż drugi największy bank w Polsce.* Available at: https://businessinsider.com.pl/gielda/wiadomosci/cd-projekt-kurs-wycena-kapitalizacja-wieksza-od-pekao-sa/yl56n32 [accessed: 9 January 2020].

CD Projekt (2019a). *GWINT na iOS już accessny w Apple App Store!* Available at: https://pl.cdprojektred.com/news/gwint-na-ios-juz-dostepny-w-apple-app-store/ [accessed: 9 January 2020].

CD Projekt (2019b). *Management Board Report on CD Projekt capital group activities between 1 January and 30 June 2019* (accessed 9 January 2020).

CD Projekt (2019c). *Premiera gry Wiedźmin 3 na Nintendo Switch!* Available at: https://pl.cdprojektred.com/news/premiera-gry-wiedzmin-3-na-nintendo-switch/ [accessed: 9 January 2020].

Czakon, W. (2006). "Łabędzie Poppera – studia przypadków w naukach o zarządzaniu", *Przegląd Organizacji*, 9, 9–12.

Czakon, W. (2013). "Zastosowanie studiów przypadku w badaniach nauk o zarządzaniu", in W. Czakon (ed.), *Podstawy metodologii badań w naukach o zarządzaniu*, Warszawa: Oficyna a Wolters Kluwer business.

LABportal.pl (2015). *Innowacyjność to także miara sukcesu firmy.* Available at: ww.labportal.pl/news/innowacyjnosc-takze-miara-sukcesu-firmy [accessed: 9 January 2020].

Lee, A. (1989). "Case Studies as Natural Experiments", *Human Relations*, 42(2). DOI: 10.1177/001872678904200202. Available at: www.bankier.pl/gielda/notowania/akcje/CDPROJEKT/wyniki-finansowe [accessed: 9 January 2020].

www.cdprojekt.com/pl/ [accessed: 9 January 2020].

www.money.pl/gielda/spolki-gpw/PLOPTTC00011.html [accessed: 9 January 2020].

PwC (2015). *Inicjatorzy innowacji nagrodzeni*. Available at: www.pwc.pl/pl/media/2015/2015-06-01-inicjatorzy-innowacji-nagrodzeni.html [accessed: 9 January 2020].

Torchała, A. (2019). "CD Projekt większy niż Pekao. Nowy rekord notowań", *Bankier.pl – Polski Portal Finansowy*. Available at: www.bankier.pl/wiadomosc/CD-Projekt-wiekszy-niz-Pekao-Nowy-rekord-notowan-7794809.html [accessed: 9 January 2020].

Wańtuchowicz, P. (2018). "Seria Wiedźmin ze sprzedażą na poziomie 33 milionów egzemplarzy", *eurogamer.pl Daily*. Available at:www.eurogamer.pl/articles/2018-03-22-seria-wiedzmin-ze-sprzedaza-na-poziomie-33-milionow-egzemplarzy [accessed: 9 January 2020].

Yin, R. (1984). *Case Study Research: Design and Methods*, Thousand Oaks: Sage Publications, .

7 Conclusion

The topic of digital business models presented in the monograph is holistic and complex. The dynamic development of the digital economy results in the constant emergence of new concepts that revolutionise modern business. Digitalisation covers a growing range of activities of companies and individual users, and both of these areas must form mutual synthetic relationships. The condition for the development of the concept of the new economy is the increased universality of mobile devices; then the range of access to new services is almost unlimited. The multitude of technological solutions leads to the increased likelihood of creating an attractive digital business model. This results in a great deal of activity in the sphere of searching for innovative value delivery solutions. The issues presented in the monograph lead to the formulation of a number of conclusions, recommendations, and suggestions regarding the development of issues related to digital business models, particularly in the context of monetisation processes. Attention should be paid to the need to balance economic and social goals, which determines the creation of value economy assumptions. The value economy satisfies social expectations by confirming that success in the digital economy should be built on solid principles of social dialogue and community satisfaction. Any strategy based on dishonest intentions can be quickly discovered and the value provider within the digital business model can be rejected by a specific part of the user community. Therefore, the relationship between the effectiveness of monetisation formulas and the resulting financial performance must be compared with the expectations of stakeholders in ethical and ecological terms. Digital business models significantly affect these non-economic effects through global impacts. At the same time, great opportunities to optimise the use of natural resources and goods and encourage traditionalists to reflect are created. Current trends and concepts greatly undermine the achievements of the classical economy. Their understanding requires a slightly different look than before. The priority of profitability as a crucial goal of companies is increasingly not applicable, and the most important issue is to develop social aspects, including community building. New possibilities resulting from the use of innovative technological solutions make modern concepts serve people in the first place – they are humanistic and ordered. In this context, we are not only talking about the customer, but more broadly about the user. The classic value chain is hardly used as a result, because the proposed solutions broaden the range of considerations and applications. Thus, new approaches and paradigms are created. This approach means that not only phenomena which affect the creation of value, but which can also threaten to bring about losses in this regard, must be taken into consideration. A condition of implementing an effective monetisation strategy will be an appropriate community that will financially support the digital business model through its activities. The digital business ecosystem is based not only on the traditional value chain but also on the complex system of actors' relationships in the network over time. It should be noted that the roles of individual actors result from the accepted logic of value delivery and the adopted monetisation formula. An important role is also played by the aspect of building a community that makes mutual relationships dynamic and initiates actions and reactions. Monetisation, meaning transforming something (assets, e.g. business model, data sets, etc.) into money, is a crucial component of digital business models. Micropayments are, to a large extent, a condition for success and determine the provision of cash flows in the digital economy. Monetisation formulas should be effective, primarily due to the unique features of the digital business model, which should convert the value created into steady sales. The attractiveness of the digital business model will be crucial in this respect. The fundamental condition for achieving the monetisation of a business model will be attracting a large volume of recipients of the proposed business solution. The concept of monetisation is not the same as the concept of data monetisation, although these concepts must overlap in the digital economy. The dynamic development of Big Data sets results in the creation of cashable additional resources as a by-product, in addition to the factors responsible for value creation. This new formula for using new resources is a challenge for the managers of digital business models. When using these data, ethical and legal aspects should be highlighted, as they may give rise to a number of controversies that require new legal regulations now and in the future. Particular attention should also be paid to the theoretical conditions for the monetisation of digital business models. The monetisation formulas of digital business models illustrate the relational nature of the functioning of the modern global economy. A transition is occurring from the transactional model to the relational model, which creates broad opportunities for the development of indirect monetisation formulas. Monetisation as a concept of generating revenue is strongly associated with the concept of the scalability of the digital business model. Scalability means the ability of a system (usually IT) to maintain performance while increasing the load by increasing the number of components. Scalability is a crucial parameter which determines the company's ability to grow; it is based, among others, on the statement that not every unit of revenue is generated by an equal unit of cost. The adaptation of scalability to the monetisation formula generates economic opportunities for the digital business model.

As regards the monetisation strategy, the following conclusions, recommendations, and suggestions should be indicated:

- An effective monetisation formula is a condition for the success of the digital business model.
- The digital business model is configured by using components such as a value proposition area, a data set area, a technology area, an organisation and management area, a value visualisation area, a customer (user) relationship area, and a business analytics area, among others.
- The main achievements responsible for the success of the digital business model include the profitability of the digital business model by applying the optimal effective monetisation formula and achieving the expected volume of digital business model users. The number of users is a condition for the success of the business model and its monetisation.
- As regards the recognition of the digital business model as a complex system, there is a strong relationship between the selection of the monetisation formula, the implementation of the monetisation strategy, and the choice of the configuration of digital business model components.
- The process of designing the monetisation formula for the economisation of the digital business model should have the character of a technical design using a system of tests, measurements, and validation of the proposed solutions.
- The monetisation controlling process plays a crucial role in the exploitation of the digital business model, which is an important element in supporting the design and monitoring of the effectiveness of the monetisation formulas of digital business models.

Referring to the theoretical issues presented in the monograph, many recommendations, suggestions, and conclusions which verify the adopted assumptions are presented as well.

The main purpose of the scientific discussion was to present, from a multi-dimensional and holistic perspective, the mechanisms of the conceptualisation and operationalisation of digital business models in terms of their monetisation. The implementation of the assumed goal of the work confirmed that the design of digital business models is based on other assumptions than the design of traditional business solutions. The prevailing factor in the case of digital business models is relationship networks, which bond all related elements together. People, business, cloud computing, and things create the configuration of the ecosystem within which a network of relationships with a unique structure is created. They are of an organisational and technological nature. Technological relationships are built through interfaces and result from the technology used, while organisational relationships result from the designed component-based digital business model. Thus, technology and dynamic interaction between actors in the network play a crucial role in digital business models. In the context of the scientific problem posed and the identification of the cognitive gap, attention was paid to the need to identify a set of factors responsible for the effective use of the monetisation formulas of digital business models in the conditions of globalisation. Theoretical and practical factors have emerged against the background of this concept, which determine the high level of effectiveness of the monetisation formulas of digital business models. From an economic point of view, the condition for the survival of a given business model is the need to fulfil three conditions:

- Actors gathered around the business model must recognise the benefits of the value proposition delivered within the business model.
- Actors must accept the proposed monetisation method.
- The cash flow does not have to be adequate in volume to the value delivery scheme.

Monetisation will also depend on the adopted concept of the new economy, such as the concepts of the Sharing Economy, the Circular Economy, or Big Data set systems. In each different approach to value creation, monetisation will be based on different assumptions, which will refer to the concept of business model dynamics.

The cognitive goals of the monograph included:

1. The identification of the main scientific theories based on which digital business models are designed.
2. The description of key concepts of the so-called new economy, their assumptions and limitations.
3. The assessment of the impact of the concept of the new economy on the emergence of digital business models.
4. The assessment of the relationship between the configuration of digital business models and the effectiveness of the monetisation formulas they use.

The main theories which are the basis for the digital economy are the ecology theory, the complex network theory, the actor–network theory, the spectral graph theory, the competing values theory, Claudio Ciborra's theory, the theory of evolution, the resource-based theory, and the Markov chain theory. All these theories highlight the complexity of the systems that underpin the modern digital economy. The combination of the theory of sociological sciences and technical sciences defines the interdisciplinary nature of the digital economy. It is also impossible to indicate one leading theory of science because only a combination of many theories is able to explain the complex relationships between phenomena occurring in digital business. New economy concepts such as the Sharing Economy, Big Data, the Circular Economy, the Platform Economy, and other concepts make the digital economy a tool for implementing revolutionary ideas that would not have emerged without the development of innovative technologies. These concepts make the process of the emergence of digital business models dynamic, and at the same time these models create a business ecosystem which is different from previous conditions.

There is a relationship between the configuration of digital business models and the effectiveness of their monetisation formulas. This relationship emerges in the form of restrictions on the use of selected monetisation formulas. In many cases, other monetisation formulas can be used for computer games and still others for business models of companies in the Sharing Economy. Obviously, there will be such schemes that are universal, but the formula and context of their application may differ significantly in the context of the various concepts of the new economy and the digital economy industries. The effectiveness of monetisation formulas will strongly depend on the attractiveness of the digital business model, which will be largely responsible for the expected increase in the volume of users. The greater the volume of users, the more effective the monetisation formula will be, while maintaining the principles of the scalability of digital business models.

As regards methodological and utilitarian goals, the configuration of factors which describe digital business models was presented and strategic recommendations for the development of digital business models in terms of their monetisation were developed. A canvas was designed for the description of digital business models, which covered quantitative and qualitative aspects. Such a dual description of digital business models allowed for the identification of factors related to the scalability of business models as well as determinants which characterise their configuration. The quantitative attributes included the volume of recipients (users), company market value, as well as the scope of market impact (local/global). The qualitative parameters of the description of digital business models, in turn, include the sector where the given company operates, the core technology of the digital business model, the key attributes of business model innovation, the core functionality, the core concept of the new economy within which the digital business model operates, and in particular the monetisation formulas used. To illustrate the specificity of digital business models, digital business models which represent three key concepts of the new economy, namely the Sharing Economy, Big Data, and the Circular Economy, were described using the above approach. The monograph answers the main research questions that have been transformed into theses:

- The effectiveness of monetisation formulas results from the compilation of other components of digital business models.
- There is a synergy between the chosen concept of the new economy and the potential for the monetisation of the digital business model.
- The sector where a given company operates, the core technology of the digital business model, the key attributes of business model innovation, the core functionality, the core concept of the new economy within which the digital business model operates, the volume of recipients (users) and monetisation formulas constitute a set of components which form a

consistent digital business model capable of achieving the expected level of monetisation.

As indicated before, due to the multidimensionality and holistic nature of the functioning of digital business models, the subject of scientific considerations requires raising issues related to the theory of management science, economics, and finance, as well as the theory of technical sciences. The complexity of digital business model issues prompts researchers, business analysts, and managers to seek knowledge from many areas of science and practice. The monograph confirms that digital business models have changed the contemporary conditions of doing business, and the foundations based on which traditional business principles were shaped have changed radically. Economic factors must interact with social expectations, in particular those focused on the specific ideas of communities of people who are increasingly transferring their lives, emotions, and values to the virtual world.

Index

Note: Page numbers in *italics* indicate figures and in **bold** indicate tables on the corresponding pages.

For Product Safety Concerns and Information please contact our EU
representative GPSR@taylorandfrancis.com
Taylor & Francis Verlag GmbH, Kaufingerstraße 24, 80331 München, Germany

www.ingramcontent.com/pod-product-compliance
Lightning Source LLC
LaVergne TN
LVHW011130300926
849160LV00008B/589
9780367548520